Lipi Begum is Programme Leader in Fashion Management at the Winchester School of Art, University of Southampton and former lecturer in Marketing and Branding at the London College of Fashion, University of the Arts London. She has worked as a United Nations global consultant for the ready-made garment sector in Bangladesh and has developed fashion education globally. She is a Fellow of the Royal Society of Arts and currently Open Space editor for the International Journal of Fashion Studies (Intellect).

Rohit K. Dasgupta is a lecturer in Media and Cultural Studies at the Institute for Media and Creative Industries, Loughborough University. He is the co-editor of *Friendship as Social Justice Activism: Critical Solidarities in a Global Perspective* (2017); *Rituparno Ghosh: Cinema, Gender and Art* (2015) and *Masculinity and its Challenges in India* (2014). Most recently he was the lead investigator on the Wellcome Trust UK funded project 'Mobile-ising for Sexual Health'.

Reina Lewis is Professor of Cultural Studies at London College of Fashion, University of the Arts London. Her books include: *Muslim Fashion: Contemporary Style Cultures* (2015); *Rethinking Orientalism: Women, Travel and the Ottoman Harem* (2004); *Gendering Orientalism: Race, Femininity and Representation* (1996). Edited volumes include: *Modest Fashion: Styling Bodies, Mediating Faith* (2013); *Gender, Modernity and Liberty: Middle Eastern and Western Women's Writings: A Critical Reader* (with Nancy Micklewright 2006); *Feminist Postcolonial Theory: A Reader* (with Sara Mills 2003); *Outlooks: Lesbian and Gay Visual Cultures* (with Peter Horne 1996). Reina Lewis co-edits two books series: Dress Cultures with Elizabeth Wilson; and Cultures in Dialogue with Teresa Heffernan.

'This is a very much needed collection with a great range of highly original ethnography and a helpful spread across the region ... The material is fascinating and ready to be picked up by comparativists working in China, Southeast Asia, the Middle East and so on.'
– Caroline Osella, SOAS, University of London

Series Editors: Reina Lewis & Elizabeth Wilson

Advisory Board: Christopher Breward, Hazel Clark, Joanne Entwistle, Caroline Evans, Susan Kaiser, Angela McRobbie, Hiroshi Narumi, Peter McNeil, Özlem Sandikci, Simona Segre Reinach

Dress Cultures aims to foster innovative theoretical and methodological frameworks to understand how and why we dress, exploring the connections between clothing, commerce and creativity in global contexts.

Published and forthcoming:

Branding Fashion: Bridging the Self and the Social Consumer
by Anthony Sullivan

Delft Blue to Denim Blue: Contemporary Dutch Fashion
edited by Anneke Smelik

Dressing for Austerity: Aspiration, Leisure and Fashion in Postwar Britain
by Geraldine Biddle-Perry

Experimental Fashion: Performance Art, Carnival and the Grotesque Body
by Francesca Granata

Fashion in European Art: Dress and Identity, Politics and the Body, 1775–1925
edited by Justine De Young

Fashion in Multiple Chinas: Chinese Styles in the Transglobal Landscape
edited by Wessie Ling and Simona Segre Reinach

Fashioning Indie: Popular Fashion, Music and Gender
by Rachel Lifter

Modest Fashion: Styling Bodies, Mediating Faith
edited by Reina Lewis

Niche Fashion Magazines: Changing the Shape of Fashion
by Ane Lynge-Jorlén

Sinophilia: Fashion, Western Modernity and Things Chinese after 1900
by Sarah Cheang

Styling South Asian Youth Cultures: Fashion, Media and Society
edited by Lipi Begum, Rohit K. Dasgupta and Reina Lewis

Thinking Through Fashion: A Guide to Key Theorists
edited by Agnès Rocamora and Anneke Smelik

Veiling in Fashion: Space and the Hijab in Minority Communities
by Anna-Mari Almila

Wearing the Cheongsam: Dress and Culture in a Chinese Diaspora
By Cheryl Sim

Wearing the Niqab: Fashioning Identities among Muslim Women in the UK
by Anna Piela

Reina Lewis: reina.lewis@fashion.arts.ac.uk
Elizabeth Wilson: mail@elizabethwilson.net
At the publisher, **Philippa Brewster**: philippabrewster@gmail.com

Styling South Asian Youth Cultures

Fashion, Media & Society

edited by
Lipi Begum, Rohit K. Dasgupta and
Reina Lewis

BLOOMSBURY VISUAL ARTS
LONDON · NEW YORK · OXFORD · NEW DELHI · SYDNEY

BLOOMSBURY VISUAL ARTS
Bloomsbury Publishing Plc
50 Bedford Square, London, WC1B 3DP, UK
1385 Broadway, New York, NY 10018, USA

BLOOMSBURY, BLOOMSBURY VISUAL ARTS and the Diana logo
are trademarks of Bloomsbury Publishing Plc

First published in Great Britain 2018 by I.B. Tauris & Co. Ltd.
Paperback edition published 2020 by Bloomsbury Visual Arts

Copyright Editorial Selection © Lipi Begum, Rohit K. Dasgupta, Reina Lewis, 2018

Copyright Individual Chapters © Kaustav Bakshi, Lipi Begum, Rohit K. Dasgupta,
Sunil Gupta, Sandya Hewamanne, Raisa Kabir, Sneha Krishnan, Tereza Kuldova, Reina Lewis,
Arti Sandhu, Sarah Shepherd-Manandhar, Charan Singh, Paul Strickland, Priya Swamy, 2018

Lipi Begum, Rohit K. Dasgupta and Reina Lewis have asserted their rights under the
Copyright, Designs and Patents Act, 1988, to be identified as Editors of this work.

For legal purposes the Acknowledgements on p. xv constitute
an extension of this copyright page.

All rights reserved. No part of this publication may be reproduced or
transmitted in any form or by any means, electronic or mechanical,
including photocopying, recording, or any information storage or retrieval
system, without prior permission in writing from the publishers.

Bloomsbury Publishing Plc does not have any control over, or responsibility for,
any third-party websites referred to or in this book. All internet addresses given
in this book were correct at the time of going to press. The author and publisher
regret any inconvenience caused if addresses have changed or sites have
ceased to exist, but can accept no responsibility for any such changes.

A catalogue record for this book is available from the British Library.

A catalog record for this book is available from the Library of Congress.

ISBN: HB: 978-1-7845-3917-7
PB: 978-1-3501-5407-0
ePDF: 978-1-8386-0918-4
eBook: 978-1-8386-0917-7

Series: Dress Cultures

Typeset by OKS Prepress Services, Chennai, India

To find out more about our authors and books visit
www.bloomsbury.com and sign up for our newsletters.

CONTENTS

List of Images — vii
List of Plates — ix
Contributor Notes — xi
Acknowledgements — xv

Style, Fashion and Media in South Asian Youth Cultures — 1
Lipi Begum, Rohit K. Dasgupta and Reina Lewis

1. Street Style vs. Style on the Street?: Two Interpretations of Indian Street Fashion — 30
   Arti Sandhu

2. Style-ish Girls and Local Boys: Young Women and Fashion in Chennai — 49
   Sneha Krishnan

3. Rituparno Ghosh, Sartorial Codes and the Queer Bengali Youth — 65
   Rohit K. Dasgupta and Kaustav Bakshi

4. In/Visible Space: Reflections on the Realm of Dimensional Affect, Space and the Queer Racialised Self — 86
   Raisa Kabir in conversation with Lipi Begum and Rohit K. Dasgupta

5. Faces of Subversion: Queer Looks of India — 96
   Sunil Gupta and Charan Singh

6. Designing for 'Zippies' and the Madness of *Bhootsavaar*: On Commercially Inflected Artistic Nationalism and Branded 'Subcultures' — 102
   Tereza Kuldova

7. Trouser Wearing Women: Changing Landscape of Fashion among Free Trade Zone Factory Workers and Contemporary Political Tensions in Sri Lanka 124
   Sandya Hewamanne

8. Changing Fashions of Bhutanese Youth: Impacts on Cultural and Individual Identity 146
   Paul Strickland

9. Matching Clothes and Matching Couples: The Role of Dress in Arranged Marriages in Kathmandu 165
   Sarah Shepherd-Manandhar

10. 'Of Course It's Beautiful, but I can't Wear It!': Constructions of Hindu Style among Young Hindustani Women in Amsterdam 183
    Priya Swamy

11. Bras are not for Burning: The Bra and Young Urban Women in Delhi and Bombay 202
    Lipi Begum

Index 223

LIST OF FIGURES

Figure 1.1 Camel traders wearing their traditional attire at the annual cattle fair in Pushkar. From the blog post titled *Camel Traders of Rajasthan*, 11 August 2014, wearabout.wordpress.com. Image courtesy of Manou.   39

Figure 1.2 Fashion designer Anand Kabra on Day 2 of Lakmé India Fashion Week 2010, wearing a T-shirt from Topman, shirt from CK Jeans, self-designed waistcoat and pants from Fabindia. From a blog post dated 9 March 2010, wearabout.wordpress.com. Image courtesy of Manou.   44

Figure 3.1 Rituparno Ghosh playing Rudra in *Chitrangada* (2012). Image courtesy of Shri Venkatesh Films.   74

Figure 3.2 Rituparno at Kolkata Fashion Week 2009. Image courtesy of Abhishek Datta.   78

Figure 3.3 Rituparno with actress Deepti Naval in *Memories in March* (2012). Image courtesy of Shri Venkatesh Films.   80

Figure 6.1 Kalki Koechlin for *Hello India*, 27 May 2015. Image courtesy of *Hello India*.   107

Figure 6.2 Nitin Bal Chauhan, New Delhi, 2012. Image courtesy of Arash Taheri.   110

Figure 6.3 Rishi Raj, a stylist, *Bhootsaavar*, 2013, Crescent Mall. Image courtesy of Nitin Bal Chauhan.   115

Figure 6.4 Ritika Singh, a singer, *Bhootsavaar*, 2013, Crescent Mall. Image courtesy of Nitin Bal Chauhan.   117

Figure 8.1 Foreign road workers in Bhutan, 2016. Image courtesy of Paul Strickland. 148

Figure 8.2 Western influence on youth fashion: dressed for going out at the weekend, 2016. Image courtesy of Paul Strickland. 150

Figure 8.3 His Majesty Jigme Khesar Namgyel Wangchuck and Queen Jetsun Pema, 2011. Image courtesy of *Yeewong* Magazine. 152

LIST OF PLATES

Plate 1 Sita, Raisa Kabir, 2014. 35mm film, type C prints, paper montage, 64 cm × 45 cm, from the series (In)visible Space. Courtesy of Raisa Kabir.

Plate 2 Ungendering Prayer, Raisa Kabir, 2014. 35mm film, type C prints, paper montage, 64 cm × 45 cm, from the series (In)visible Space. Courtesy of Raisa Kabir.

Plate 3 Maryam, Raisa Kabir, 2014. 35mm film, type C prints, paper montage, 64 cm × 45 cm, from the series (In)visible Space. Courtesy of Raisa Kabir.

Plate 4 Girl in Hijab, Raisa Kabir, 2014. 35mm film, type C prints, paper montage, 64 cm × 45 cm, from the series (In)visible Space. Courtesy of Raisa Kabir.

Plate 5 Nikita, Raisa Kabir, 2014. 35mm film, type C prints, paper montage, 64 cm × 45 cm, from the series (In)visible Space. Courtesy of Raisa Kabir.

Plate 6 Raju, Raisa Kabir, 2014. 35mm film, type C prints, paper montage, 64 cm × 45 cm, from the series (In)visible Space. Courtesy of Raisa Kabir.

Plate 7 Raju detail, Raisa Kabir, 2014. 35mm film, type C prints, paper montage, 64 cm × 45 cm, from the series (In)visible Space. Courtesy of Raisa Kabir.

Plate 8 Yasmin/Girl with Hijab detail, Raisa Kabir, 2014. 35mm film, type C prints, paper montage, 64 cm × 45 cm, from the series (In)visible Space. Courtesy of Raisa Kabir.

Plate 9 *Arti, Greater Kailash, M-Block Market*, from the series *Mr Malhotra's Party*, Sunil Gupta, 2007–2012. Courtesy of the artist and SepiaEye.

Plate 10 *Anusha, Jawaharlal Nehru University*, from the series *Mr Malhotra's Party*, Sunil Gupta, 2007–2012. Courtesy of the artist and SepiaEye.

Plate 11 *Mario, Golf View Apartments*, from the series *Mr Malhotra's Party*, Sunil Gupta, 2007–2012. Courtesy of the artist and SepiaEye.

Plate 12 *Sonal, Yusuf Sarai*, from the series *Mr Malhotra's Party*, Sunil Gupta, 2007–2012. Courtesy of the artist and SepiaEye.

Plate 13 *Untitled #5*, from the series *Kothis, Hijras, Giriyas and Others*, Charan Singh, 2013–2014. Courtesy of the artist and SepiaEye.

Plate 14 *Untitled #6*, from the series *Kothis, Hijras, Giriyas and Others*, Charan Singh, 2013–2014. Courtesy of the artist and SepiaEye.

Plate 15 *Untitled #1*, from the series *Kothis, Hijras, Giriyas and Others*, Charan Singh, 2013–2014. Courtesy of the artist and SepiaEye.

Plate 16 *Untitled #2*, from the series *Kothis, Hijras, Giriyas and Others*, Charan Singh, 2013–2014. Courtesy of the artist and SepiaEye.

CONTRIBUTOR NOTES

Lipi Begum is Programme Leader of Fashion Management at the Winchester School of Art, University of Southampton and former lecturer in Marketing and Branding at the London College of Fashion, University of the Arts London. She has worked as a United Nations global consultant for the ready-made garment sector in Bangladesh and has developed fashion education globally. She is a Fellow of the Royal Society of Arts and currently Open Space editor for the *International Journal of Fashion Studies* (Intellect).

Rohit K. Dasgupta is a lecturer in media and cultural studies at the Institute for Media and Creative Industries, Loughborough University. He is the co-editor of *Friendship as Social Justice Activism: Critical Solidarities in a Global Perspective* (2017); *Rituparno Ghosh: Cinema, Gender and Art* (2015) and *Masculinity and its Challenges in India* (2014). Most recently he was the lead investigator on the Wellcome Trust UK funded project 'Mobile-ising for Sexual Health'.

Reina Lewis is Professor of Cultural Studies at London College of Fashion, University of the Arts London. Her books include: *Muslim Fashion: Contemporary Style Cultures* (2015); *Rethinking Orientalism: Women, Travel and the Ottoman Harem* (2004); *Gendering Orientalism: Race, Femininity and Representation* (1996). Edited volumes include: *Modest Fashion: Styling Bodies, Mediating Faith* (2013); *Gender, Modernity and Liberty: Middle Eastern and Western Women's Writings: A Critical Reader* (with Nancy Micklewright 2006); *Feminist Postcolonial Theory: A Reader* (with Sara Mills 2003); *Outlooks: Lesbian and Gay Visual Cultures* (with Peter Horne 1996). Reina Lewis co-edits two books series: Dress Cultures with Elizabeth Wilson; and Cultures in Dialogue with Teresa Heffernan. Reina convenes the public talk series Faith and Fashion: http://www.

arts.ac.uk/research/current-research/ual-research-projects/fashion-design/faith-and-fashion/.

Arti Sandhu is Associate Professor in Fashion Design at the School of Design in DAAP, University of Cincinnati. Her research is mainly centred on contemporary Indian fashion and related design cultures. She is the author of *Indian Fashion: Tradition, Innovation, Style* (2014).

Sneha Krishnan has a doctorate in Development Studies from the University of Oxford, where she is currently a Research Fellow at St John's College. Her research interests lie at the intersection of youth, gender and agency. She has previously researched masculinity and nationalism in India and continues to research gender and youth in Tamil Nadu.

Kaustav Bakshi is Assistant Professor in English at Jadavpur University, India. He is the co-editor of *Anxieties, Influences and After* (2009) and *Rituparno Ghosh: Cinema, Gender and Art* (2015). Most recently he received the Charles Wallace India Trust research grant to further his research in the UK on Sri Lankan expatriate fiction.

Raisa Kabir is a multidisciplinary artist, weaver and writer who uses contemporary textiles, sound and photography to interrogate and question concepts around the politics of dress in connection to gender, race, and sexuality. Trained as a weaver at Chelsea College of Art, University of the Arts London, she exhibits and curates work globally and has undertaken creative residencies in Mexico, Bangladesh and the UK – www.raisakabir.com, www.in.visiblespace.co.uk.

Sunil Gupta is a photographer, artist, educator and curator based in London and New Delhi. Born in New Delhi (1953) and educated at the Royal College of Art (London, 1983) he has been involved with cultural activism and independent photography as a critical practice for many years. He is currently Visiting Professor at University of the Creative Arts, Farnham. His recent books include *Wish You Were Here* (2008) and *Queer* (2011).

Charan Singh lives and works from New Delhi and London. He is currently a PhD candidate in Photography at the Royal College of Art, London. Singh's photographic practice is informed by HIV/AIDS work and community activism in India, along with a formal study of the history of art and photography. The principal common threads of his works are memory, story-telling, and masculinity. His work has been exhibited at Vadehra Art Gallery, New Delhi (2014), The Photographers Gallery, London (2015), FotoFest, Houston (2015), GFEST, London (2015) and SepiaEye, New York (2016).

Tereza Kuldova is a post-doctoral fellow at the Department of Archaeology, Conservation and History, University of Oslo, and a Social Anthropologist. She is currently part of the HERA II Enterprise of Culture research project. Among her recent publications are the co-edited *Urban Utopias: Excess and Expulsion in Neoliberal South Asia* (with Mathew A. Varghese, 2017), her monograph, *Luxury Indian Fashion: A Social Critique* (2016) and an edited volume, *Fashion India: Spectacular Capitalism* (2013). She is Editor-in-Chief for the *Journal of Extreme Anthropology* (University of Oslo).

Sandhya Hewamanne has worked as an assistant professor of Anthropology at University of Essex, UK and Wake Forest University, USA. She received her MA and PhD in Anthropology from the University of Texas, Austin. Her research interests include globalisation, identity, cultural politics and feminist and postcolonial theory. She is the author of *Stitching Identities in a Free Trade Zone: Gender and Politics in Sri Lanka* (2008) and *Sri Lanka's Global Factory Workers: (Un) Disciplined Desires and Sexual Struggles in a Post-Colonial Society* (2016).

Priya Swamy holds a BA in World Religions from McGill University and an MPhil in Asian Studies from Leiden University. Her doctoral research explored the emergence of a public Hindu identity in relation to temple building processes in Amsterdam Southeast. Her postdoctoral research at the Royal Netherlands Institute of Southeast Asian and Caribbean Studies (KITLV) in Leiden examines the relationship between active citizenship and Surinamese Hindu identity in temples in Amsterdam.

Paul Strickland is a lecturer and course coordinator for tourism, hospitality and event management programmes within the La Trobe Business School in Melbourne, Australia. Paul has extensive industry experience and has taught hotel management in Bhutan. Paul's research areas include ethnic restaurants, Bhutanese studies, wine and event tourism. Paul is currently a PhD candidate in wine events and innovation.

Sarah Shepherd-Manandhar is currently a PhD candidate in the Anthropology department at the University of Illinois at Chicago where she is a Graduate Research Fellow. She has spent the last ten years travelling back and forth between Nepal and the USA. Her primary research interests include gender, performance theory, consumption and material culture.

ACKNOWLEDGEMENTS

This book would not have been possible without the dedication of the contributors, editors and readers. We thank them greatly for being part of this book. Particular thanks to Amrit Kumar and Mriga Kapadia for the cover image; the copy-editor, indexer, reviewers and series editor Philippa Brewster at I.B.Tauris for her professional advice throughout. Thanks to the London College of Fashion, University of the Arts London and the University of Southampton, Winchester School of Art for kindly supporting us with funding. Finally, thanks to the anonymous peer reviewers for their detailed feedback and comments. We would also like to thank our friends, family and colleagues who have continually motivated and inspired us throughout the process.

STYLE, FASHION AND MEDIA IN SOUTH ASIAN YOUTH CULTURES

Lipi Begum, Rohit K. Dasgupta and Reina Lewis

For the part of the world commonly known as South Asia, fashion and consumption has come to play an increasingly important role in the lives of young people and in the formation of youth cultures. Afghanistan, Bangladesh, Bhutan, India, Maldives, Nepal, Pakistan and Sri Lanka have all, in related and distinctive ways, seen a growth of the middle class: this, along with the increased reach of globalised consumer cultures and a surge in youth population, has produced an increase in the demand for fashion consumption. The region is the most youthful of Asia's sub-regions; it is home to 26 per cent of the entire world's youth (the under 25s) and is set to maintain its peak till 2030 (www.social.un.org/youthyear 2011). Collectively, and in different ways individually, countries discussed in this book have been constituted as important 'emerging' markets for lifestyle goods and services in general, and for fashion in particular. At a time when established fashion markets (amongst them the UK, USA and Japan) are exploring the impact of the world's increasingly older population, we draw attention to the impact and implication of demographic shift in South Asia and its related diasporas which have seen a growth of young people compared to older generations (Chakma 2014).

Focusing as much as possible on the South Asian region and its diasporas, this book builds on existing scholarship on youth cultures and style in the region (Lukose 2009; Nakassis 2016), which to date has mostly focused on India's consumer cultures. Market research too has focused on the size of the Indian market, where the annual expenditure on apparel has consistently risen over the last decade. However, the growth of fashion markets and practices within other South Asian regions is less well-documented, and one of our aims with this book was to put into articulation under the rubric of 'South Asia' far more of the nations in the region than are usually the focus of study, bringing in new scholarship on Bhutan, Pakistan, and Nepal.

Whilst there is an intrinsic value to providing some of the first studies of particular countries, regions or populations, as is the case most spectacularly with Bhutan, our purpose goes beyond a desire to be geographically comprehensive. Framed by a historically informed critical engagement with the constructed entity of South Asia, the geographical scope of this book brings opportunities for new comparative studies that value the intra-South Asian transmission of styles and cultural forms alongside a nuanced understanding of multiple and interlinking diasporas in diverse postcolonial contexts. We hope that the reader will be able to see over-arching themes in relation to youth cultures – generation, age, market, sexuality, religion, caste, ethnicity, gender, media, the body – in ways that enliven the understanding of local, national, international and transnational convergences in and contestations over cultural values and identity.

WHY SOUTH ASIA AS A REGION?

The interconnectedness and differences within the South Asian region have long demonstrated an ongoing modernity, characterised by distinctive combinations of traditionalism and neoliberalism (Begum and Dasgupta 2015; Tarlo 1996), which shape the sartorial identity of youth across South Asia as explored in this book. Within a comparative frame our contributors both supply new case studies and bring new critical frames to the study of those regional fashion practices that have previously received research attention.

We propose that studies of contemporary youth cultures and fashion need to be both specific and comparative, avoiding the tendency of approaches to regional studies that often disregard the specificities of different South Asian nations (Dasgupta 2007: xxii). In this way, our use of the term 'South Asia' does not seek to homogenise the different perspectives found within the region, but to identify and evaluate the intra-regional influences, conflicts, and possibilities produced by shared colonial histories and entwined cultural landscapes. South Asia is not merely a geographic classification coincident with Southern Asia, though geography is implicit in its appellation. Nor is it a political entity to be only identified through its more economically powerful regions, often defined as the Indian sub-continent (India, Pakistan and Bangladesh). Very few people would give South Asian as their primary form of identification. Most commonly people name themselves in terms of nation; as Afghanis, Bangladeshis, Bhutanese, Indians, Maldivians or Pakistanis. Yet, as diaspora politics have shown, the components that make these sometimes essentialised national identities are themselves shifting (Gopinath 2005) in relation to changing patterns of globalisation and economic fluctuation.

Although the inter-connected regional focus of the book celebrates multiple cultural identities, the increasing primacy of national identities in South Asia arising from postcolonial tensions has fuelled xenophobic brands of nationalist rhetoric whose worldview often erases commonalities of rich cultural exchange. Spivak has argued that it is important to not let the plurality of South Asia (or Asia as she describes) be studied according to the national distinctions favoured by western political policies. She argues: 'the pluralised Asia I am thinking of not only respects, but attempts to know the differences within Asia as imaginatively as possible' (Spivak 2008: 2). In this light, the chapters of this book provide an exercise in imagining the plurality of the region in terms of dress cultures, clothing and media politics, in conjunction with responses to the specificity of individual situations. This interaction between ideas of nationalism(s) and communities (Anderson 1991) is further discussed by Partha Chatterjee (1993) in the opening chapter of his book *The Nation and its Fragments*, maintaining that nationalisms in the postcolonial world do not necessarily choose their 'imagined community'; questioning the extent to which models premised on western norms can be applied to postcolonial nations in South Asia.

Whilst there has been some study of South Asian fashion and dressing cultures within history, anthropology (Banerjee and Miller 2003; Kuldova 2016; Lukose 2009; Nakassis 2016; Srivastava 2007; Tarlo 1996), cinema (Dwyer 2000; Wilkinson-Weber, 2014), diaspora (Bhachu 2004; Mani 2003; Reddy 2016) and in relation to orientalist transnational implications (Niessen et al. 2003), there has been little work that has looked directly at transnational implications through a contemporary youth perspective for the various South Asian regions. As Emma Tarlo (1996) has argued, dress in India and more largely South Asia has been and is used to instigate change, question national identities and assert power. Building on Tarlo's important intervention into Indian dress and identity, this collection looks at the South Asian region as a whole and focuses specifically on contemporary youth cultures.

For youth in South Asia, the experience of youth as a life stage is distinctive in a number of ways, framed by gendered codes of respectability. South Asian young people encounter, and contribute to, a network of formal and informal surveillance, whose effects are themselves formative of and formed by discourses of gender, sexuality, religion, ethnicity and class. As a liminal life phase in which behaviours that transgress norms of gender, sexuality and respectability may be temporarily permitted, the exceptionalism of young adulthood simultaneously reaffirms the status of those norms as essential to 'adult' sociality. Across the region and in the diaspora, degrees of fitting in and/or standing out are subject to the regulatory gazes of schools, employers, government, states, and religions.

COMPARATIVE FRAME: TEMPORAL, SPATIAL LINKS AND DISSONANCES

The complexity of globalisation and economic change marked by transnational cross-flows, disjuncture and difference (Appadurai 1996), and the destabilising power of nation-states, gives way to exciting forms of identity and self-making through digital cultures, globally connected employment within the fashion, media and textiles sector and increasing access to transnational flows of creative education (Mora et al. 2014). For Kuldova and Varghese, neoliberalism in South Asia is leading to a culture of both excess and expulsion, proposing that 'special economic zones, the GDP-centred developmentalism, the corporate state, the liquidation of public spaces, and the increase of the spectacular and excessive can be all seen also as the signs of the materialization of exclusions' (2017: 7).

We hope that our inclusive South Asian comparative frame will have intrinsic value for regional specialists of South Asia, as also for those specialising in other emerging fashion regions, whether post-Soviet Russia, Latin America, and East and Central Asia, or MENA, and sub-Saharan Africa. In the mix of approaches and critical frameworks utilised by our authors we also see the richness of cross fertilisation between related research fields. Conceptualising youth cultures as historically and spatially located, our contributors provide corollaries for and correctives to the canon of subcultural youth studies initially formulated in relation to western, male and white youth cultures. In locating youth cultures in relation to regional economies and state cultural policies, the essays here feed into several strands of postcolonial cultural studies, framed by an understanding of multiple and alternative modernities (Breckenridge 1995; Eisenstadt 2000; Gaonkar 2001), situating class in relation to caste and religion, and identifying how experiences of gender, as of generation, are similarly intersectional.

We have chosen contributors from a number of different fields, finding richness in their range of critical registers and methodological approaches. Readers will find a creative tension in the use of terms and concepts; whilst we endeavour in this introduction to provide a sufficiently cohesive explanation of key terms and concepts and the different ways in which they are used to help navigate the book, in the chapters that follow our contributors – driven in part by the distinctiveness of their particular case studies – may utilise terms and disciplinary frames in different ways. Our contributors use a variety of visual, literary, and material sources and generate a range of data in their research field. This includes ethnographic interviews and observation and several approaches to visuality, space and the dressed body. As well as more conventional forms of data gathering and presentation, we also feature two photo essays, allowing creative practitioners to provide different observations on the processes and politics of styling for representation of the South Asian body. If the resultant images aimed to intervene into a variety of related pictorial codes, so too do their conditions of production – as discussed here – intervene into the gendered, classed, and religiously marked spaces of South Asia and its diasporas, revealing the socialising impact of spatial relations and the spatialisations of society (Massey 1994).

CONSTRUCTING YOUTH: GENERATION, CLASS, GENDER, RELIGION

As with the best work in popular and media studies, the case studies in this book demonstrate the ways in which South Asian youth cultures relate to and reframe the multiple cultural forms and social conventions of South Asian societies. This collection's insights into how the South Asian and diaspora context often foregrounds religious and religio-ethnic components of individual and group identity provides a valuable antidote to the secularist presumptions that have often underpinned studies in youth and popular culture, as in fashion studies. Rather than regard religion as a specialist research field and an inevitably minority experience, our contributors elegantly integrate the myriad ways in which religious and spiritual cultures and beliefs inform the dressing, styling, presentation, and reception of bodies, matching this to the consideration of other intersectional factors, each spatially and temporally located.

Whilst many in the West are concerned with, or celebrating, the perceived return of religion to the public square (whether by recognising as religion new practices and beliefs or detecting apparently unchanged the reactivation of previous modes of religious behaviour (Hoelzl and Ward 2008; Woodhead and Catto 2012), the fact that, in parts of the world including South Asia, religion never went away has long provided questions for the secularisation thesis. Religion has not remained static, and this book provides several compelling examples of how youth cultures are framed by religion and belief in South Asian and diaspora contexts; including the navigation of codes of honour and shame, changing attitudes to the body and its representation, and the use of fashion media – especially the increasingly affordable and available mobile smart devices of digital fashion social media. In attending to religious and religio-ethnic cultures and practices, the differences between co-religionists and the policing of boundaries against those considered heterodox reveal fault lines that go beyond national or political boundaries.

In all of this, social class plays a distinctive role, given that in South Asian regions such as India class is foregrounded in caste. At present it is clear that the access created to symbolic capital through increasing means of consumption, production and labour force mobility have weakened caste ties (Beteille 1996; Sheth 1999), and further studies looking at the interconnections of social class and caste, especially in relation to dress and embodiment, remain urgent. Studies on youth and class in the region, particularly India and Nepal, establish that middle-class-ness is a contested category, not easily definable or homogenous (Liechty 2003; Mazarella 2006; Osella and Osella 1998), particularly as South Asian regions move away from savings-ethics towards consumption and consumer cultures (Srivastava 2007; Jeffery 2010). In the context of modernism, liberalism and rapid economic growth (varying across the region), our contributors reveal the many shifting, contested, and competing sub-categories of 'middle-class' that characterise the South Asian context, explicating, for example, the nuanced distinctions between lower-middle-class and middle-middle-class as gendered as well as age-related classifications. As Nisbett cautions, an overly inclusive definition of middle-class status 'that includes "schoolteachers in the moffusil" [small towns] and jet-setting corporate executives assumes too many similarities between the social norms, status, ambition and means of a very disparate group of people' (Nisbett 2009: 32). Crucially, as Mazarella (2006) has written, the problem is not how the term middle-class is used but why it has come to dominate; 'what is more interesting is to attempt to understand how the concept structures and enables a certain set of imagined identities – both utopian and dystopian – to be articulated' (Mazarella 2006: 3). This is particularly of relevance to sartorial identities, as class has come to be continually and dynamically practiced by 'doing fashion' (Liechty 2003: 135–140). In the Indian, and now wider South Asian, context, doing fashion is often conceptualised in relation to the contrast between style and 'ishtyle' (Nakassis 2016; Srivastava 2007). Ishstyle, the north Indian borrowing of the English term style and fashion now commonly used in Bangladesh, Pakistan and Sri Lanka, is often used to suggest the fashion choices of the rural or non-middle-class population characterised as gaudy and excessive in contrast to the 'more sophisticated' aesthetic embodied by the cosmopolitan upper-middle classes and consecrated by fashion advertising and editorial (Srivastava 2007: 227). Osella and Osella (1998) note how ishtyle serves as a referent for the film-driven vernacular aesthetic of working-class taste.

The growing liberalisation of Indian fashion, retail, media and advertising since the 1990s (Athique 2012), includes an increased focus on social mobility and the acquisition of social status through the consumption of material goods in fashion blogs, beauty magazines, to retail advertising (Mazzarella 2006). As elsewhere, clothing continues to function as a visual indicator of class status, cultural capital, and is imbricated in forms of social belonging and exclusion (Bourdieu 1984). The formation of social identity through consumption of global and local consumer goods in South Asia is intertwined with and shaped by the long history of social and religious hierarchies and colonisation of the region dating back to the sixth century (Shukla 2008). This is complicated by the interconnectedness between rural and urban geographies, class, gender and larger processes of globalisation and nationalism.

The doing of style is both spatially and temporally contingent and differentially available to men and women. As well as being a characteristic of youth as a life stage, the concept of 'waiting', or 'timepass' (Jeffrey 2010), is itself a key dimension of doing style, in the setting of offices, colleges, shopping malls, and cinemas, that make middle-class youth highly visible. This is particularly relevant for men who are more visible than women in public spaces within the region. Class differences are prevalent in the way that lower-middle-class male youth engage with fashion and style. Threats to middle-class power in India are often especially keenly felt by lower-middle-class educated men excluded from secure employment (Nisbett 2009: 9), and therefore educated employed men feel they need to pass time in new ways, with simply hanging around doing style (Nakassis 2016) emerging as a method for negotiating not being left behind but engaging with material representations of masculine success (Osella and Osella 1998).

For female youth, everyday dress practices are shaped by a multiplicity of moral codes of dress, closely linked to religious, familial and community expectations of heterosexuality, including South Asian traditions of arranged marriages (Liechty 1995). Social expectations of how one should dress and behave are frequently framed by the recurring theme of shame (*lajja/lojja/laaj*) and honour (*izzat/ijat*). South Asian youth of both genders use 'code-switching' appearance management techniques to dress differently for familial domains or social scenes, switching between traditional clothes for the home and family events and western clothing for school or the workplace (Bhachu 2004).

Most prominent in women's dress, sartorial code-switching is an ambivalent mode of appearance management. Code-switching is not always a choice nor a conscious system of dressing and, similar to other non-south Asian regions, is symbolic of wider regimes of patriarchal power enacted upon the female body and sexuality (Entwistle 2000). In the South Asian region however, this is complicated further by the history of anti- and post-colonial and national struggles against western forms of modernisation inseparable from western capitalism.

The dichotomous meanings attached to traditional and western clothes going back to the Gandhian *Swadesi* (self-rule) independence movement, have left an ongoing and gendered legacy. In a paradoxical anti-consumption independence narrative, the boycotting of western consumer goods was promoted alongside the consumption of more local products. The *Swadesi* movement did not simply boycott foreign clothes and western clothes on economic grounds; they were also to be disavowed as symbols of western capitalism and sexual hedonism (Hardiman 2003; Trivedi 2007). Local patriarchies meant that this moral consumption discourse impacted differently on Indian women than men. Where men adopted western clothing after Indian independence, women were expected to retain traditional dress choices to mark their role as guardians of nationhood (Tarlo 1996). To this day, in many parts of South Asia, western clothing is associated with western modernity in ways strongly linked to cultural loss and hyper-sexuality, whilst traditional clothes are more routinely associated with chastity, nationhood and cultural and religious purity (Begum and Dasgupta 2015; Tarlo 1996). In countries such as Pakistan and Bangladesh, these patriarchal and nationalistic meanings are further complicated by Islamic codes of modest dressing (also see Cook 2005).

As several of our contributors reveal, the meanings of code-switching between western and traditional dress are shifting. Switching to western clothes is no longer mostly perceived as symbolic of western values and western capitalism, but may also be perceived as forms of fashioning resistance related to becoming, performativity, desire and comfort.

Early associations of style and subculture (whether mods, goths, or punks) with forms of resistance and youth (Davis 1992; Hebdige 1979; Polhemus 2010), are now under review with attention to 'adult' participation in subcultures as a potentially ongoing life-project (Bennet and Hodkinson 2012). In the context of South Asia, when rural ishstyle (Srivastava 2007) is adopted by affluent upper-middle-class hipsters, what may seem like resistance may also be a 'counterculture insult' – an anti-fashion movement that integrates easily with mainstream fashion, despite being an anti-fashion statement (Davis 1992).

Whilst South Asian subcultural trends have been under-researched, there are a number of similarities to the interplay of resistance and appropriation and accommodation identified in research on non South Asian subcultures. In this book some of the dress choices that South Asian youth are making reflect emerging movements of resistance against socio-political power structures similar to those previously documented by South Asian and non-South Asian scholars of the region, such as the Taqwacore Punk Pakistani Muslim scene (Murthy 2010), Hip-Hop Desis in the USA (Sharma 2010), Asian Kool of the 1990s in the UK (Sharma 2006), British Bhangra Style (Dudrah 2016) and 'freak style' in Tamil Nadu (Osella and Osella 1998).

The people described in the chapters of this book are able to play with their dress choices to varying extents, mixing and matching South Asian and non-South Asian styles as they negotiate conventional or prevailing classifications of gender and sexuality, moving between resistance and control. Indian feminist demands for sexual freedom linked to the freedom to choose what to wear are heartening resistant tactics; (Menon 2012; McRobbie 2000) yet the violence that underlies socially-sanctioned eve teasing combines with class-based divisions of public space to produce persistent and structural forms of gender, class, and caste exclusion.

As this book demonstrates, it is not enough simply to widen the frame of fashion to include South Asian styles, bodies, and markets: it is imperative that these new examples and the new understandings they bring are used to recalibrate the still often universalised norms that underwrite fashion practice, marketing, media, and, sometimes, academic fashion studies. One such instance is the often-thoughtless sanctification of the street as a zone of fashion innovation and style in global fashion media and in some academic studies. The varying degrees of access to, and comfort and discomfort in, the space of the street discussed in these South Asian contexts will doubtless find parallels in studies of other non-western and emerging markets, as too in the dis/comfort of migrant, refugee, and minority populations in the long-standing Euro-American and Australian capitals of the 'fashion world'.

Fashion cultures may be closely linked to attempts by minority groups and religious groups to distinguish themselves. We see this with North-American 'turban chic', an assemblage of heterogenous discourses about 'religious identity, fashionability, terrorism and pathologized South Asian immigrant bodies and labour' (Reddy 2016: 209). In queer youth cultures, we note how the particularities of queer youth differ from adult queer concerns (Pullen 2014). In the context of a colonial legal legacy and postcolonial struggles over the morality of the individual qua the nation, key sites of struggle in queer life such as coming out, education and bullying are compounded by the lack of historical documentation of queer South Asian communities. Into this gap, this book uses visual and cultural analysis of photography and film to explore how queer South Asian youth within South Asia and its diasporas perform their sexual identities by breaking gendered norms of dressing (see Chapters 4 and 5). As studies of sexuality and histories move away from their Eurocentric focus, also prompted by critical studies of heteronormativity and multiple modernities and histories of sexuality, future research is yet to develop on queer youth cultures across the South Asian regions. It should be noted that Nepal has become the first state in South Asia to enshrine anti-discriminatory provisions for sexual minorities, a big statement when its near neighbours India and Pakistan still criminalise queer people (Dasgupta 2017; Dasgupta 2014; Dasgupta and Gokulsing 2014). Scholarship on queer youth cultures has mostly focused on popular and independent cinema, however there is scope to examine self-making through sartorial depiction of queer youth cultures within creative practices such as online magazines, Tumblr pages and graphic arts; for example, in 2015, Boys of Bangladesh, the country's largest gay rights group, launched '*Dhee*' Bangladesh's first lesbian comic strip to raise awareness against lesbian discrimination.

FASHION AND STYLE-PRODUCTION AND CONSUMPTION IN THE SOUTH ASIAN CONTEXT

It is evident in this book that South Asian youth are increasingly taking part in style-production as well as consumption. Networks of fashion production and consumption have both deepened and widened in South Asia with easier access to modes of production such as digital media and, on a grand scale, garment manufacturing and global free trade zones across the region. Since the 2000s, the economic success of the region's garment manufacturing sectors linked to outsourcing of fast fashion manufacturing from the West has generated competition within the region to stabilise large orders from global fashion retailers.

Countries like Pakistan and Sri Lanka, which have been overshadowed directly by separatist independence movements from India (see Chakma 2014) have launched their own successful international fashion weeks and have taken part in London Fashion Week's International Fashion Showcase, a platform that includes other emerging fashion regions such as Latin America and Africa (http://design.britishcouncil.org/projects/ifs/). Participation in such events is part of national development strategies to promote the country as a high quality, reliable destination for outsourcing, making and manufacturing. Global fashion events demonstrate the complicated and multiple ways in which cultural imperialism is reproduced and re-orientalised (Niessen et al. 2003) through the need to compete with Eurocentric standards of fashion. However, these competitive activities can also create countertrends and opportunities for agency, indicating the complex relationships between indigenous local 'costumes' and colonial modes of dress (Banaji 2006; Roach and Eicher 2007; Wilson 2005), as traditional codes of dressing are reframed by globalised conditions of economic change. In the case of Pakistan and Sri Lanka, access to global fashion networks and access to formalised creative education has prompted local designers to research and showcase 'lost' sartorial identities erased by religiously inflected nationalist and colonialist movements. This complicates classical orientalist theoretical frameworks (Niessen et al. 2003; Said 1978) that would suggest power relations as only oppressive and flowing from West to East.

In the early years of economic liberalisation in Nepal, as Liechty's study in the mid 1990s demonstrated, it was young people in particular who began to frame themselves in terms of materiality and consumer culture (Liechty 1995). At that point, aspiration for consumer lifestyles was both generic and framed in relation to global youth cultures which were then becoming more accessible through new forms of media transmission such as satellite television. Similarly, in the lesser documented regional consumer cultures of Bhutan, the recent global popularity of the Bhutan Street Fashion blog[1] illustrates how strict national dress codes imposed since the 1990s in Bhutan are becoming blurred by the availability of western-style clothing influenced by a larger global youth culture made accessible through the proliferation of Internet access through mobile phones (Newbold 2016). However, these countries are marked by an inability to accommodate satisfactorily local aspirations and diverse social and political agendas within the national agendas of the different constituent countries. This can be seen in a number of ways, such as the new constitution of Nepal in 2015 which, despite its progressive attitudes over certain issues such as secularism, has been marked by widespread protest over the refusal to recognise class and minority status in Bhutan (see Rizal 2015).

Popular Indian cinema has nearly always been the referent for style coverage in South Asian media (Dwyer 2000; Gokulsing and Dissanayake 2012). Bollywood, having overtaken any other form of Indian and South

Asian cinema, remains a potent site for interrogating diverse histories of style and fashion within the subcontinent. In Hindi cinema actors and actresses switch seamlessly between western and regional styles without the dichotomous connotations of Indian dress as traditional and modern dress as western. It is not to say that orientalist legacies or the pressures of globalisation tied to Americanisation (Lukose 2009) within sartorial styles across South Asia have disappeared. However, the increasing revival of local dress within its own non-western fashion system as a site of fantasy and desire, productive of pleasure, challenges and complicates hegemonic western and non-western fashion systems which render local fashions as other to and inferior to the West or the rest.

Cinema has conventionally been linked to the music industry in the region (not least through revenue from music sales (Dudrah and Malik 2017; Gokulsing and Dissanayake 2012), and the growing digital landscape means that music cultures themselves play an increasing role in the development and spread of style cultures. South Asian singers such as Ali Zafar from Pakistan, Neeti Mohan and transnational diaspora artists such as rapper Heems (USA), singers Alo Wala (USA) and M.I.A (UK) and Shapla Salique (UK) are changing the listening experience and emerging as style icons. The connection between popular music and individual personality is not just limited to pop artistes: rather, as Frith (1996: 185) has argued, 'as listeners we assume we can hear someone's life in their voice'. Most of these artists are regular fixtures on music programmes produced by MTV, Coke Studio and The Deewarists, representing aspirational cultural and social capital on programmes that endorse luxury consumer lifestyles only accessible to a middle-class target audience.

As in other regions, 'fashion, blogging, and photography as technologies of the self come together through a fourth technology of the self, a contemporary space of individual expression: the computer screen' (Rocamora 2015: 414). In South Asia the extension of Internet infrastructure and the increased affordability of mobile smart devices (phones, tablets) brings interactive social media and e-commerce into the reach of vastly more of the population. As elsewhere, the opportunity to become a social media 'influencer' can be a major reputation building opportunity and potential income stream for designers and creatives. Several well-known South Asian designers such as Neeta Lulla, Manish Malhotra, Shivan and Naresh all have a strong online and social media presence. The reach of social media allows youth brands such as NorBlack NorWhite (NBNW) to reach out and sell to a mixture of South Asian, South Asian diaspora and non-south Asian fans outside of India through their online store.[2] A strong Instagram presence, fashion gifs, video blogs and posting of the designer's studio life and collections inspired by black North-American and Caribbean cultures are some of the ways NBNW followers engage with the brand's strong transnational and diaspora Indian strategy. In Pakistan, the popular online brand Secret Closet[3] features regular blog columns and videos. In India, *Vogue India* regularly publicises successful Indian fashion bloggers who have developed cult followings around the world. These online platforms, like digital fashion cultures across the world, are not just entrepreneurial enterprises, or a means to ship products across trade barriers; they serve as platforms that tell transnational stories exploring brand cultures, street-style and local events and youth cultures. Digital platforms allow South Asian bloggers to stage a presence and compete in the global fashion industry.

South Asian sartorial practises of code-switching are revisited, played out and blurred on online platforms. For example, Myntra.com (accessed 20th April 2018), an online shopping platform for designer lingerie, allows young Indian women to purchase lingerie in private and away from traditional male vendors and at the same time allows them to publicly engage with their sexuality through personal profiles and discussion groups available on the site. Where once South Asian youth would pursue courtship through love-letters and arranged marriages, these online shopping practices reflect some of the changing attitudes that youth in South Asia have towards marriage, gender, sexuality and companionate marriage (Dasgupta 2017; Nisbett 2009), indicating how dominant codes of gender and sexuality are being challenged, resisted and also reconfigured through sartorial practices. For young people, the discretion afforded by mobile devices permits social media participation unmonitored (less monitored) by the passing eye of parents and elders: young women may find themselves stalked and trolled online in ways that re-exert pre-existing codes of shame and honour, and may themselves surveille the social media profiles of prospective marriage partners.

Personal fashion blogs as gendered spaces of introspection and surveillance, have also enabled those traditionally excluded from fashion imagery to enter its visual scape (Rocamora 2015: 414).

Further changes to creative practice and production are also marked by global shifts within the fashion and textiles sector making fashion imports more readily available. In the case of Bhutan, increasing tourism correlates with increased imports of western fashion brands. In Bangladesh, production of global fast fashion brands through its ready-made garment sector has fostered the critical debate around the production and consumption of sustainable fashion.[4]

Bangladesh, once derided as an economic basket case by western economists, is now hailed as a best practice scenario for India and its regions, in terms of re-connecting with inherently positive gender values and activism (Begum and Anjum 2018) to develop a successful ready-made garments sector (Drèze and Sen 2013). It is also home to a rich history of a crafts and textiles industry that is pioneering development and sustainable design processes (Parker 2011) such as artisan and designer collaborations using natural dyes[5] and intergenerational practices to ensure the preservation and revival of heritage fabrics and their respective artisan weaving communities.[6] Yet, the exponential growth of Bangladesh's ready-made garment sector in the past twenty years, now the second largest in the world after China, has also produced challenges connected to exploitative capital flows of the western fast fashion industry (Fletcher 2016), including factory fires, precarity, gendered divisions of labour, un-sustainable mass-migration and low pay (Begum and Anjum 2018; Hewamanne 2008; Saxena 2014).

Evidence from recent research on the creative industries in Bangladesh highlights the potential for rapid growth in the areas of fashion and design as a result of the country's growing ready-made-garment sector (British Council 2013) and increasing numbers of second and third generation diaspora youth pursuing art and design education pathways (Begum and Anjum 2017). In Britain, Lipi Begum has been working with the creative collective Oitij-jo[7] to promote the creative industries, including the fashion design and textiles creative industries of Bangladeshi heritage in Britain and Bangladesh. A large part of the project involves intergenerational skills-sharing between young diaspora designers working with craft communities in Bangladesh. These sustainability projects bring into the South Asian artisan theatre a set of British-born, diaspora subjects who themselves consider the cross generational transmission of skills and dispositions as essential to their success. In Britain, Reina Lewis has been working with a group of industry professionals to establish the British Asian Fashion Network, a pan-Asian organisation intended to celebrate and promote the contribution of Asians to fashion and textiles in Britain and to the British Asian fashion industries.[8] In Pakistan, the creative industries are an important contributor to the country's employment base, providing opportunities for skills development, entrepreneurship and business start-up – though with the notable exception of fashion design (British Council 2014). However, for youth from lower socio-economic backgrounds in South Asia and its diasporas, success within the fashion industry and the creative industries continues to be challenged by eurocentric cultural and creative policy, lack of access to creative education, social capital and, to an extent, the finance necessary for local creative start-up businesses, including fashion start-up businesses (Begum and Anjum 2017; Dudrah and Malik 2017). This is comparable to other regions of the global south where, as in MENA, poor employment prospects for artisan work (many of whom are South Asian migrant workers from South Asia) mean that youth do not see the value in continuing family artisan businesses. Within the British South Asian fashion industry many first-generation designers, who have themselves maintained relationships with artisans in the sub-continent over decades, report concerns that younger designers, Asian and non-Asian, lack knowledge about what artisan skills can do and often lack the social capital necessary for brokering successful working relationships with small artisan businesses. This combination, they fear, threatens and compounds the ongoing reduction within South Asia of the artisan skills base.

CHAPTER OUTLINES

In a book concerned with youth cultures and fashion it is refreshing to see an understanding of temporality that can situate reportage about youth cultures and fashions of the moment in relation to the styling of youth from the past. The photo essay by Sunil Gupta and Charan Singh looks back at their earlier agenda-setting projects, providing the inside scoop on the conditions of production that allowed the work to go forward. For Gupta, seeking to provide for India a documentation of contemporary queer cultures post-economic liberalisation and the absence of a 'queer public street' became central to the staging of educated, middle-class alternate sexualities. For Singh, the gravitas of portraiture served to bring into the studio the non-elite youth usually disregarded by the posterity-creating gaze of commemorative visual culture. Their reflections on process and on their changing relationships with sitters bring the creative visual arts into developments in post-subcultural studies: no longer regarded as a temporary youthful phenomenon, forms of subcultural knowledge and capital can be understood as carried through life and transmitted in both directions between generations. For queer subcultures this is especially apposite; the photographers' ability to situate their intervention in relation both to the western norms that so often underwrite ideas of a 'gay international' and to histories of gender in South Asian visuality bring rich insights.

The photographic engagement with mass media forms in the manufacture and staging of queer masculinities, highlighted by Singh, dovetails with the account of how Indian auteur and media personality Rituparno Ghosh was variously and variably visible as queer to his diverse audiences across a long career. Making adroit use of gossip that circulated at the time to create knowledge for those who knew what to look for, Rohit K. Dasgupta and Kaustav Bakshi argue that Ghosh deliberately used his embodied public presence on and off screen to validate effeminate forms of masculinity as an alternative to dominant heteronormative definitions of proper manliness. Emblematic to many gay men in the decades before he came out, the subcultural competencies required to share in the gay pleasures of insider knowledge are learned through immersion into a cultural world that historically, and still now, has often been disregarded, trivialised, and stigmatised.

In contexts where codes of honour and shame produce forms of surveillance that intersect with caste, class, gender, religion and nation, the changeable mixture of religious cultural norms, as Lipi Begum elaborates in her account of advertising and retail in the bra sector in

India, suffuses the spaces of representation and the spaces of the market. Discourses of female respectability and sexuality, reframed by rising Hindu nationalism, produce a circuit of culture in which where and from whom you buy your bra (male vendors at 'Chinese' market stalls or the privacy of e-commerce) can have as much impact on the purchase choice as brand advertising featuring Bollywood actresses. Tracking the discursive life of the garment in the construction of modern urban femininities, Begum draws out how young and youngish women demonstrate micro-generational change in attitudes to the body, with discussions about bra selection creating conduits for the production and transmission of knowledge about sex and reproductive health.

Two of the sequences in Raisa Kabir's photo essay articulate and re-imagine the regulatory powers of religiously coded spaces, restaging the prayer spaces of Islam in ways that render illusory the idealised egalitarianism of the mosque. For one woman, the segregation of women within the mosque can be subverted by replacing the headscarf or *hijab* – seen as symbolic of female seclusion – with a beanie cap that stands in for the man's topi or prayer cap. But for another female worshipper the dangers of the mosque space are beyond recuperation. Collaborating to create a sacralised mosque-like space for a non-binary identified individual to pray safely, Kabir's image connects the specifics of a London South Asian diasporic experience to an alternative Muslim imaginary which, often under the rubric of progressive Islam, seeks (off and online) to house inclusive interpretations of the faith for the supranational multi-ethnic umma or community of believers.

The accounts by the three photographers foreground the importance of relationships with artists and attachments to cultural producers for social subjects otherwise culturally marginalised or disenfranchised. Like the possessive pleasure of 'knowing' about Ghosh's queerness before he came out, the connections with artists equipped to 'see' the queer body perform important personal, social, and political as well as artistic cultural work. For young Hindu Surinamese women in the Netherlands, as Priya Swamy discusses, mediatised cultural representations are differently valued by successive generations and micro-generations. Fashions and related models of femininity for which Bollywood movies previously provided diaspora inspiration are viewed critically by young women, selectively rejecting or adapting the movie industry's predominant modes of Indian or Hindu or Hindustani femininity.

In generally heteronormative South Asian postcolonial contexts, youth is constituted for many social groups as a period of freedom before marriage. Dressed embodiment and youth cultural practices provide opportunities for the development of forms of capital and agency that – in contingent and constrained ways – can be used by young people to challenge the limits of permissibility and to create social assets with the potential to be transformative in future adult life. The ways in which youthful dress and behaviours are spatially and temporally relational to both the lifespan of the individual and to wider political and social change are illustrated by Sandya Hewamanne's ethnographic study of Sinhalese Buddhist rural women workers in a Sri Lankan clothing factory. Transgressing gender norms in trousers and assertively refusing to adhere to middle-class aesthetics in their valorisation of colour and embellishment, newcomers are inducted, sometimes pressured, into distinctive group dress practices that forge collective identities and loyalties in a work context that outlaws collective trade union associations. Subject to surveillance by local men working in the Free Trade Zone (FTZ) of Katunayake, the women maintain village dress conventions on visits home because they will have to dress in this way when they move back, often, ideally, to get married, after the temporary young adult experience of living in the city for work. Social capital developed in the FTZ may be strategically re-developed in the village setting, to build new networks essential to surviving married life in sometimes their husband's village.

Code-switching between multiple co-existent fashion and dress systems is revealed in this book as a widely honed skills set among South Asian young people, deployed both to dress and style their own bodies and to read and evaluate those of others. Regarded as not yet fully responsible, youth may be permitted heightened flexibility in wardrobe choices, which as Sarah Shepherd-Manandhar discusses in relation to young women of 'marriage' age in Nepal, provides opportunities to operationalise fashion capital to gain leverage in arranged marriage processes. Moving between garments designated locally as 'modern' (jeans, imported garments) or 'traditional' (*saris* for married women or *kurta surawel* for unmarried) available in the Kathmandu consumption-scape, young women utilise fashion judgements to read consumption practices as indicators of their potential futures with husbands and their families. It is well established that the dressed embodiment and visible consumption practices of women are seen as an indicator of, or threat to, the social status of families or kin; fascinating here is how the extension of the surveilling gaze to digital communications opens vistas for young women to intervene, as with one young woman who mobilised women elders in her rejection of a suitor as insufficiently modern for her future when their online investigation revealed that he was never pictured on Facebook in jeans.

The ways in which young people consciously stage their dressed embodiment in relation to an understanding of themselves as owner of and subject to the regulatory gaze on and offline is brought forward across the book. If one young man in Kathmandu may be disappointed to discover that the aspirational western commodities featured on his bride's social media were fake, and that she is not engaged in the level of status-building consumption he desired for his family, other young people in Bhutan collaborate to share valued western goods in the collective achievement of cool. As Paul Strickland reports, the interest shown by young people in western and imported fashion in the context of government mandated 'national' dress raises concerns about losing authentic Bhutanese identity. Here, point of origin blurs the divide between western and Asian styles and commodities, so that jeans manufactured in China or India may hover between categories for Bhutanese consumers aware of unequal power relations with neighbouring Asian superpowers. In addition to a fluid classification system, it is also clear that the processes by which western clothing is indigenised represent an adaptation of existing local customs and of western clothes: youth lend costly western garments, building the social capital of conventional family and kin affiliations into youth based friendship networks that, underwritten by Buddhist ethics of sharing, allow them to pool fashion goods in a collective project of staging modern Bhutanese identities.

Collective understandings of what counts as cool underwrite the complex mechanisms of style in Sneha Krishnan's account of student life in Chennai. The co-ordinates of space and time essential to the doing of 'style' – hanging out, performing leisure by doing nothing, in public places – are gender and class specific with finely nuanced distinctions between lower- and middle-class young people demarcated by choice of clothes and place of display. The politics of the gaze – looking, constituting oneself as object of gaze, and gazing oneself – bring significant risk for young women in South Asian urban spaces where the flâneur's loitering is likely to bring police attention for gender deviant behaviour. In addition to formal regulation, so called 'eve teasing' recurs across the book as a determinant of and impediment to women's access to public spaces and public transport with male peers as well as elders regulating young women's behaviour. Yet, young women may sometimes be able to turn routinised eve teasing into banter, co-opting the college bus-stop as temporary stage for the presentation of scene where they nonchalantly flick hair whilst sizing up passing boys, ready to appear ironic and self-knowing and using big sisterly mocking to puncture the posture of youthful male cool.

Arti Sandhu reflects on her difficulties in dressing for the street of Delhi fashion week when public transport is a hazard and the physical environment outside of the gated commercial space of the fashion week provides a very different set of interlocutors for the style efforts now mandated as industry standard for attendees. In India, the fashion discourse of street style reframes both constituent terms. Street is reconceptualised in relation to the recently created privatised spaces of consumption and elite/middle-class leisure which protect affluent dressers from dirt, noise, and the general public gaze, and for women, the persistent sexual harassment of eve teasing. Style is also repositioned as a component of the post-liberalisation economy; emblematised by the new liberal subject of the 'global Desi', the Indian at ease with transnational consumer goods and consumer behaviours. Whilst style is performed for the media and fashion public in the corralled spaces of Delhi fashion week, the urbanised fashion elite reify the dress of subaltern bodies excluded from the temporality and spatiality of modernity, commodifying traditional, regional, or folk style, and artisan techniques, colours, and textiles as aesthetic inspiration.

The contrast between the shabby chic of the youthful fashion elite and the real holes in the clothing of the poor underlies Tereza Kuldova's polemic. Identifying participation in esteem-enhancing fashion events, such as designer Nitin Bal Chauhan's fashion shows 'street cast' from the cohort of fashion insiders and avant-garde creatives who make up his brand 'family', she discusses how the younger generation are pivotal to the construction of the ideal consumer citizen of the post-liberalisation Indian economy. Glorified as emblematic of Indian success yet chided for irresponsible spending by financially prudent parents, corporate social responsibility recalibrates consumption as a moral obligation, despite that the subaltern makers and craftspeople are rarely appropriately rewarded.

FUTURE DIRECTIONS

In the past decade young people in South Asia have become important participants in popular culture narratives, consumerist market economies, the fashion and textile sector, and media cultures. Young people through their several modes of representation have challenged us to re-think and re-imagine youth cultures (also see Boyce and Dasgupta 2017). In this book we see how the South Asian youth fashion landscape is increasingly changing as local dress cultures collide with global fashion cultures, and subcultural styles collide with styles on the street. Complex patterns of change do not follow a simple pattern of western imperial mimesis. Classificatory binaries of modern/traditional, Asian/western, male/female, artisan/designer have not disappeared, but are rapidly changing and increasingly understood as ambiguous as a result of globalisation, trade liberalisation and multivalent mediated processes between South Asia and rest of the world.

South Asia may be still shaped by the dichotomising classifications of what it is to be traditional and be modern. Yet increasingly scholars studying South Asia and dress cultures, including authors in this book, seek to acknowledge alternative modernities (Breckenridge 1995; Gaonkar 2001) with future work likely to incorporate attention to the long history of men and women's fashion in South Asia that pre-dates classification systems of modern and traditional (Begum and Dasgupta 2015; Shukla 2008; Vanita 2014). Our authors mark a shift beyond Bollywood towards online and digital platforms such as street-fashion blogs, YouTube videos and online fashion stores. Future work exploring technology and digital cultures is still required to understand virtual identity amongst a youth demographic group which has the highest digital media usage in South Asia (Athique 2012). This is likely to further emphasise the heterogeneity of South Asian sartorial identity, a heterogeneity that this book strongly points towards.

Future research that can document and analyse the intra-South Asian and diaspora social relationships which underlie globalised fashion production in the South Asian context will be essential to new understandings of the fashion industry, disallowing orientalist east/west collectivist/individualist binarisms by demonstrating the complex workings of capital and culture within a network of multiple modernities and postmodernities. A desire to mitigate fashion's role in contributing to social and environmental damage is now prevalent among fashion students, designers, creative entrepreneurs, and consumers: cautioning against simplistic good intentions, this book provides evidence and analysis of the network of business, government, NGO, and diaspora relationships, including the role of postcolonial elites which foster or inhibit success in sustainable fashion. We hope that this volume's attention to different national, ethnic and cultural business cultures, and to complex layers of collectivism and individualism will provide demonstrable value to the research field in fashion marketing and studies of the creative industries more widely.

One significant change since we started working on this project has been the constitution of Muslims as a global consumer segment, an expansion of previous ethnic marketing into the faith sector. It is well established that in South Asia the creation of class identities and pursuance of class interests intersect with regionally specific divisions of caste and 'tribe' as well as with local variants of gender, sexuality, and age. The role of religion as a factor in communal, regional and national politics is also evident in scholarship to date as in this volume, whilst the incorporation of religious distinction into the formation of regional consumer cultures has been discussed in ground-breaking studies by Mazarella (2006). Yet, whilst marketing activity has so far focused on the petro-dollar, super-rich consumers of the Gulf, and on the growing middle classes of Indonesia and the Philippines, the availability of Muslim consumers with spending power in parts of South Asia will raise different opportunities and challenges: despite that the so-called 'Muslim world' contains within it many non-Muslims. What will it mean to hail as Muslim consumers in India, where they form the second largest religious group in a country governed at the time of writing by Modi's Hindu nationalist Bharatiya Janata Party (BJP)? Will South Asia provide a catalyst for global brands to commodify other forms of institutional religion? Given that marketing does not merely reflect pre-existing forms of social identity but is itself generative of new forms of identity, what might be the impact of the commodification of religious dispositions on the syncretic blending of traditions that makes up daily religious practice (Ammerman 2007; McGuire 2008) for so many in the region? At a point when the extension to South Asia of Islamic branding and Muslim marketing to South Asia looks inevitable we hope this volume will be of value to researchers in critical marketing studies. The rich heterogeneity of the studies here come through from the intersectional and multi-disciplinary background of our authors, illustrating sartorial codes and fashion practices across the spectrum of gender, class, race, sexuality and religion, which are often homogenised in academic fashion studies pertaining to this region. Nonetheless, we encountered limitations: further work is required to advance understandings of caste and its relation to youth cultures and dress. Geographically, we were unable to cover equally the richness of style across all the South Asian regions: Afghanistan, Pakistan and the Maldives remain absent from this collection but we believe that initiating the dialogue on youth and style cultures in emerging fashion markets like Bhutan, Bangladesh and under-researched South Asian diaspora communities can only encourage further research and add to the existing dress cultures knowledge for this complicated region, enabling consumer culture theorists, scholars of dress cultures and cross-cultural marketers across the world to better understand alternative formations of South Asian identity.

NOTES

1. See www.facebook.com/BhutanStreetFashion. Accessed 20th April 2018.
2. See www.norblacknorwhite.com. Accessed 20th April 2018.
3. See www.secretcloset.pk/blog. Accessed on 20th April 2018.
4. See www.fashionrevolution.org. Accessed 20th April 2018.
5. See www.aranya.com.bd. Accessed on 20th April 2018.
6. See www.bengalfoundation.org. Accessed 20th April 2018.
7. See oitijjofdtc.wordpress.com. Accessed 20th April 2018.
8. See www.bafn.org.uk. Accessed 20th April 2018.

REFERENCES

Ammerman, Nancy T. (2007) 'Introduction: Everyday Religion: Observing Modern Religious Lives', in N.T. Ammerman (ed.), *Everyday Religion: Observing Modern Religious Lives*, Oxford, New York: Oxford University Press.

Anderson, B. (1991) *Imagined Communities*, London: Verso.

Appadurai, A. (1996) *Modernity at Large: Cultural Dimensions of Globalization*, Minneapolis: University of Minnesota Press.

Athique, A. (2012) *Indian Media*, London: Polity.

Banaji, S. (2006) *Reading 'Bollywood' The Young Audience and Hindi Films*, London: Palgrave Macmillan.

Banerjee, M. and Miller, D. (2003) *The Sari*, Oxford: Berg.

Begum, L. and Dasgupta, R.K. (2015) 'Contemporary South Asian Youth Cultures and the Fashion Landscape', *International Journal of Fashion Studies*, 2(1).

Begum, L. and Anjum, M. (2017) 'Beyond the Creative Class, Mapping the Collaborative Economy of Bangladeshi Creative Industries: Case Study of Oitij-jo', in R. Dudrah and K. Malik (eds), South Asian Creative Industries Special Issue, *South Asian Popular Culture* 14(3): 137–153.

——— (2018) 'Friendship Networks as a Mode of Survival and Activism in the Bangladesh Ready-Made-Garment Sector', in N. Banerjea, D. Dasgupta, R. Dasgupta and J. Grant (eds), *Friendship as Social Justice Activism: Critical Solidarities in a Global Perspective*, Chicago: The University of Chicago Press/Seagull India.

Bennett, A. and Hodkinson, P. (eds) (2012) *Ageing and Youth Cultures. Music, Style and Identity*, London & New York: Berg.

Beteille, A. (1996) *Caste in Contemporary India, Caste Today*. C.J. Fuller (ed.), Delhi: Oxford University Press, pp. 1–31.

Bhachu, P. (2004) *Dangerous Designs: Asian Women Fashion the Diaspora Economies*, London: Routledge.

Bourdieu, P. (1984) *Distinction: A Social Critique of the Judgement of Taste*, Cambridge: Harvard University Press.

Boyce, P. and Dasgupta, R.K. (2017). 'Utopia or Elsewhere: Queer Modernities in Small Town West Bengal', in T. Kuldova and M. Varghese (eds), *Urban Utopias: Excess and Expulsion in Neoliberal South Asia*, London: Palgrave Macmillan, pp. 209–225.

Breckenridge, C.A. (ed.) (1995) *Consuming Modernity: Public Culture in a South Asian World*, Minneapolis: University of Minnesota Press.

British Council (2013) *Fashion Industry Mapping in Bangladesh*, British Council: United Kingdom.
British Council (2014) *Cultural and Creative Industries in Pakistan*, British Council: United Kingdom.
Chakma, B. (2014) (ed.) *South Asia in Transition: Democracy, Political Economy and Security*, London: Palgrave Macmillan.
Chatterjee, P. (1993) *The Nation and its Fragments*, New Delhi: Oxford University Press.
Cook, N. (2005) 'What To Wear, What To Wear?: Western Women and Imperialism in Gilgit, Pakistan', *Qualitative Sociology* 28(4): 351–369.
Dasgupta, R.K. (2017) *Digital Queer Cultures in India: Politics, Intimacies and Belonging*, London: Routledge.
——— (2014) 'Articulating Dissident Citizenship, Belonging and Queerness in Cyberspace', *South Asian Review* 35(3): 203–223.
Dasgupta, R.K. and Banerjee, T. (2016). 'Exploitation, Victimhood and Gendered Performance in Rituparno Ghosh's Bariwali', *Film Quarterly* 69(4): 35–46.
Dasgupta, R.K. and Gokulsing, K.M. (2014) *Masculinity and its Challenges in India*, Jefferson, NC: Mcfarland.
Dasgupta, S. (2007) *A South Asian Nationalism Reader*, New Delhi: Worldview.
Datta, S., Bakshi, K. and Dasgupta, R.K. (2015) *Rituparno Ghosh: Cinema, Gender and Art*, London: Routledge.
Davis, F. (1992) *Fashion Culture and Identity*, Chicago: The University of Chicago Press.
Drèze, J. and Sen, A. (2013) *An Uncertain Glory: India and its Contradictions*, Princeton: Princeton University Press.
Dudrah, R. (2016) '"Balle-Balle, Balle-Balle": Fashion – British Bhangra Style', *Atlantic Studies* 13(4): 491–511.
Dudrah, R. and Malik, M. (2017) *South Asian Creative Industries*, Special Issue, *South Asian Popular Culture*.
Dwyer, R. (2000) 'The Erotics of the Wet Sari in Hindi films', *South Asia: Journal of South Asian Studies* 23(2): 143–159.
Eisenstadt, S.N. (2000) 'Multiple Modernities', *Daedelus* 129(1) Winter: 1–29.
Entwistle, J. (2000) *The Fashioned Body: Fashion, Dress and Modern Social Theory*, Cambridge: Polity Press.
Fletcher, K. (2016) *Craft of Use: Post-Growth Fashion*, London: Routledge.
Frith, S. (1996) *Performing Rites: On the Value of Popular Music*. Cambridge: Harvard University Press.
Gaonkar D.P. (2001) *Alternative Modernities*, Durham: Duke University Press.
Gokulsing, K.M. and Dissanayake, W. (2012) *From Aan to Lagaan and Beyond: A Guide to the Study of Indian Cinema*, Staffordshire/London: Trentham/IOE Press.
Gopinath, G. (2005). *Impossible Desires: Queer Diasporas and South Asian Public Cultures*, Durham: Duke University Press.
Hardiman, D. (2003) *Gandhi: In His Time and Ours, the Global Legacy of His Ideas*, New York: Columbia University Press.
Hebdige, D. (1979) *Subculture: The Meaning of Style*, Routledge: London.
Hewamanne, S. (2008) *Stitching Identities in a Free Trade Zone: Gender and Politics in Sri Lanka*, Philadelphia: University of Pennsylvania Press.
Hoelzl, M. and Ward, G. (2008) *The New Visibility of Religion: Studies in Religion and Cultural Hermeneutics*, London: Bloomsbury.
Jeffrey, C. (2010) 'Timepass: Youth, Class, and Time Among Unemployed Young Men in India', *American Ethnologist* 37(3): 465–481.

Kuldova, T. (2016) *Luxury Indian Fashion: A Social Critique*, Bloomsbury: London.
Kuldova, T. and Varghese, M. (2017) 'Introduction: Urban Utopias – Excess and Expulsion in Neoliberal India and Sri Lanka', in T. Kuldova and M. Varghese (eds), *Urban Utopias: Excess and Expulsion in Neoliberal South Asia*, London: Palgrave Macmillan, pp. 1–15.
Liechty, M. (1995) 'Media, Markets and Modernisation: Youth Identities and Experience of Modernity in Kathmandu, Nepal', in V. Amit-Talai and H. Wulff (eds), *Youth Cultures: A Cross Cultural Perspective*, New York: Routledge, pp. 185–202.
Liechty, M. (2003) *Suitably Modern: Making Middle-Class Culture in a New Consumer Society*, Princeton: Princeton University Press.
Lukose, R.A. (2009) *Liberalization's Children: Gender, Youth, and Consumer Citizenship in Globalizing India*, Durham: Duke University Press.
Mani, B. (2003) 'Undressing the Diaspora', in N. Puwar and P. Raghuram (eds), *South Asian Women in the Diaspora*, Oxford: Berg, pp. 117–136.
Massey, D. (1994) *Space, Place and Gender*, Cambridge: Polity Press.
Mazzarella, W. (2006) *Shoveling Smoke: Advertising and Globalization in Contemporary India*, Durham: Duke University Press.
McGuire, M.B. (2008) *Lived Religion: Faith and Practice in Everyday Life*, Oxford, New York: Oxford University Press.
McRobbie, A. (2000) *Feminism and Youth Culture*, 2nd edn, London: Palgrave Macmillan.
Menon, N. (2012) *Seeing Like a Feminist*, India: Zubaan.
Mora, E., Rocamora, A. and Volonte, P. (2014) 'The Internationalisation of Fashion Studies: Rethinking the Peer Review Process', *International Journal of Fashion Studies* 1(1): 3–16.
Murthy, D. (2010) 'Muslim Punks Online: A Diasporic Pakistani Music Subculture on the Internet', *South Asian Popular Culture* 8(2): 181–194.
Nakassis, C. (2016) *Doing Style: Youth and Mass Mediation in South India*, Chicago: The University of Chicago Press.
Newbold, A. (2016) 'Bhutan Fashion: The Unique Street Style Scene in a Country with a National Dress Code', *Telegraph UK Online*. Available at http://www.telegraph.co.uk/fashion/style/bhutan-fashion-surveying-the-unusual-street-style-scene-in-a-cou/ (accessed on 01/06/2016).
Niessen. S., Leshkowich, A.M. and Jones, C. (2003) *Re-orienting Fashion: the Globalization of Asian Dress*, Oxford: Berg.
Nisbett, N. (2009) *Growing up in the Knowledge Society: Living the IT Dream in Bangalore*, New Delhi: Routledge.
Osella, C. and Osella, F. (1998) 'Friendship and Flirting: Micro-Politics in Kerala, South India', *Journal of the Royal Anthropological Institute* 4(2): 189–206.
Parker, E. (2011) *Steps towards Sustainability in Fashion: Snapshot Bangladesh*. L. Hammond, H. Higginson and D. Williams (eds), London College of Fashion, University of the Arts London.
Polhemus, T. (2010) *Street Style*, London: PYMCA.
Pullen, C. (2014) *Queer Youth and Media Cultures*, London: Palgrave.
Reddy, V. (2016) *Fashioning Diaspora: Beauty, Femininity and South American Culture*, Philadephia: Temple University Press.
Rizal, D. (2015) *The Royal Semi Authoritarian Democracy of Bhutan*, Lanham: Lexington Books.
Roach, M.E. and Eicher, J.B. (2007) 'The Language of Personal Adornment', in M. Barnard (ed.), *Fashion Theory: A Reader*. London: Routledge, pp. 109–121.

Rocamora, A. (2011) 'Personal Fashion Blogs: Screens and Mirrors in Digital Self-Portraits', *Fashion Theory* 15(4): 407–424.
Said, E. (1978) *Orientalism*, New York: Pantheon.
Saxena, S.B. (2014) *Made in Bangladesh, Cambodia, and Sri Lanka: The Labor Behind the Global Garments and Textiles Industries*, United States: Cambria Press.
Sharma, N.T. (2010) *Hip Hop Desis: South Asian Americans, Blackness, and a Global Race Consciousness*, Durham: Duke University Press.
Sharma, S. (2006) 'Asian Sounds', in N. Ali, V.S. Kalra and S. Sayyid (eds), *A Postcolonial People: South Asians in Britain*, London: Hurst and Co.
Sheth, D.L. (1999) 'Secularisation of Caste and Making of New Middle Class', *Economic and Political Weekly* 34(34/35): 2502–2510.
Shukla, P. (2008) *The Grace of Four Moons Dress, Adornment, and the Art of the Body in Modern India*, Indianapolis: Indiana University Press.
Spivak, G. (2008) *Other Asias*, Oxford: Blackwell Publishing.
Srivastava, S. (2007) *Passionate Modernity: Sexuality, Class and Consumption in India*, New Delhi, Routlege.
Tarlo, E. (1996) *Clothing Matters: Dress and Identity in India*, London: Hurst and Co.
Trivedi, L. (2007) *Clothing Gandhi's Nation: Homespun and Modern India*, Indianapolis: Indiana University Press.
Vanita, R. (2014) 'Foreword', in R.K. Dasgupta and K.M. Gokulsing (eds), *Masculinity and its Challenges in India*, Jefferson, NC: Mcfarland, pp. 1–3.
Wilkinson-Weber, C. (2014) *Fashioning Bollywood: Costume and Culture in the Hindi Film Industry*, London: Bloomsbury.
Wilson, E. (2005) *Adorned in Dreams: Fashion and Modernity*, New Brunswick: Rutgers University Press.
Woodhead, L. and Catto, R. (eds) (2012) *Religion and Change in Modern Britain*, London: Routledge.

1
STREET STYLE VS. STYLE ON THE STREET?

Two Interpretations of Indian Street Fashion

Arti Sandhu

In 2013, while conducting field research on Indian fashion and designers in New Delhi I had the opportunity to attend *Wills Lifestyle India Fashion Week*[1] (WLIFW S/S 2014, October 2013). The venue for this bi-annual fashion event was the expansive exhibition and convention centre Pragati Maidan. In spite of its central location — accessible by arterial main roads [sic] and various means of public transport — Pragati Maidan suffers from traffic congestion and general infrastructure issues that are characteristic of all urban centres in India.

Despite being aware of the platform India fashion week would offer for showing off trendy and experimental fashion, my personal style choices ended up in the fairly practical and understated realm. This was due to the fact that I had decided to make use of the Delhi Metro to commute to and from the venue, and hence needed to dress suitably for public transport and the transition from public to private space and vice-versa. Navigating several traffic crossings in South Delhi without any sidewalk access, pedestrian crossings or designated traffic signals, along with ongoing construction sites all around, further affirmed the appropriateness of my clothing choices. However, on seeing a number of women belonging to the labouring classes working on these construction sites — lifting bricks, shifting rubble, mixing concrete — dressed in once vibrant but now dusty ghaghras and short cholis, wearing flimsy rubber chappals on their weathered feet that were adorned with dull silver payals, I could not help but reflect on my own discomfort in wearing a more flamboyant ensemble in a similar public street setting.

Immediately outside *WLIFW's* venue at the entry ticket counters a nervous group of young fashion bloggers giggled and chatted about the styles of well-known fashion personalities — models, fashion editors and designers — as they hastily walked past. This group of mostly female bloggers openly spoke about their own hopes of being 'spotted' by other more prominent fashion bloggers, journalists and 'street style' photographers based on what they had chosen to wear that day.

Once inside, the transformation from Delhi's heat, dust, traffic, and unruly and uneven streets to a place where one could realise one's potential for taking fashion risks was instantly noticeable. Notable fashionistas hung about designer stalls, eating at Delhi Smoke House Grill's makeshift cafe, sampling coffee and doughnuts at the newly launched Dunkin' Donuts stall, while at the same time regularly taking selfies and posing for photographers in these spaces or during their 'ciggie' breaks outside the main hall. The queues for the back-to-back runway shows additionally presented a new assortment of fashionable industry professionals and guests each day, many of whom had made the effort to style themselves in accordance to the designer show they were waiting to attend.

The overall styles worn at *WLIFW* were a stark contrast to the basic everyday clothing worn by the urban classes in public spaces such as at metro stations and local markets. At *WLIFW* neon see-through Louis Vuitton bags, Zara skorts, men in skirts and lungis, Péro designer saris worn in interesting drapes, Kallol Datta's amorphous dresses, Oxford shoes, Cambridge satchels, kedia tops, jodhpur pants, colorful stockings, tribal jewellery, and copious layers of draped scarves were all the norm.

INTRODUCTION

The vignette above highlights how certain protocols emanating from established fashion capitals are now universal norms of a globalised fashion industry. In addition to designer runway shows, personal style statements by fashion enthusiasts and industry professionals en route to catwalk shows — classified as contemporary 'street style' — not only garner significant media attention in London and Paris, but also in non-western fashion centres and at events such as New Delhi's bi-annual fashion week.

The central aim of this chapter is to investigate the concept of street style as it relates to contemporary Indian dress and fashion, and the different interpretations that can be drawn while examining this phenomenon within India. In doing so, the chapter first examines the aforementioned displays of personal fashion that occur off the actual street at fashion weeks and other fashion related events by cosmopolitan Indians belonging to the upper middle and elite classes.[2] Here the discussion not only highlights how these sartorial displays align with the parameters of contemporary global street style, but also how such localised interpretations allow for the establishment and assertion of a unique Indian fashion identity. Following from this, the chapter offers another interpretation that can be made when one studies the clothing worn by those belonging to lower or labouring classes and rural communities that inhabit India's real streetscapes. Such instances of unstaged and unintended style on the street are often considered more authentic representations of Indian street style or fashion by local designers and industry professionals, which points to the constructed and contested classification of the term. Taken together, both interpretations highlight the resurgence of orientalist viewpoints in the way fashion is designed and visually promoted on blogs and fashion magazines (Sandhu 2014) – all of which invariably leads to the othering of a significant portion of India.

INDIA'S GLOBAL *DESI* STREET STYLE

A survey of personal *style statements* at India fashion week as well as those documented on blogs like Manou's *wearabout*, Santu Misra's *devil wore* and on the pages of various Indian editions of international fashion magazines like *Elle*, *Vogue*, and *Marie Claire*[3] points to the first interpretation of the term 'street style' that can be made in the context of India. Usually comprising quirky and experimental ensembles worn by trendy upper-middle-class or elite Indians, such street style can be observed at art fairs, literary festivals and other fashion events, featured on personal blogs, or reserved solely for display at exclusive private parties (Tewari 2014).[4]

The format of these sartorial presentations bears semblance to the display of personal style by well-known fashion personalities and industry professionals in western fashion capitals like London and New York. Made popular by its documentation by equally hip photographers like Scott Schuman for the blog *Sartorialist*, for example, this type of street style is a marked shift from earlier linkages to subcultural style statements that were more obviously about resistance to dominant culture (Evans 1997). Rocamora and O'Neill (2008) note how displays of contemporary street fashion and its documentation are now extremely commonplace, where interestingly

> not only do [fashion] journalists offer selective definitions of the fashionable city subject, but they simultaneously construct and define their own roles. Although concessions are made to the creative style and the authorship of the people, readers are reminded that true expertise remains the attribute of fashion journalists.
> (Rocamora and O'Neill 2008: 194)

There is also a shift away from the representation of 'the people, the real and the street', as '[t]he figures they depict are far from ordinary ... while the settings are confined to fashionable districts' (Rocamora and O'Neill 2008: 195–196).

The general pattern and composition of this interpretation of Indian street style follow aforementioned formats emanating from western fashion centres. This is firstly evident in the style of documentation by fashion journalists and photographers using 'straight-up shots' (Rocamora and O'Neill 2008) with emphasis on highlighting the juxtaposition of various garments and brands, along with a list of items (purchases) worn. Through these images the journalist's role is elevated as an arbitrator of good taste and style. This type of street style also lies firmly in the domain of those who have adequate fashion pedigree, hailing from India's elite or upper middle classes, or have aspirations to the same.

Other similarities are evident in the way these cosmopolitan style statements juxtapose international high-street brands – such as Zara and Forever 21 that are recent entrants into the Indian market – with thrifted [sic] items or edgy pieces from emerging local designers. The general lack of elaborate Indian traditional couture garments in contrast to the predominance of high-street branded clothing does not disqualify these personal style statements from being worthy of recognition from the leading fashion magazines I mention above. This is because of the cultural capital associated with many of these brands, which in some cases has accumulated over a number of years even prior to their availability in the Indian market, as well as due to the fact that they retail at price points (and locations) that are accessible only to upper-middle-class and elite shoppers.

Another key point of difference is that most of these displays occur completely off-the-street. This can be attributed to the chaotic and congested nature of Indian streetscapes[5] and the absence of prestigious shopping districts such as Avenue Montaigne in Paris or Fifth Avenue in New York. In addition, a significant portion of India's elite can afford to lead lives out of view of the wider population of India — in that they reside in gated communities, shop in exclusive malls, and socialise in clubs, bars, hotels, etc. that restrict general public entry.

Despite being closeted, highly curated and off-the-street, the medium and label of 'street style' is an exciting platform for sartorial self-expression for urban fashionistas in a post-liberalised era — a time period that has witnessed significant socio-cultural and economic shifts as a result of the financial reforms initiated in the 1990s by the Indian government. These reforms directly led to the rise of an increasingly globalised and cosmopolitan elite and middle class, who are now in a position to lead lifestyles on a par with many of their global counterparts. Understandably, this also had implications for fashionable dress in urban centres — where we see greater acceptance of western clothing as well as easy availability of global brands alongside Indian designer wear. The boom experienced within Indian fashion retail in recent years as well as the rise of a local fashion design industry has meant that New Delhi and Mumbai are now counted amongst the world's top global fashion cities (Global Language Monitor 2014). Also impacting fashion and strategies of self- and collective-fashioning amongst the urban classes is the overall sense of positivity experienced as a result of India's economic gains that have led to a sharp rise in patterns of conspicuous consumption. The mushrooming of numerous shopping malls, private clubs, luxury resorts, etc., in all major urban centres alongside online formats of fashion blogging further aid the consumption and display of material possessions including fashion goods, and have led to a significant change in the way fashion is worn and performed in urban settings. The overall shift away from India's older nationalist ideals that emphasised austerity has also meant that there are now fewer stigmas attached to openly showing off material possessions and related lifestyles. In tandem with these attitudinal changes, all forms of visual media actively promote idealised constructions of upper-class lifestyles where luxury products, designer and branded items are seen as markers of success.

While there is much criticism within India from various social commentators about this shift in mentality and the general public image it has created, Fernandes notes that a distinctive feature of India's prospering urban classes (in particular, those she and popular media platforms refer to as the 'new' middle class)[6] is their position as a 'new class' of entrepreneurs 'who are potential leaders of the Indian nation with a new global outlook' (Fernandes 2000: 92). This is evident in the way all forms of visual and print media openly celebrate their individual achievements and collective contributions towards the nation's economic success. Fernandes sees this group additionally charged with the role of cultural mediation between India and the rest of the world, which hinges on their ability to

> negotiate India's new relationship with the global economy in both cultural and economic terms; in cultural terms by defining a new cultural standard that rests on the socio symbolic practices of commodity consumption, and in economic terms as the beneficiaries of the material benefits of jobs in India's 'new economy'.
>
> (Fernandes 2000: 91)

This results in the culmination of the very popular media construction dubbed the global Indian or global *desi* – an idealised representation of cosmopolitan Indianness that many urban Indians can relate to and aspire to (Sandhu 2014).

Most media publications tend to portray the global *desi* as the 'ideal Indian consumer who is young, hip, and conscious of his or her sense of locality and simultaneously aware of global trends, while being socially mobile and financially able to indulge in them' (Sandhu 2014: 106). This is immediately noticeable in the way street style is performed and documented, as today's fashionable global *desis*' individual fashion statements are indicative of their acquired fashion capital and cosmopolitanism, either as a result of their social standing combined with experiences of travelling overseas, styling for magazines and blogs, etc., or their aspiration for these lifestyle markers.

Fashion for the global *desi* as promoted by leading fashion magazines is characterised by a heightened interplay between local and global trends, designer brands, and dress practices. This confluence, which is a natural outcome of contemporary globalisation and can be observed in other non-western centres (Jones and Leshkowich 2003), is more complex and multi-layered than a simple case of 'East meets West' or westernisation of Indian clothing; especially as liberalisation brought with it a renewed sense of anxiety about the preservation of Indian identity in the wake of global influences (Sandhu 2014), which I discuss in a little more detail later in this chapter. The heightened emphasis on class, status, and the consumption and display of material goods means that branded high-street and designer clothing and accessories that are now available in India take on extra prominence in the performance of global *desi* street style. A point of difference, which I have already mentioned, is that while leading examples of western street style as promoted by the global fashion press rely less heavily on high-street brands, and instead include an eclectic mix of high-fashion and luxury items, in India, international high-street brands tend to be more popular in cosmopolitan displays of street style online, at fashion events, and in fashion magazines.

Finally, due to its display off-the-street it is clear that the 'street' in the construction of cosmopolitan street style is not so much a real space but a conceptual space where fashion forward Indians can present their own individual takes on fashion to a global audience. This is increasingly possible through the medium of fashion blogs (where much of contemporary global street style comes to be recorded), which act as virtual sites for challenging the Eurocentric frameworks of fashion that have historically excluded non-western centres of dress from the definition of 'fashion'. Even though western fashion capitals of London, Paris, New York and Milan continue to remain the leading sources of global fashion trends, recent years have witnessed significant shifts in the way fashion opinion leadership has become decentralised through the popularity of blogs and the opportunity they present to bloggers to provide 'the narrative and meaning for fashion that had previously been the domain of traditional fashion media' (Berry 2010a). Street style blogs in particular 'encourage a global dialogue' and through 'their photographic coverage of emerging fashion cities, [they] have also contributed to an extension of the democratisation of fashion through the decentralisation of elite capitals of style' (Berry 2010a). In this way it is possible to see how crucial the role of fashion blogs and related discourse on non-western street style is to asserting India's presence globally as a potential fashion and design capital.

THE 'OTHER' INTERPRETATION

Interestingly, during my field research in 2013 in Delhi and Mumbai, the existence of cosmopolitan Indian street style was always met with a firm denial by leading fashion professionals – designers, stylists, magazine editors, etc. Much of their disagreement centred on issues of authenticity. In some cases this interpretation of Indian street style was seen to be blindly mimicking western exemplars and in others was considered not as good as the same. Yet, as most saw little stylistic merit in what I had witnessed at WLIFW, for example, they countered by emphasising the richness of real and un-staged style on Indian streets. In doing so, they were referring to clothing worn by those belonging to lower segments of society, namely the labouring classes, rural villagers and tribal groups seen on urban and rural streets and roadsides across India. While by no means lacking in individualism, creativity and in many cases aesthetic sophistication, such styles of dress – composed of various types of regional and/or tribal clothing as well as weathered workwear worn by segments of society who do not have the means or access to high-fashion – offer a stark contrast to the carefully orchestrated street style I had witnessed at fashion week.

Many of these styles along with their wearers have in recent years been pushed further out of view from India's newly developed metropolitan sites, yet in all my conversations with noted designers, stylists, writers and fashion commentators these were categorised as 'authentic' Indian street fashion.

According to these fashion professionals, items of dress like Rajasthani men's turbans, cattle herders' outfits (see Figure 1.1), a fisherwoman's *sari*, or the construction workers' *ghagharas* I mentioned at the start of the chapter, were all accurate representations of Indian style in the truest sense and deeply influential in shaping the design of contemporary high-fashion and couture. This was clearly evident in the catwalk presentations at WLIFW S/S 2014 for example, where I noted a proliferation of design references to tribal dress and regional drapes, not only in the garments showcased but also in the general styling of models and their jewellery, footwear, and other accessories. At times this influence also stretched to the physical setting and props on the catwalk, where on occasion tribal performers, dancers or street scenes were presented to the audience.

Fashion photographer and blogger Manou records instances of authentic Indian street fashion alongside posts on 'fashion-obsessed regulars' (Manou cf. Anon. 2011) on his extremely popular blog *wearabout*. He travels across India and parts of the South Asian subcontinent to smaller towns and cities like Salem, Pushkar, Jodhpur and Shillong, to venues ranging from roadside bazaars, cattle fairs, local festivals, etc., in search of diverse clothing styles and dress practices worn by communities that have been pushed further out of view from upscale urban settings in cities such as Delhi and Mumbai. He says, 'geographically speaking, I've found the best [street style] in small towns, or in beaten down areas, mostly the poorest people' (Manou cf. Anon. 2011). His posts often capture multiple styles of one garment type or a regional style as well as feature images of clothing worn by vagrants and homeless people photographed in great detail.

Posts such as the one titled *The Last People* (Manou 2012) or those from his recent travels to Pushkar (Figure 1.1) and Nagaland appear to be an attempt towards not only providing thorough documentation of local dress practices but also a way of bringing to the forefront fading traditional styles and asserting India's fashion lineage. According to Manou, what sets Indian street fashion apart from the rest of the world is that it is 'unexpected, inconsistent, and sometimes improvised' and 'more individualistic, at times effortless, [and] out of basic necessities'. Interestingly, he notices 'a strong connect between style of the poorest and the chic-est [sic]' in the way both groups tend to juxtapose and improvise mismatched items of clothing (Manou cited in Anon. 2011).

Figure 1.1 Camel traders wearing their traditional attire at the annual cattle fair in Pushkar. From the blog post titled *Camel Traders of Rajasthan*, 11 August 2014, wearabout.wordpress.com. Image courtesy of Manou.

The strong following enjoyed by Manou's blog posts – evident in the long comment threads and multiple re-posts that have even appeared on international news and fashion websites – points to the fascination India's cosmopolitan classes and global audiences have with these fashions. Through reviewing his posts it is clear to see that many of Manou's photographs are reminiscent of those taken by tourists who regularly travel to India in search of inspiration and document their fascination with the 'exotic' quality of Indian costume, crafts, and clothing, that appear untouched by the forces of globalisation or are worn in unabashed ignorance of global fashion trends. It is also possible to see parallels between his desire to record a plethora of authentic indigenous styles and the methodological documentation of unique sartorial [native] styles in conjunction with the diversity of castes and ethnicities encountered in India by British photographers, anthropologists, illustrators and artists during colonial times. At times Manou's photographic stance and style of selection and representation of his subject matter mimics what Pinney categorises as the 'salvage paradigm' of photography that emerged in India during the nineteenth century, 'which was applied to what were perceived to be fragile tribal communities' (Pinney 1997: 45). In addition, cosmopolitan Indians' penchant for the authentic dress practices featured on Manou's blog is similar to the way the British felt a strong connection to Indian artifacts due to their ability to remind them of their own distant 'primitive' pre-capitalist past (Mathur 2007: 19) – as a result of which attempts were made to study, classify and make detailed records of these artifacts.

In colonial times, the popularity of photographic collections of indigenous people that offered visual documentation of a range of physical attributes, including dress and adornment practices – such as those presented in the infamous eight volume study entitled *The People of India*, compiled by John Forbes Watson and John William Kaye during the late nineteenth century[7] – further 'distinguish[ed] the civilized from the primitive, the leisured tourist from the commodified Other, the spectator from the object of sight seeing gaze' (Strain 1996: 96). The renewed interest in the documentation of clothing worn by indigenous groups or those hailing from lower segments of society in contemporary times, and its classification as Indian street fashion once again labels them as Other.

Only this time it is not through the colonial lens but through that of fashion and re-orientalism.

NOSTALGIA AND RE-ORIENTALISM IN INDIAN FASHION DESIGN AND STREET STYLE

The resurgence of orientalist viewpoints in contemporary couture and high-fashion is a key characteristic of India's emerging fashion identity, and worth noting in this section as it is not only evident across a number of designer collections showcased at fashion weeks, but also influences the way cosmopolitan Indians fashion themselves.

Fashion designers like Sabyasachi Mukherjee, Ritu Kumar and JJ Valaya, to name but a few, regularly refer to India's royal past, traditional styles, local crafts, forgotten textiles, and embroidery motifs for their collections as well as promotional materials such as photoshoots, catwalk shows, etc. Kondo (1997) links such design strategies to the lasting legacy of the imbalances and viewpoints established by orientalism itself, that led to the labelling of India and Indian artifacts as timeless, 'exotic, luxurious and "Other," [when compared] to a more rationalist, industrializing Europe' (McGowan 2005: 265). She proposes the concept of re- or self-Orientalising for describing those methods of design and self-fashioning, whereby fashion designers internalise the Orientalised western gaze and begin to regard their own culture, traditions, past, dress, crafts and people as exotic sources of inspiration (Kondo 1997: 57).

Jones and Leshkowich (2003) consider re-orientalising strategies of design to be logical outcomes of globalisation and have observed similar trends in other centres of non-western fashion. In India they can be attributed to changes occurring post-liberalisation and the broader identity based anxieties experienced by urban classes about the preservation of Indian traditions – where for example, the tastes of the younger generations, especially in clothing, food, films and music, for a large part are no longer identifiable as solely 'Indian'. In some cases they are indistinguishable (at least on the surface in terms of clothing and fashion) from their global counterparts, thereby creating an inherent fear of homogenisation and the deep desire to retain a point of difference, without turning back the clock of globalisation. Hence, concurrent to the enshrining of western and global brands there is also a growing interest in the meaning and value of local identity amongst the urban classes. This ranges from a renewed interest in the study, preservation and revival of Indian traditions and related rituals, vernacular cultural forms and traditional dress practices, which include clothing styles, textiles and craft techniques – evident at India's fashion weeks.

The strategy of self-orientalising design and fashion could be misread as a position of inferiority when read outside of the context of India as it reaffirms and recreates western fantasies of the 'oriental other' and related stereotypes of viewing Indian dress and textiles; and yet it still relies on western frameworks, i.e. western styles of clothing, trends, catwalk shows and print media to legitimise it as 'fashion' (Kondo 1997: 78). Furthermore, since such approaches to design were further emphasised over the past century by western designers – who worked with Indian and other non-western cultures as exotic inspiration for their collections – these have also come to determine the framework within which Indian designers come to find themselves. Within India, however, the idea that 'one's own heritage and culture have become an important stepping-off point in the design process' (Teunissen 2005: 11) is extremely successful with local consumers and popular across all fields of design. In the case of fashion, much like the way traditional dress allowed for non-western cultures like India to maintain crucial points of difference from the West during colonial rule, the deliberate celebration of 'anti-[western]-fashion' (Niessen 2003) in contemporary times not only promotes local resources and design innovation, but is also an assertion of local distinction towards the establishment of India as a legitimate fashion capital.

Not only do contemporary designers internalise the Orientalised western gaze, the same also is evident in the way cosmopolitan Indians fashion their own personal looks. Their style experimentations, which fit under the first category of cosmopolitan street style I discussed earlier, highlight their ability to draw from current global fashion cues, yet at the same time present their own individual stance that often draws upon familiar traditional dress practices.

As is evident on Manou's blog that also documents the elite version of Indian street style, the other India is yet again a valuable source of inspiration as *lungis, gamchas, dhotis, cholis,* ankle bracelets, nose rings and *banyans* get re-fashioned and combined with high-street and high-fashion brands in order to create vibrant, playful and original outcomes (see Figure 1.2). In this way not only are the two interpretations of street style highlighted in this chapter linked because of strategies of sartorial juxtaposition, they are also visually connected due to the way cosmopolitan Indians borrow from the clothing styles they see on the street.

As I have discussed in greater depth elsewhere,[8] such strategies of fashion fusion are practiced at differing levels across all social strata in India as they allow for the preservation and maintenance of traditional values, beliefs, cloth and clothing that Indians are so fiercely proud of, alongside the possibility of enjoying highly attractive modes of experiencing modern lifestyles that are on par with the rest of the world. Much like the re-orientalising strategies employed by designers, ensuring the compatibility of Indian and western garments as a strategy for personal and collective styling also acts as a medium for maintaining a point of difference while experiencing a sense of national pride — a strategy that is strongly encouraged in the way contemporary fashion is represented in fashion magazines and on blog posts.

Important to note also is that current strategies for design and self-fashioning that rely on nostalgia for India's past as well as a fascination for the 'other' India that has been pushed further away or out of sight from contemporary cosmopolitan lifestyles subdue any negative elements — such as dirt, dust or poverty — that could be associated or experienced in real terms. Instead these are turned into pleasurable experiences that can be consumed, as well as symbols that reinforce identity and belonging, and act as markers of distinction from the rest of the world.

CONCLUSION

Despite Edensor's observation of the Indian street as a 'spatial complex' that 'provides for a meeting point for several communities' and functions as a 'gregarious environment, which privileges speech', announcements, demonstrations on what he refers to as a 'temporary stage', with the

Figure 1.2 Fashion designer Anand Kabra on Day 2 of Lakmé India Fashion Week 2010, wearing a T-shirt from Topman, shirt from CK Jeans, self-designed waistcoat and pants from Fabindia. From a blog post dated 9 March 2010, *wearabout.wordpress.com*. Image courtesy of Manou.

exception of some staged photo opportunities, most fashion forward Indians are uncomfortable displaying their interpretations of street style in these settings (Edensor 1998: 206–207). And while it is possible to view Indian streets as 'centres of social life, of communication, of political and judicial activity, of cultural and religious events and places for the exchange of news, information and gossip' (Buie 1996 cited in Edensor 1998: 206), there exists a wide and un-scalable physical gap between 'authentic' style on the streets and fashionable displays of cosmopolitan street style in idealised spaces (where most of India has been airbrushed out). This gap reflects the heightening polarity between India's rich and poor subsequent to liberalisation and the resulting sense of 'split public', especially in media constructions (Rajagopal 1997 cited in Kumar 2010), where Indian society is demarcated; with the well-presented, well-networked classes (and their idealised representations) on one side, and the rest as other.

Yet, as the discussion in this chapter has shown, despite the two distinct interpretations of street style that can be drawn in India, visually and stylistically the two are often linked through sartorial strategies of juxtaposition as well as the borrowing of style cues from the lower segments by those in elite segments, who come to view these dress practices as exotic. However, through the lens of re-orientalism and that of the fashion journalist's camera, the othering of a significant portion of India persists.

Nonetheless, through its popularity and success, mostly via fashion blogs as well as magazine features, it is possible to see how the 'street' for the cosmopolitan display of street style is a crucial conceptual and virtual space to assert a sense of distinction for Indian style – that additionally has the ability to challenge the stereotypes and Eurocentric frameworks that have historically excluded India as a legitimate fashion centre.

As an endnote, I offer another observation – one that does not really fit with the chapter's intention but became apparent as I closely examined fashion photographer and blogger Manou's posts on Indian street style vs. style on the streets. Edensor notes the allure and 'sensuality' of Indian streets settings that can be likened to early modern European metropolitan streets. Hence these are, once again, conducive to the roaming of the flâneur, as originally theorised by Baudelaire, as one 'wallowing in flux, observing the fleeting and the transitionary, witnessing unique juxtapositions and incidental meetings' (Edensor 1998: 217). More recently Berry (2010b) has also linked fashion blogging and street fashion photography to the notion of the twenty-first-century flâneur due to the way these mediums 'provide an alternative urban space to observe fashion that expands the boundaries of the city into cyberspace, to be experienced by visitors from across the globe' (Berry 2010b). The distinctive nature of Indian streets, combined with virtual formats of fashion blogging allow for both the old and new interpretations of flânerie to be applied to Manou's street fashion blog as he roams across the country in search of stylish samplings of the other India and posts them online for India's urban cosmopolitan classes to appreciate and re-fashion.

NOTES

1. During the time of my field research (2013) Wills Lifestyle was the main sponsor for Wills Lifestyle India Fashion Week, New Delhi. In 2015, Amazon India took over sponsorship of this event. Held in partnership with FDCI (Fashion Design Council of India), Amazon India Fashion Week (AIFW) and Lakmé India Fashion Week (LIFW, held in Mumbai) are the two main bi-annual fashion weeks in India's fashion calendar.
2. For the purpose of this discussion I refer to a report generated by McKinsey Global Institute (MGI) in 2007 that classifies Indian households earning within Rupees 200,000 to 10 lakh per year as middle class, and those earning more than Rupees 10 lakh a year as [elite] 'global Indians'. The chapter's reference to India's upper middle class, elite and global-*desis* relates mainly to the second segment and the upper rung of the first segment outlined in MGI's report. MGI's report also projects that the 'global Indian' segment will account for two per cent of India's total population by the year 2025. While it may appear to be a small percentage, this elite segment in actual numbers is greater than the entire population of Australia.
3. No longer in print as of July 2013.
4. Bandana Tewari, *Vogue India* Fashion Features Director, in a personal conversation with the author in 2014.
5. Choosing what to wear for open street spaces in India relies on making the distinction between public vs. private, modes of transport and the time of day or night, among other things. Hence most street settings in India tend to better suit clothing that *Grazia* India's editor Ekta Rajani describes as 'simple and convenient' (Rajani cited in Sandhu 2014: 5). The dilemmas for women are even greater when it comes to making personal clothing choices, and subsequently their styles of dress can differ significantly when comparing what is acceptable in private or

domestic spaces to what is safe or appropriate for openly public spaces. See Säävälä (2012) for a discussion on the demarcation between the domestic and public sphere when it comes to women's dress in India – where at home or in more private social settings women from middle-class or upper-class social groups may be comfortable wearing shorts, mini-skirts and dresses, while they are more conservative in wider open settings.

6. The use of the word 'new', commonly employed when referring to India's growing middle class, for the most part, is not to signify that it is a new social class but that it is 'novel' in the way that new segments of society and professions now make up this class (Fernandes 2000; Säävälä 2012), and secondly, due to their shared experience of changing lifestyles and social status following India's economic reforms (Sääävälä 2012).

7. The People of India: a series of Photographic Illustrations, with Descriptive Letterpress, of the Races and Tribes of Hindustan by Great Britain. India Office; Kaye, John William, Sir, 1814–1876; Taylor, Meadows, 1808-1876; Watson, J. Forbes (John Forbes), 1827–1892. Publication date 1868. These collections were a reflection of an overall effort to ensure there existed reference points by which various physical characteristics and related material artifacts could be better understood and authenticated (Pinney 1997), as a result of which 'minute material aspects of their supposedly "untouched" culture were focal points of the photos... Additionally, many photos appeared to appeal to a certain romanticism about "a simpler age"' (Strain 1996: 92).

8. See Sandhu (2014: 16–21).

REFERENCES

Anon. (2011) 'Interview with Manou', 11 August 2011. *Blogadda: Blog*. Available from http://blog.blogadda.com/2011/08/11/manou-wear-about-street-fashion-india-interview (accessed 13 August 2014).

Berry, J. (2010a) 'Street-Style: Fashion Photography, Web Logs and the Urban Image', in R.F. Jacque-Lynn Foltyn (ed.), *Fashion: Exploring Critical Issues*, Oriel College, Oxford: inter-disciplinary.net. Available at https://www.academia.edu/6621403/Street-Style_Fashion_photography_weblogs_and_the_urban_image_Jess_Berry/ (accessed 10 October 2017).

―――― (2010b) 'Flâneurs of Fashion 2.0'. *SCAN | journal of media arts culture*, 7(2). Available from http://scan.net.au/scan/journal/print.php?journal_id=152&j_id=20 (accessed 12 September 2014).

Edensor, T. (1998) 'The Culture of the Indian Street', in N.R. Fyfe (ed.), *Images of the Street: Planning, Identity, and Control in Public Space*, London, New York: Routledge, pp. 205–221.

Evans, C. (1997) 'Street Style, Subculture and Subversion', *Costume* 31, pp. 105–110.

Fernandes, L. (2000) 'Nationalizing "The Global": Media Images, Cultural Politics and the Middle Class in India', *Media, Culture and Society* 22: 611–628.

Global Language Monitor (2014) *Annual Report*. Available from http://www.languagemonitor.com/ (accessed 30 November 2014).

Jones, C. and Leshkowich, A.M. (2003) 'What Happens When Asian Chic Becomes Chic in Asia?' *Fashion Theory* 7(3/4): 281–300.

Kondo, D. (1997) *About Face: Performing Race in Fashion and Theatre*, London: Routledge.

Kumar, S. (2010) *Postcolonial Identity in a Globalizing India: Case Studies in Visual, Musical and Oral Culture*. University of Iowa.

Manou (2012) The Last People. *wearabout: Blog*. Available from https://wearabout.wordpress.com/category/the-last-people-2/ (accessed 12 December 2012).

Mathur, S. (2007) *India by Design: Colonial History and Cultural Display*, Berkeley, Los Angeles, London: University of California Press.

McGowan, A. (2005) '"All that is Rare, Characteristic or Beautiful" – Design and the Defense of Tradition in Colonial India, 1851–1903', *Journal of Material Culture* 10(3): 263–287.

McKinsey Global Institute (2007) *The 'Bird of Gold': The Rise of India's Consumer Market*. Available from http://www.mckinsey.com/insights/asia-pacific/the_bird_of_gold (accessed 19 September 2011).

Niessen, S. (2003) 'Afterword: Re-Orienting Fashion Theory', in S. Niessen, A.M. Leshkowich and C. Jones (eds), *Re-Orienting Fashion: The Globalization of Asian Dress*, Oxford, New York: Berg.

Pinney, C. (1997) *Camera Indica?: The Social Life of Indian Photographs*, Chicago: The University of Chicago Press.

Rocamora, A. and O'Neill, A. (2008) 'Fashioning the Street: Images of the Street in the Fashion Media', in E. Shinkle (ed.), *Fashion as Photograph: Viewing and Reviewing Images of Fashion*, London; New York: I.B.Tauris, pp. 185–199.

Säävälä, M. (2012) *Middle-class Moralities: Everyday Struggle over Belonging and Prestige in India*, New Delhi: Orient Blackswan.

Sandhu, A. (2014) *Indian Fashion: Tradition, Innovation, Style*, London; New York: Bloomsbury Academic.

Strain, E. (1996) 'Exotic Bodies, Distant Landscapes: Touristic Viewing and Popularized Anthropology in the Nineteenth Century', *Wide Angle* 18(2): 70–100.

Teunissen, J. (2005) 'Global Fashion/Local Tradition: On the Globalisation of Fashion', in J. Brand and J. Teunissen (eds), *Global Fashion/Local Tradition: On the Globalisation of Fashion*. Arnhem: Terra, pp. 8–23.

The People of India, Freer Gallery of Art and Arthur M. Sackler Gallery Archives. Smithsonian Institution, Washington, D.C., Purchase. Available from https://transcription.si.edu/project/6587 (accessed 10 October 2017).

2

STYLE-ISH GIRLS AND LOCAL BOYS

Young Women and Fashion in Chennai

Sneha Krishnan

Amma, wake me up	Mother, wake me up
Kalai-ile nine o'clock	At nine in the morning
Shopping poganum	I have to go shopping
Lip-gloss vaanga	To buy lip-gloss
Ten o'clock friend varaa	A friend of mine is coming over at ten
Ten-thirty share auto	At ten-thirty we're taking a share-auto
Three hundred change kudu	Give me change for three hundred (rupees)
Breakfast vendam	I don't want breakfast
Daddy-tte solladhe	Don't tell Daddy
Sayankaalam late aagum	I'll be late this evening
Engay ponaalum	Wherever I go
Boys, baba, boys	There are boys, baba, boys

From *Vathikutchi* (The Matchstick, 2013)

Few of the young women I met in Chennai would actually be able to tell their mothers the audacious truths of their wandering in the city and they certainly would not boast about the ubiquity of 'boys, baba, boys' in their lives. In reality, a few hours of mall-going are usually won in exchange for babysitting siblings, or more often, stolen away when parents think their daughters are attending extra classes. Except for this difference, this song and its video ring endearingly close to home. It begins with a group of young women who meet in a middle-class locality and go to a popular mall in the city. They wear the dark leggings and tunics that were popular among girls of this age and class during my fieldwork period; accessorised with a *pottu* (mark on the forehead), watch, as well as ballerina slippers and counterfeit fake-leather handbags, bearing such haute couture labels as Gucci and Louis Vuitton. They take pictures of each other in posh shops, giggling in the dressing room, wearing clothes they would never be able to afford, and also never dare to wear out: halter tops and backless dresses.

This song, which gained great popularity with youth in the city, is representative of a fantasy of youth nursed by many young women: of waking up late, going shopping for make-up with their friends, and being surrounded by romantic opportunity. Such fantasies, as a wide scholarship now suggests (Mankekar 1999; Favero 2003; Lukose 2009), are means of imagining global modernities centred on idioms of style, fashion and consumption. This chapter draws on ethnographic fieldwork conducted towards a doctoral thesis to examine the performance of *style* as a local idiom in Chennai, by young lower middle-class women attending colleges in the city. Nakassis (2010) connects *style* with the exteriority that has been historically associated with male youth in Chennai (see also Rogers 2008): to do *style* is to situate oneself exterior to notions of 'adult' middle-class hierarchy. Doing *style* is the mark of youth rather than status-bearing adulthood. The performance of *style* is also exterior in that it is usually physically located in public spaces and solicits viewing publics for its performance. This typically places young women *doing style* in a precarious position vis-à-vis prevailing norms of middle-class femininity. In this chapter I demonstrate that nevertheless, young women use *style* in two ways. First, they often use it to negotiate status among peers. Secondly, style also mediates young women's claims to both discursive and physical spaces of 'youth'.

SETTING AND CONTEXT: COLLEGE AND FASHION IN CHENNAI

This chapter is based on research I conducted with college-going women in Chennai in 2012 and 2013. I call the colleges I spent time in

Church College and NT College. Besides this, I also lived in a women's hostel, as accommodation for students is popularly called in this region. Central and Southern Chennai – from about Anna Nagar in the west of the city to Adyar in the southern end of the city – tended to be the primary areas where the women I met spent their time. This was the area in which hostels were located and it was also regarded as the 'safe' centre of the city.

The young people that this study focuses on all identified as 'middle class', a category that forms as much part of the problematic that this study investigates as one of its parameters. To be 'middle class' in India, it has been suggested, is increasingly a balancing act (Radhakrishnan 2011) between the 'backward' failure to enter global modernity associated with the working classes and the elites' disregard for 'Indian culture'. As Mankekar (1999: 9) writes: 'If the middle classes seemed eager to adopt modern lifestyles through the acquisition of consumer goods, they also became the self-appointed protectors of tradition.' Seeing themselves, then, as representatives of a global nationalism (Gilbertson 2014: 121), the middle classes seek to consolidate this position through a range of strategies: for instance, the acquisition of education, jobs in the private sector and consumption, to prevent downward mobility. At the same time, they seek to be 'appropriately Indian' (Radhakrishnan 2011) through strategies of moderated consumption and a resurgent politics of traditionalism (Säävälä 2010).

Further, the disproportionate weight of this balancing act falls on women, particularly young women (Gilbertson 2014), who are called on to demonstrate their ability to straddle both a 'global' world of education, work and economic opportunity, as well as a family-centric 'India world', as one student I met put it. It is within consumption's precarious place in making middle-class subjectivity, and particularly a gendered middle-class subjectivity for young women that I locate the arguments laid out in this chapter.

A small but growing body of work has examined 'college culture' among youth in Chennai (Nakassis 2013, 2010; Rogers 2008), focussing primarily on men. While this literature draws attention to everyday practices that mark youth for men, in engagement with the college, it leaves room to further this line of enquiry in the context of young women's lives.

As Nakassis (2013) indicates, women are often under a far greater deal of surveillance than men, whether at home or in their colleges and student residence halls. As the debates that occur on the topics of dress codes for women in college, women's safety, and questions of love and sex every year in Chennai's newspapers and television outlets suggest, women's participation in 'college culture' is a site where middle-class modes of life are contested and produced in the city.

'Youth' and 'childhood' as social categories of experience in India, it has been suggested (Nakassis 2013; Jeffrey 2010), are located at the intersection of age, kinship hierarchies, position relative to institutions of schooling and marriage, and since liberalisation, media discourses that have produced a range of cultural products addressing this category. As such, 'youth' is often described in terms of time stretching endlessly, a lack of responsibility, combined with freedoms that were inaccessible during childhood, and access to consumer products such as motorbikes, MP3 players, and mobile phones.[1] 'College' is about 'freedom'. 'Youth' it has also been suggested is widely seen as male by default (Nakassis 2010, 2013), and women's access to the practices, spaces and temporalities that define 'youth' remain tenuous. Closely connected to 'youth' is the notion of a 'youth culture', or as Osella and Osella (1998) define it, 'college culture'. Usually connected with practices of fun, friendship and mischief, these practices are seen as subversive to though not transformative of the adult world order. Seen widely within Tamil culture as natural and even expected and conducive for the development of adult masculinity (Mines 1994), young men are encouraged to leave the home and engage in some 'mischief' with friends.

In laying claim to 'youth culture' young women, I will demonstrate, increasingly enact ambivalent and conflicting practices that challenge prevailing norms of class and gender on the one hand, while consolidating these hierarchies and their own positions within middle-classness. These technologies and practices, as I will show, allow for forms of un-heroic and everyday agency that allow young women to disturb and question dominant social paradigms without necessarily upending them or causing transformative change. Shopping, fashion and a politics of display popularly termed 'style' is here presented as one of a number of practices young women engage in that allows them to lay claim to a 'youth culture' otherwise marked male, while also positioning themselves as subjects of a globalised urban middle-class milieu.

'STYLE' AND GENDER

When I asked students in Chennai – largely between the ages of 18 and 23 years – what they most closely associated with their lives as college-goers, the answers I usually got centred on fun and friendship. *Oor sutharathu* – to wander about the city – seemed to be the iconic practice that marked youth and the time of leisure associated with it. It was the one thing that to many was impossible when adulthood struck, whether in the form of graduation from college, marriage or holding a job. Associated closely with 'doing nothing' and indeed often used synonymously with this mark of youthful leisure was the practice of 'doing style'. Typically referring to acting 'stylish' – i.e. dressing in fashionable clothing, and engaging in practices of display by standing around on public streets – youth practices of 'doing style' are often central to a spatial politics of youth in the city, as well as to young people's deployment of consumption as a means to claim a global identity and culture.

'Style' as Nakassis (2013: 251) writes: 'crystallises and diagrams youth's liminality, functioning as the register through which young men's ideas of status come to be expressed and negotiated as a double distancing from childhood and adulthood'. Through 'style', in this formulation, youth is imagined as a liminal period, between childhood and adulthood, during which youth is 'exterior' to their families and is away from the surveillance of kin. *Style* is also exterior in that the doing of style is usually physically located in public spaces and solicits viewing publics for its performance. Young men 'do style' by wearing jeans and T-shirts with brand names prominently displayed on them, and standing around near women's colleges.

'Style', as Nakassis (2013) goes on to establish, is a means of differentiating oneself from the peer group: to stand out, and display one's uniqueness. Through this, youth disturbs traditional value systems in which this form of individualism might be seen as a form of undesirable arrogance (*timir*), that is disruptive to society (Mines 1994). To 'do style' therefore is to set up an alternative value system that disturbs notions of respectability and propriety. In this, it resembles Osella and Osella's (1998) 'college culture', which is similarly predicated on youth breaking the 'rules' of middle-class society: for instance negating physical distance by sharing cigarettes and engaging in unproductive uses of time such as simply standing around and staring. It is worth noting that such practices have been studied largely in the context of men by scholars like Osella and Osella (1998) who describe young men in rural Kerala who go *vaaya nokkan* – literally a phrase meaning 'to stare at the mouth' but connoting practices of wandering about and looking at girls, and Lukose (2009) who examines youth practices of 'wasting time' by riding bikes, sitting around in beer parlours and purchasing and publicly wearing fake branded clothes.

Despite young women's increasing participation in these activities, for many I spoke to, wandering about the city and 'doing style' are predominantly masculine practices, in which their participation is a pleasurable act of transgression. One major reason for this is that loitering remains a laden and difficult practice for young women to engage in. As Phadke et al. (2011) amply demonstrate, women in Indian cities typically do not feel free to wander about without purpose, feeling watched and sexualised simply for their presence in public spaces, as well as positioned as 'loose' or 'immoral' women if they are seen to be simply loitering without actually going somewhere. A number of women I met talked about how they would be stopped by policemen who would want to enquire why they were out and about in the middle of the day: Didn't they have homes to return to if classes were finished? If they didn't want to go home right away, why not go to a mall? One of my roommates, was having some fun late one afternoon, hanging around on the road 'doing style' by simply flicking her hair back and forth, and walking up and down while enjoying the looks of appreciation she got from young men, when she was stopped by a policeman, and aggressively asked what she was doing out at this time. When she said she had attended an afternoon seminar and was just returning home, the policeman asked her how he could be sure she was telling the truth – might she not be a sex worker soliciting. Practices of standing around in public, and staring are also widely banned in women's colleges, where staff routinely round up students sitting around under trees or in the canteen, and send them back to classes. At NT College, the 'Home Ministry' of the student parliament takes on this policing duty: members of this ministry routinely check the canteen for students 'bunking' – i.e. skipping classes – and send them back, or interrogate them about why they are there. At college gates, security guards typically hurry students along so they do not hang around, often just staring at passers by, and assessing the men standing that day at the bus stop, while they wait for more friends to arrive.

Concepts of *maanam* (honour) and *karpu* (chastity) were often brought into play in this context and women feared that they might be seen as arrogant – having 'head weight' – and the perception of 'arrogance' always exposed a woman to some mechanism of disciplining. That these concepts circulate popularly among youth today is obvious among students in the city. Soon after my arrival in Chennai for ethnography in 2012, a song called *Clubbu-le Mabbu-le* (in the club), by a local band named *Hiphop Tamizha* gained popularity on social network websites and YouTube. In this song a male singer bemoans the loss of his *maanam* at the mere sight of Tamil women in revealing clothing at clubs, performing 'transgressive' acts such as drinking, smoking and engaging in casual flirtation. Both in everyday conversation and on the comments of the song's YouTube page, a number of young people, both male and female defended the song, arguing that *karpu* and *maanam* appear threatened in the face of rapid urban transformation and advancing consumer culture. It does not address 'all women' was the explanation I was often given, but only 'bad girls, who do dirty things'. It is worth noting that the song was often described as 'style-*ana*' – i.e. bearing or having style – and the lead singer's movements in the song – raising his collar, wearing sunglasses, and standing around, while a group of women sigh in his direction – as being 'stylish'. These practices mark 'style' as being located in the domain of masculine display and a spatial politics of male youth. As Kapur (2012) points out, however, it would be wrong to be too hasty and judge this within a unilateral framework that allows no place for the expression of women's agency and desire. Instead, we might explore the street as a place of possibility.

Young women's engagement in 'doing style' further also disturbs the narrative of women's agency on the street as being located in demure and feminine acts that nevertheless constitute instances of conscious self-positioning (Osella and Osella 1998). When young women dress in fashionable – often also 'western' – clothing and stand around in public spaces, they are drawing attention to themselves, and positioning themselves as active agents in an economy of gazing. As opposed to the demure play of gazes that Osella and Osella (1998) describe – which is also a widely occurring phenomenon – when they 'do style', young women occupy what is otherwise marked as a masculine place of self-conscious and visible positioning. 'Doing style' can be, for many young women, a means of gaining attention and becoming popular among their peers. The ability to 'do style', one group of women told me, shows 'boldness': a girl who does style is widely regarded as a challenge to men around her, and unlike the demure play of gazing, the purpose of 'doing style' is not to start a romance but to flirtatiously question young men's occupation of public spaces, and their usually exclusive and gendered claim over 'youth culture'.

'Doing style' also skirted the boundaries of tomboyish play in young women's lives. Elsewhere, I have shown that young women sometimes 'play male' in joking situations with other women, allowing them to engage in surrogate practices of flirting, and erotic touching that are all passed off as parody, even as they suggest queer potentials (Krishnan 2016). In public, young women rarely engage in erotic play of this kind: rather the street is recreated in the hostel, and boyish style is exaggerated into picaresque caricature in the safety of the hostel's intimacies. This was not so much straightforwardly 'doing style' as a self-conscious parody of young men's uninhibited 'style': it was not meant to subvert these masculine performances publicly, but instead created a space of mocking and flirtation in a space of safety.

In some ways, 'style' and its forms of playful subversion are only enabled by the boundary young women occupy between childhood, and its transgressive possibilities, and respectable adulthood. Even as young women were under a lot of pressure to demonstrate respectability, they also saw their college-going years as a final period of childish playfulness, during which such transgressions were tacitly permitted. Here, playing the male 'rowdy' and doing 'style' in imitation of male filmstars was childish and funny, rather than inappropriate for a young woman. 'Boldness' is a good thing within this context, because it is a way of engaging playful possibilities that young women often want to make the most of, before the responsibilities of adulthood close in on them.

'I DON'T NEED TO DO STYLE': NEGOTIATING HIERARCHY

Style serves also as a site of social differentiation, producing caste and class through a visual aesthetic. Women inhabiting an upper-middle-class 'English-medium' world, thus saw *doing style* as a definitive aspect of lower-middle-class 'popular culture'. Many of these students tended to wear crumpled cotton *kurta*, with either jeans, or baggy *pyjamas*, in imitation of the style popularised by students of more elite universities like Delhi's Jawaharlal Nehru University – a popular graduate school destination for many – and which was described often to me as the nation's 'intellectual uniform', worn by journalists, NGO workers, and students alike. Ironically of course, these clothes – often made of hand-spun cotton, and featuring 'ethnic' prints – much as they are made to look unassuming, are more expensive than the flashy usually chiffon or polyester *style*-ish clothes less privileged peers tend to wear. As Nakassis (2010) notes correctly, one does not have to *do* style, when one already *has* style. In their refusal to acknowledge their own transcendence of *style*, in many ways these students were the sought after ideal. They also typically did not stand around at bus stops, or even go to malls, to engage in *sight adikkarathu* – gazing – more often than not having access to social spaces where they could meet, interact with, and 'date' within western idioms of this term, young men of their own age and social class. Some of these women described *sight* and *style* to me, as 'juvenile' and not clued into global discourses of erotics and romance.

This might be unpacked as a politics of scale, in which the aesthetically reimagined 'local' and 'authentic' increasingly displaces communities that do not have access to the global economies in which this re-imagination is embedded. Emma Tarlo (1996) makes an illustrative argument in her discussion of the social history of Delhi's Hauz Khas village – formerly an actual village now converted into an elite antique-shopping destination. Tracing the story of Bina Ramani, one of the first designers to set up at Hauz Khas, Tarlo (1996) describes how the 'ordinary' Indian clad in an everyday polyester sari or tight shirt and jeans came to be ignored as 'un-Indian' and profoundly westernised in the tourist lens of the elite. Instead, the village, and the labourer, taken out of their context, and placed in glass-windowed, air-conditioned shops were celebrated as the 'real India' in its global avatar. This recovered 'ethnic chic' (Tarlo 1996: 295) 'which displayed only the decorative aspect of tradition without any of its associated hardship or discomfort' (Tarlo 1996: 304) was only accessible to a globalised upper-middle and elite class. To others this still represented what the modernising impulse had bid them leave behind and move out of.

For the lower middle-class woman in Chennai, wearing striped jeans and giggling with her girlfriends about boys in the mall is what represents a 'modern' India. Whereas to the upper-middle-class urban woman, wearing rumpled Fabindia tunics and traditional hard-leather *kolhapuri* sandals while singing along to Bollywood's latest risqué number that mimics the elite imagination of working-class life and ribaldry might better represent the same ideal of modernity. As an upper caste and elite male student in the city put it: 'If you're trying too hard, then you're not happening.' Seeking to go to a club or wanting a Vespa whilst one was still distant from being able to realise these desires was the position of the person who is *doing style*.

Scene podarathu is a practice very closely related to 'style' and suggests attracting attention to oneself by publicly performing something. So for instance, when Kumari walked in to college one day and announced, in a melodramatic tone, recalling the heroines of dramatic Tamil cinema: '*Intha kaadhaley oru thalavali*' (This love is a headache), one of her friends turned to the others, and mockingly said, '*scene podara paaru*' (look – she's making a scene). Similarly, we would be standing at the bus stop, and one of the young women in the crowd would start to do something attention-drawing like swishing her loose, long hair around, as she noisily used her mobile phone, or even posed, say one leg out, hips thrust to one side. The others would then declare that she was doing *scene podarathu*. The purpose of the *scene* was usually to attract the attention of those present, making oneself visible albeit in an ironic gesture. If one did a *scene* without meaning to – i.e. came off as being overly melodramatic with no intent of drama – others then pointed out that this was a *scene*, thus rendering it ridiculous and vulnerable to friendly mocking.

Scene podarathu was also used mockingly by young women of the middle and lower middle classes to describe the attention-drawing practices of upper middle-class and elite students who were their peers. So for instance, sunglasses are, in Chennai, often the singular commodity sign of *scene* – students typically do not wear them even at the height of summer in 40 degrees centigrade or over, unless they are trying to do *scene*. In Tamil films, typically, the 'hero' whips out his sunglasses in a scene where he is showing off, either to impress the heroine or to intimidate villains. In Rajni Kant's iconic films, the moment where the 'hero' puts on his sunglasses typically also presages an eventful scene. To wear sunglasses, then, is to presume that one has the status of the 'hero' – the ability and panache to carry off this very loaded commodity. Hence, when occasionally middle- or upper middle-class students turned up in college in cars, and wearing sunglasses, others pointed and said '*scene podara paaru*' (Look, she's making a scene). In mocking those who possessed these much sought-after symbols of class status, those who do the mocking suggest that they in fact cannot carry them off: that they look ridiculous trying. Through 'style' and the practices associated with it, young women therefore negotiate hierarchies of class and caste, which otherwise fracture and deeply complicate experiences of being middle-class.

'EVE TEASING': 'STYLE' AS AGENCY

Flirtation and 'doing style' with each other, also sometimes pales into the territory of 'eve teasing' as sexual harassment on the streets is often called. So ubiquitous that most young women now carry pins or umbrellas with sharp tips when they board buses, to ward off the roving hands of male passengers, eve teasing is an experience many connect to the dangers of simply 'hanging out' in places. As Rogers (2005) suggests, for young men, eve teasing is often both an aspect of masculine competition with other young men, as well as a means of exercising control over women who are seen as being arrogant, or otherwise transgressing the bounds of femininity.

As Kapur (2012) writes, women in Indian cities are ogled and sexualised in any context where they are present in public spaces: whether as shoppers, workers or students. Following the death of a student in a road traffic accident that was directly related to this form of harassment in Chennai, the Tamil Nadu government passed the Prohibition of Eve Teasing Act (1998) that recognises this practice as a crime, carrying a sentence of up to ten years' imprisonment for particularly heinous forms of harassment. In the years that I conducted fieldwork – 2012 and 2013 – 'eve teasing' was back in the focus in the context of renewed debates on dress codes in Chennai's colleges. Institutions often also used 'eve teasing' as justification for imposing dress codes on students. College authorities typically argued that 'undignified behaviour' by young women was a cause for 'eve teasing' on the streets. In particular, an NT College teacher argued that the 'type of girls' who enrolled in her college these days – i.e. lower middle-class and lower caste students – appeared not to care about the 'type of men' they might attract by wearing revealing clothing. In positioning sexual harassment on the streets as a problem centered on the public presence of subaltern bodies, this teacher echoes a widely heard middle-class opinion in Chennai and elsewhere.

In the everyday lives of young women, 'eve teasing' often occupies a murky boundary between the aggressive banter that characterises flirtatious games and sexual harassment as a form of violence. It indexes forms of play between young men and women where young men use a challenging, hypermasculine tone in addressing women they wish to flirt with. As Osella and Osella (1998: 194) suggest, the effect of this is most often 'to rupture social distance, reducing formality and restraint and bringing the girl and the youth into the same space'. The context is most often left ambivalent; allowing the young woman and her friends either to accept the invitation to banter, or to interpret it as harassment, and in this latter case, usually walk away. And, confusingly, in this dynamic, sometimes 'no' does mean 'yes'.

Young women often used the idioms of *scene* and *style* to mock men who would woo them, thus embarrassing these young men in front of their friends. In these cases, to point these practices of class out as *style* or *scene* is in fact to lower their status and value, and reduce them to mere bravado. In doing so, young women assume considerable agency over the practice of *sight adikkarathu* — often using this to deflect overtures that may not have been welcome or pleasant, and turning them back on the men who made them, by embarrassing them. One common way in which some women did this was by addressing the man who made this overture as a brother, with mockingly exaggerated ignorance as to his erotic intent. This, by nullifying the possibility of romantic attachment, embarrasses the young man, snubbing him in the moment of the making of his gesture. Kalaiselvi, a serious athlete, often found herself in this position. For various reasons, Kalaiselvi had decided she did not want to engage in any romantic attachments with boys around her. She told me she found them immature: they were *chinna pasangka* — 'little boys' — and she wanted a 'man' — *a periya aal*. She was, nevertheless, often the object of *sight adikkarathu* for the young men around her. She added that many gathered to watch and comment on her body or *figaru* — a widely used Tamil modification of the English 'figure' — as she did her long jumps.

While she ignored them most of the time, she said she sometimes enjoyed bantering with them and then eventually snubbing them, calling them *tambi* (little brother) or *pasangkala* (children), so they did not seriously pursue her. Often this bursts the *style* or *scene* balloon, rendering these young men ridiculous for having assumed a status that they did not possess. However, interestingly, Kalaiselvi described her own performance as *style* as well. In acting cool — and demonstrating her status over the young men who were *sight*-ing her, Kalaiselvi had assumed *style*, in a way that did not do a *scene*, or make a ridiculous figure of her. Kalaiselvi had also, in doing so, managed to appropriate control of the space of the act of *sight*-ing and refigure it in her own terms. During this time, she would also *sight* some men in her own right. However, by snubbing them, she left herself invulnerable. Kalaiselvi managed, thus, to create a space for erotic expression without letting herself feel precarious in a public space. In this, Kalaiselvi's friends considered her 'smart' — using the English word.

Another often-used tactic was to position oneself as being above 'style', by declaring the man doing 'style' as *cēri*. Literally referring to the Dalit settlements outside villages, *cēri* has now migrated from a literal meaning to being a deeply casteist metaphor for anyone whom youth regard as 'uncool' or in the more interesting translation, 'local'. Here the word 'local' refers not merely to proximity of 'location' but to something that is the opposite of 'global'. *Cēri* and local boys, I was told, wear fakes, and do not have global cultural references. They are imagined to be 'backward' and 'uneducated', even if they are fellow college-students. Style when it goes 'over-ā' or is seen to cross a boundary to being 'too much' – here referring usually to the murky boundary crossed between aggressive masculine self-positioning and sexual harassment – is then often declared '*cēri*' or 'local'. Such men, I was often told, are 'unused' to 'fashionable girls' and to 'style-*āna*' clothes, such as jeans, tight T-shirts, and sunglasses. It might be worth noting here that women often draw on certain discourses of power – here caste and class – to counter sexual threat, and to position themselves as being beyond reproach and within a 'safe' zone. By marking the men who threaten them as '*cēri*' or 'local', the young women here reinforce caste-inflected ideologies about which men are 'safe' to flirt with, and who is 'dangerous', while simultaneously expressing dissent against the normalised practice of 'eve teasing'.

CONCLUSION

In this chapter I have shown that 'style' as an idiom is useful to examine the ways in which young women practice forms of everyday agency, whether in negotiating hierarchies with peers or in countering the threat of sexual harassment on the street. These forms of agency, as I have shown, are ambivalent, often reinforcing some dominant discourses even as they resist others. 'Style' has also been shown to be a means for young women to stake claims to an otherwise masculine 'youth culture' in which, unlike their male counterparts, they face a great deal of surveillance.

As a playful appropriation of young men's cultural practice, 'style' allows young women to occupy an ironic site of critique vis-à-vis the social norms through which they are gendered, as well as made respectable and middle class. In this, 'style' allows young women to play 'rowdy' and inhabit masculine forms of comportment, as a means of ironically interrupting scripts of demure respectability. This itself is enabled mostly because young women – particularly college-going women – occupy a middle ground between childhood innocence and adult respectability. So, for instance, Masters students that I met in Chennai did not engage in such practices. Many of them wanted to be married soon, and saw the play of 'style' as a childish preoccupation. Similarly, the numerous 'working women' – usually young graduates in their early twenties – who live in women's hostels, do not engage in 'style', and even feared that they might be seen as being too playful and improperly adult both in the hostel and in public if they did so.

The boundary of 'style', therefore, was adulthood, marked by graduation from college and entry into a world of respectable futures, in which marriage featured brightly. In marking 'style' as childish, young women who had recently graduated from college marked themselves above college culture, and ready for a life of responsibility.

NOTE

1. While this paper is focused more on the space and embodied politics of style, we might note that gendered experiences of time are also central to the different ways in which young men and women think of leisure and even of the performance of style. In a paper recently delivered at the American Anthropological Association's Conference (2016), I argued that young women experience time as fleeting: their youth is widely imagined and described as a 'blink' and a 'breath'. Ironically, the only way to make the most of this fast-moving time is to 'waste' it by engaging in practices that are normatively imagined as non-productive, such as wandering around the city, and window-shopping. This is the temporal framework in which we might locate young women's performance of 'style' as a site of subversion.

REFERENCES

Favero, P. (2003) 'Phantasms in a "Starry" Place: Space and Identification in a Central New Delhi Market', *Cultural Anthropology* 18(4): 551–584. Doi: 10.1525/Can.2003.18.4.551.

Gilbertson, A. (2014) 'A Fine Balance: Negotiating Fashion and Respectable Femininity in Middle-Class Hyderabad, India', *Modern Asian Studies*, 48(1): 120–158.

Jeffrey, C. (2010) 'Timepass: Youth, Class, and Time Among Unemployed Young Men in India', *American Ethnologist* 37(3): 465–481.

Kapur, R. (2012) 'Pink Chaddis and SlutWalk Couture: The Postcolonial Politics of Feminism Lite', *Feminist Legal Studies* 20(1): 1–20.

Krishnan, S. (2016) 'Agency, Intimacy, and Rape Jokes: An Ethnographic Study of Young Women and Sexual Risk in Chennai', *Journal of the Royal Anthropological Institute* 22(1): 67–83.

Lukose, R.A. (2009) *Liberalization's Children: Gender, Youth, and Consumer Citizenship in Globalizing India*, Durham: Duke University Press.

Mankekar, P. (1999) *Screening Culture, Viewing Politics: An Ethnography of Television, Womanhood, and Nation in Postcolonial India*, Durham: Duke University Press.

Mines, M. (1994) *Public Faces, Private Voices: Community and Individuality in South India*, Berkeley: University of California Press.

Nakassis, C.V. (2010) 'Youth and Status in Tamil Nadu, India', PhD, Anthropology, University of Pennsylvania.

—— (2013) 'Youth Masculinity, "Style" and the Peer Group in Tamil Nadu, India', *Contributions to Indian Sociology* 47(2): 245–269.

Osella, C. and Osella, F. (1998) 'Friendship and Flirting: Micro-Politics in Kerala, South India', *Journal of the Royal Anthropological Institute* 4(2): 189–206.

Phadke, S., Ranade, S. and Khan, S. (2011) *Why Loiter? Women and Risk on Mumbai Streets*, New Delhi: Penguin.

Radhakrishnan, S. (2011) *Appropriately Indian: Gender and Culture in a New Transnational Class*, Durham: Duke University Press.

Rogers, M. (2005) *Tamil Youth: The Performance of Hierarchical Masculinities: An Anthropological Study of Youth Groups in Chennai, Tamil Nadu, India*, Unpublished DPhil thesis, Department of Anthropology, University of Sussex, Sussex.

—— (2008) 'Modernity, "Authenticity", and Ambivalence: Subaltern Masculinities on a South Indian College Campus', *Journal of the Royal Anthropological Institute* 14(1): 79–95.

Säävälä, M. (2010) *Middle-class Moralities: Everyday Struggle over Belonging and Prestige in India*, Hyderabad: Orient Blackswan.

Tarlo, E. (1996) *Clothing Matters: Dress and Identity in India*, London: Hurst and Co.

Vathikuchi (2013) Dir. Kinslin, Perf: Dileepan, Anjali, Saranya Ponvannan, Sampath Raj. AR Murugadoss Productions and FOX Star Studios.

3

RITUPARNO GHOSH, SARTORIAL CODES AND THE QUEER BENGALI YOUTH

Rohit K. Dasgupta and Kaustav Bakshi

INTRODUCTION[1]

In this chapter we examine Rituparno Ghosh, a queer filmmaker from Bengal, India, who left an indelible mark on the public consciousness and sartorial identity of young Bengali queer men in contemporary India. Since emerging onto the public stage with his first film *Hirer Angti* (The Diamond Ring) in 1992, and even before formally 'coming out' with visible sartorial markers, Rituparno experimented with his wardrobe through pushing male fashion to its androgynous limits. His evolving style was a manifestation of the abstract notion of an androgynous artist which he attributed to his cultural mentor, the Nobel laureate and national poet, Rabindranath Tagore (1861–1941). In a number of newspaper and magazine articles which came out following Ghosh's death on 30 May 2013, considerable space was devoted to recollecting his androgynous approach towards fashion and style. Whilst Kolkata-based designers like Sharbari Dutta are credited for popularising a flamboyant, non-western fashion aesthetic for men during the late 1990s and early 2000s, Ghosh had already set a precedent.

Based on ethnography and textual analysis of Ghosh's films and media appearances we argue that Ghosh's sartorial expressions can be read as a case of performed queer fashion at the time of an androgynous turn in the works of Indian fashion designers in the mid 1990s. The chapter includes voices of fashion designers who knew Ghosh well and contemporary young Bengali queer men who have looked upon Ghosh as a source of sartorial inspiration and encouragement to come out.

RITUPARNO

Rituparno Ghosh (1961–2013) was a cultural producer who wrote, directed and later acted in films, wrote lyrics, edited magazines, hosted television shows and became a queer style icon in India. While Ghosh was criticised for unabashedly conforming to bourgeois values and celebrating the 'good life' in the films he made, he was also widely applauded for their transgressive narratives. His stories explored transgressive social codes, marital rape, sexual desires of widows, same-sex love and moral hypocrisies of the new middle class. His films, featuring young directors, teachers, poets, career women, teenagers and queer men as protagonists, opened new windows to the 'cultured youth' of Bengal and India, straddling both tradition and modernity in the face of rapid globalisation. Ghosh's arrival in the film industry happened at a critical moment when the predominantly socialist nation state was slowly transforming into a late capitalist one, owing largely to the liberalisation of the Indian economy in the early 1990s (Dasgupta 2014; Dasgupta 2017; Dasgupta and Gokulsing 2014; Gokulsing and Dissanayake 2013). It goes without saying that Ghosh's films were informed by the social, cultural and economic changes wrought by liberalisation in the lives of the Bengali middle class. Ghosh was at once a product and producer of the schizophrenic consumerist culture effectuated by the open market (Dasgupta, Datta and Bakshi 2016). His iconoclastic decision to 'come out' officially and to associate himself with films on queer subjects was also conditioned by neoliberal discourses of sexual identity politics of a late capitalist society. However, the process of 'coming out' was long and drawn out; Ghosh's films revolving around female protagonists and their predicament within a hetero-patriarchal family betrayed unambiguous markers of queerness. His filmic critiques of arranged marriage, the commodification of women as sexual objects within the approved social structure of marriage and family, the lack of freedom they suffer from, and his endorsement of polyamory as a possible alternative to monogamous romantic associations, all insinuated a radical disposition that would culminate into liberal queer politics in his later films.

Wimal Dissanayake (2016) in his article, 'Rituparno Ghosh and the Pursuit of Freedom', while analysing *Chokher Bali/A Passion Play* (2003), which was released at least six years before Ghosh officially came out, observes; 'He was always concerned about the lack of freedom that characterised the lives of women in India and elsewhere and later began to explore issues of homosexual relations and transgender desires as articulations and effects of freedom' (49). In our personal interactions with Ghosh, we often heard him talk of how his female characters were sometimes inspired by his own life. In other words, before Ghosh actually came out, he channelled his desires, misgivings, and feelings of betrayal (in love) into the portraiture of many of his female protagonists. It was not until *Arekti Premer Golpo/Just Another Love Story* (2010) directed by Kaushik Ganguly finally pushed open the closet door, that Ghosh appeared in public, exhibiting his queerness, not only in his mannerisms but in his sartorial excesses too.

Before and after the release of *Arekti Premer Golpo/Just Another Love Story* (2010),[2] where he played a transsexual filmmaker (which was read by the audiences as autobiographical), Ghosh began appearing in flamboyant clothes and loud makeup in public. He raised a controversy in 2009 by publicly challenging a stand-up comic of Bengali television in his much acclaimed talk-show, *Ghosh & Company*:

> When you are mimicking me, are you mimicking Rituparno Ghosh, the person or are you mimicking a generic effeminate man? ... What message are you putting across? Have you ever thought that when you mimic me, you actually end up humiliating all effeminate men in Kolkata? ... You should be sensitive to the fact that you are hurting the sentiments of a sexual minority. I am objecting to your act not because I am inconvenienced myself;

rather I am objecting to it on the behalf of all those for whom I may be a representative.[3]

Ghosh reiterated several times that the lewd jokes addressed to him did not bother him as such; he was more concerned that the jokes were debilitating for other 'effeminate' men in Kolkata, who were regularly abused on the streets or within the home for being 'unmanly'. He asserted that since these men could not articulate their discomfort, he was taking up their cause with the stand-up comic who had been insulting them for years. Whilst Ghosh's films and his own sartorial choice have been instrumental in propagating the myth that all feminine men are gay and all gay men have a fascination for gender-bending apparel (due to the absence of any other equally eminent and trendsetting queer icon in the public domain to this date), it remains immutable that Ghosh's extraordinary style and visible alternative way of being came as a surprise shock to the Bengali populace and to Indians at large. But this, in our opinion, was actually Ghosh's activism – the performance of his queerness, destabilising normative assumptions about gender roles, and sexual choices. We believe that Ghosh's stardom which travelled across multiple media platforms was instrumental in also getting issues of queerness and queer identities in the Bengali mainstream public (Dasgupta and Banerjee 2016). Richard Dyer (1979), writing about stars, surmises that stars are constructed not only from their public performances but also publicity materials, magazine columns and so on. Ghosh effectively used all forms of media – television, film, Internet and print magazine – to become an important voice and 'face' of queerness in Bengal. In the following section, we locate our reading of Ghosh's fashion and its political implications within the discourses of global queer fashion that have emerged in the past two decades.

DRESSES, DRAGS AND DARE: THE POLITICS AND PRECEDENTS OF GHOSH'S WARDROBE

Dress in India, as anywhere else, plays an important role; it instigates change, questions national identities and asserts power (Tarlo 1996). The impact of colonialism upon dress in South Asia has been and continues to be twofold. On the one hand dress became a site of protest when Gandhi promoted a return to homespun *khadi* against the British clothes,[4] and on the other hand dress also signified religion and ethnicity for most Indians. Western clothing in India as Begum and Dasgupta (2015) have discussed was often associated with the contaminating forces of a heterogeneous, hyper-sexualised colonial (western) modernity whilst Indian clothes were often used to signify chastity, purity and tradition. This is still most pronounced within Indian cinema.[5] Whilst this duality has been discussed in relation to female dress and sexuality, we would argue that these dualities also affect male dress choice, especially during political protests and the Swadeshi independence movement when Indian men were encouraged to discard western clothing and return to the 'traditional' and 'pure' homespun *khadi* clothes.

Indian clothing for men, as scholars such as Vanita (2014) have argued, has been androgynous before the arrival of colonial modernity which, among many cultural changes, effectuated and advocated strict distinction between male and female ways of dressing. Representations of Hindu male gods (even the most virile ones such as *Shiva*, *Kama* and *Kartik*), for example, often have them wearing heavy jewellery, including ornate crowns or headgears, dangling earrings, navel-length neckpieces, waistbands, armlets, bracelets and bangles. They are usually portrayed as donning silken *uttariyas* over a bare body and flowing embroidered *dhotis*. The same is true of epic characters, including the most hypermasculine heroes of the *Ramayana* and the *Mahabharata*. Within Islamic cultures too, men are known to have displayed very refined sartorial tastes, as underscored by available Islamic paintings, Urdu poetry and songs from medieval India (Vanita and Kidwai 2000). Ruth Vanita, in her foreword to *Masculinity and its Challenges in India* (2014), elaborates on pre-colonial dress codes of men and women arguing that what came to be identified as feminine clothing post 1857, was not so earlier. To quote Vanita:

> Such attire was not read by Indians as signaling effeminacy or any particular sexual predilection, although it is relevant that attraction to a beautiful young person of either sex was considered par for the course and had no bearing on a man's masculinity.
>
> (Vanita 2014: 2)

The linkages between pre-colonial dressing and androgyny to contemporary queer fashion amongst Bengali males is exemplified by Ghosh who acknowledges his queer sartorial choices as an invocation and nostalgia for a precolonial/ancient Indian tradition. As Bakshi observes, 'Ghosh claimed that he was merely reviving an ancient tradition in which jewellery and the *uttariya* were integral to the male attire' (Bakshi 2013: 121). Gayatri Gopinath (2005: 21) in her seminal work on queer diasporic South Asian public cultures writes that it 'takes the form of easily "recognizable" cultural texts such as musical genres, films, videos, and novels that have a specifically transnational address even as they are deeply rooted in the politics of the local'. We surmise that Ghosh's clothes in this sense were also creating a recognisable cultural text for his Bengali queer audiences.

Ghosh saw himself as an androgynous man. He considered androgyny as a privilege for any artist. He observed that Tagore's androgyny was thematically played out in his works, for example in *Ghare Baire* (Home and the World, 1916) in which he modelled the character of Nikhilesh on that of a *birahini*, a woman who is awaiting her lover: Nikhilesh waits for his wife to come back from the path of infidelity. This, according to Ghosh, has a subversive charge as Tagore tried to create the traits of a feminine sensibility in a male character (Sarkar 2011: 83). He pointed out that even certain songs of Tagore have an ambiguous androgynous voice underneath, since 'pronouns and verbs in the Bengali language are not gender sensitive ... the mysterious and mystical ambiguity of androgyny is a treasure' commented Ghosh in an interview (Sarkar 2011: 83). His own practiced androgyny, he believed, came from this kind of influence. Androgyny, however, is not very unfamiliar in Bengali culture as at least two of the adored Bengali icons, Sri Chaitanya and Sri Ramakrishna, are widely represented as androgynous. In fact, in *Arekti Premer Golpo*, the androgynous figure of Sri Chaitanya acts as a constant symbolic reference vis-à-vis which the protagonist's gender fluidity is played out.

Interestingly, noted socialite designer Sharbari Dutta, who has been designing clothes for men since 1991, also has a similar kind of approach towards changing mindsets when it comes to dressing men.[6] According to her, Indian men are very inhibited when it comes to dressing up.

Due to the British influence and colonial hangover, Indians have always considered grey, pale blue or navy blue as masculine colours that make for smart outfits (Roychowdhury 2011: 4). In an interview, Dutta says:

> I wanted to prove that there's no clash between masculinity and bright colours. Our Indian tradition in menswear is of bright colours and *nakshas*. So why have we ignored it completely? A three-piece suit is not the only fashion statement for an Indian man. He can also make a statement in traditional Indian clothes.
> (Roychowdhury 2011)

In a way both Ghosh and Dutta seem to assert that fashion does not need to restrict itself to the socially sanctioned and culturally codified gender binaries. Fashion constitutes a major area in gender discourses as it has a 'queer' quality to itself and an ability to break conventions and set patterns. For instance Richard Dyer points out: 'Feminization of male attire [does] not mean wearing women's clothes but a readiness to wear bright or pastel colours, to put extra flounce or decoration to an outfit, to do things, in short, that only women were supposed to do' (2002: 63). Ghosh's fashion statements exemplify what Dyer says about feminisation of men's clothes.

In the case of Ghosh, his fashion statements can be seen as having the power of expanding the purview of the male wardrobe.[7] Even if Ghosh's attire is discerned as located on the borderline of cross-dressing or transvestism it causes a 'category crisis' (Garber 1992). Transvestism generally problematises, exposes and challenges the very notion of 'original' and stable identities. It also 'calls[s] attention to cultural, social or aesthetic dissonances' (Garber 1992: 16). In the same manner, Ghosh's wardrobe can be seen to demonstrate a failure of 'definitional distinction, a borderline that becomes permeable, that permits border crossing, from one (apparently distinct) category to the other' (Garber 1992: 16). In his queer films too, the costumes given to his protagonists also bordered on androgyny, highlighting this category crisis. In *Arekti Premer Golpo*, for example, Abhiroop (played by Ghosh), the queer filmmaker, is seen mostly in tops, stoles, plazo suits, pendants and colourful jackets, teamed with eye liner, lip gloss, rings and earrings, the kind of clothes and accessories Ghosh sported in real life.

In this context, it would be interesting to quote fashion connoisseur Parmesh Shahni:

> There is a new wave of androgynous dressing coming out of urban India, and I like it very much. In each case, it is a very unique form of individual expression ... I've silently admired the award-winning film director Rituparno Ghosh's several stunning public appearances in the past year. In February, at the Berlin premiere of the film *Areki Premer Golpo*, in which he makes his acting debut, Rituparno made heads turn with his turban, choker, *salwar-kameez*, lipstick and eye-liner. Was he dressing in character (he plays two roles in the film, one of a gay director and another of a *jatra* performer) – or was he just reinventing himself in the public eye? Why does it matter? He was (is!) fabulous, full stop.
>
> (Shahni 2010)

The androgyny Ghosh projected, worked towards augmenting queer visibility in media and the public sphere. As Ruth Holliday argues, 'having been invisible (or pathologized) for so long in writing, the media, law and culture more generally' now queer identities have been 'increasingly visible through a number of mechanisms' (2001: 215). She argues:

> The politics of visibility as well as the many everyday cues and codes of dress, gesture or conduct are often used to communicate identity to others of the same or different groups. For example, the development of queer styles such as butch and camp (to name but two) have become signifiers of sexuality and are mapped onto the surface of bodies, not least through clothes.
>
> (Holliday 2001: 215)

FASHION, SUBLIMATION AND GHOSH

Rituparno Ghosh's negotiation with fashion in his films is almost an act of creative sublimation, articulating his queer subjectivity. All his films display tremendous obsession with refined couture, jewellery and bridal makeup. In this context, *Chokher Bali* (A Passion Play, 2003), a period film, inspired by a Tagore novel, demands special attention; for its protagonist Binodini seems to have an unmistakable bearing on the queer characters later essayed by Ghosh. Although a narrative on female emancipation, in the film gold jewellery emerges as an object of Binodini's forbidden desire; this is because, as a widow, Binodini is socially forbidden from popular South Asian ritualistic codes of ornamentation, *shringar*. Shringar through particularly gold jewellery from early Hindu mythology to the contemporary context denotes self-adornment and a powerful means to expressing status, beauty, romantic or erotic love 'the substance of aesthetic experience' (Shukla 2008: 4).

In desiring gold jewellery and wearing it to seduce potential lovers, Binodini remorselessly transgresses a stringent social code. In an editorial piece, Ghosh wrote, 'I developed my Binodini as an extension of my own self' (Ghosh 2013). This identification with Binodini is played out explicitly in his later queer films, in terms of characterisation as well as costumes. Mahendra's adulterous affair with Binodini renders her an 'other', illegitimately intruding into the life of an apparently happily married couple and separating them. In both *Arekti Premer Golpo* and *Chitrangada: A Crowning Wish* (Ghosh 2012),[8] the queer protagonists (played by Ghosh) replicate Binodini's otherness: in their relationship with bisexual men, who prioritise and socially acknowledge their heterosexual relationships as against their same sex lovers. Ghosh's queer men suffer neglect, insult, and eventual abandonment. Ghosh's identification with Binodini is brought out through certain scenes and sartorial desires in both these films. It is important to make this connection, for it underscores how Ghosh projected his queer desires on his heroines, before he eventually came out in public.

To demonstrate this, we may allude to two similar sequences from *Arekti Premer Galpo* and *Chitrangada: A Crowning Wish* and then link them to a sequence in *Chokher Bali*. In a sequence in *Arekti Premer Galpo*, a young Chapal Bhaduri,[9] played by Ghosh, suddenly arrives at Kumar Babu's house, his mentor and lover (played by Indraneil Sengupta), in the early hours of the night. The sequence opens with a bejewelled Chapal entering the room, removing his shawl with a flourish revealing a fully ornamented get-up. This dramatic entry is followed by a conversation between them, in which Chapal, erotically reclining on the bed, teases

Figure 3.1 Rituparno Ghosh playing Rudra in *Chitrangada* (2012). Image courtesy of Shri Venkatesh Films.

Kumar, lightly reproving him for his inability to acknowledge his relationship with him. Again in the film Chitrangada, Rudra sits pensively in the dressing room, wearing elaborate jewellery just before his stage performance. His boyfriend Partho (Jishu Sengupta) finds his way to the room in an inebriated state. This is followed by an emotional altercation between the two, which finally leads to vigorous lovemaking. However, Rudra is constantly aware of the difficulty of carrying this relationship forward all along. These two characters in the abovementioned sequences find a cinematic predecessor in *Chokher Bali*. Binodini visits her love interest Bihari late at night, wearing all her jewels with the intention of seducing him. She fails, as Bihari, a sworn celibate, ignores her, despite her snide attacks on his manliness. In all three sequences an abundance of *shringar* of gold jewellery, the most desired ornamentation for unmarried and married women, dominates the narrative. By desiring and donning a forbidden object, in this case, gold jewellery, the widow as well as the queer men demand acknowledgement of their status and sexual desires which are either repressed by violence or are treated as non-existent.

GHOSH, ICONISM AND QUEER FANS[10]

Even before he began acting in queer-themed films, Ghosh had been extremely visible in the public domain, owing to the proliferation of the television industry in the early 1990s. Ghosh appeared regularly on television, sometimes hosting talk-shows, at other times as an interviewee. The clothes he wore immediately caught attention, for he was always dressed in long handloom kurtas, accessorised with a dupatta or an uttariya. In his mannerisms too he appeared different, for he never tried to hide his effeminacy. It did not take long for people to identify his uniqueness, which was visibly different from other male filmmakers who had emerged from the stable of Tollygunje.[11]

We are talking of a time, the mid 1990s, when discourses on queer sexualities and alternative registers of love and eroticism were slowly entering the public domain in Kolkata through books, American magazines, television series and films. The word 'gay' had not entered the everyday parlance; but the more informed people, particularly the English-educated metropolitan elite, had begun to realise that 'gay' no longer simply implied 'happy'; the word had a more political bearing, hitherto unknown.

In the beginning, Ghosh was not open about his sexuality. His sartorial statements were indicative of his same-sex leanings, but were not unambiguous markers. Although he was mostly seen in jeans and crew-neck T-shirts on his sets, he sported a very different style when he appeared on television or any public event. His first talk-show *Ebong Rituparno*, aired on ETV Bangla, marked him out as 'different'. However, his dressing sense often passed as carrying forward the Shantiniketani style of men's clothing, which was quite popular among the Bengali intellectuals. The Shantiniketani style, consisting of handloom kurtas (with floral patterns, large block prints or side panels, or batik prints on them), pyjamas, and jholas (embroidered or printed sling bags), originated in Tagore's ashram years back and caught up with Kolkata intellectuals from the early 1970s onwards. This style was often ridiculed by more westernised folks for being feminine. Very rarely, though, was homosexuality associated with such clothing. At the time of *Ebong Rituparno* (early 2000s), Ghosh's wardrobe flaunted an ethnic revival, which was a trend in women's fashion then. Sabarni Das, who worked as costume designer in many of Ghosh's films, has observed:

> During Ebong Rituparno, a sharp change[12] was noticed in Rituparno's fashion ... Indian fashion world was then immersed in ethnic styles: long kalidaar kurta, dogri pyajama, kantha sari, kachhi waistcoat, tie and die dupatta, ikkat blouse and what not! Regional fashion had a heyday ... In Rituparno's clothes too this influence was clearly noticeable.
>
> (Bakshi, 2013: 53)

However, among those who were more informed about queer sexualities, there used to be a lot of speculation about the possibility of Ghosh being 'gay'. Having grown up and spending a major part of our life in Kolkata, we can attest to the fact that people gossiped about Ghosh's sexuality, his habit of cross-dressing at home,[13] his alleged affairs with male film-stars, and his several idiosyncrasies, which had no verifiable evidence in public. But the pieces of gossip nonetheless circulated and were relished by the queer community, in and outside Kolkata. In an interview with us, Anindya Hazra, a queer activist based in the city, recalled that they had once invited Ghosh to a panel discussion entitled, 'Purush: Oitijhye, Sanskritite, Dharanoe Biborton' (Changing Ideas of Men and Masculinity in Tradition and Culture) in 2000, almost certain of Ghosh's sexuality. Ghosh had still not 'come out'; but they had invited him for the way in which he had redefined men's fashion, which was still not identified as specifically queer. In the same panel, Sharbari Dutta, who had remarkably transformed Bengali men's traditional wardrobe, was also invited to speak. However Ghosh declined the invitation. Hazra believes this was because Ghosh was still not ready to 'come out'. It would take another nine years for Ghosh to officially announce his sexuality. Growing up in the same city with Ghosh, people were often heard making snide remarks at men's clothes, if they were not specifically 'masculine'. An accessory, such as a *dupatta* or an *uttariya*, an ornate bag or a ring, almost certainly drew a sarcastic 'oi dekh Rituparno jachche' (there goes another Rituparno) from people on the street. Many effeminate men in Kolkata began to be identified as 'Rituparno', the term now replacing other derogatory labels like 'ladies' or *sakhi*. Much later, in his introduction to a queer journal, Hazra brought to light this phenomenon:

> I feel like asking whether that name apart from becoming a cultural icon of the feminine man is also standing-in for something else for the Bengalis. Is this name (which among many other things is also a brand of sorts for gendered performativity), unwittingly, carving out a comfort zone for the middle/upper class Bengalis? Is this name nothing but a sanitized version of such offensive terms as 'ladies', *boudi*, *sakhi* (and more recently and increasingly 'homo') ... by which the Bengali *bhadrolok* has always abused his effeminate classmate mauling the latter's self-confidence, his self-respect?
>
> (Hazra, 2011, 4)

Any visibly feminine man who has grown up in Kolkata, after Ghosh became a popular icon, would corroborate the point Hazra is making here (also see Dey 1998). However, Ghosh was silently bringing about a change in how men's clothing was to be perceived. Several queer men we interviewed remarked how Ghosh made them feel more confident about wearing androgynous clothes or even cross-dressing in public. Later, when Ghosh 'came out' in public and made his sexuality unambiguous through his sartorial statements, he simultaneously endeared and alienated his audience. While the more conservative people were scandalised, the queer-identified individuals found in him an icon to look up to. Ghosh was completely aware of this. In an interview with Bakshi, he rued:

> I have indeed estranged a section of my audience. I am aware of the loss. A lot of them are wary of my cross-dressing in public! In fact, the respect I used to command has been seriously affected by my decision to proclaim my sexuality.
>
> (Bakshi, 2013: 12)

Nevertheless, he did set an example for the queer men and women who desperately needed a local queer icon, who would tell their stories and prove to the world that homosexuality was not unnatural. Ghosh's 'coming out' was important, for he was widely revered and people could not dismiss him for being 'gay'. In 2009, a year before the release of

Figure 3.2 Rituparno at Kolkata Fashion Week 2009. Image courtesy of Abhishek Datta.

Arekti Premer Golpo, Ghosh began appearing in public, on television chat shows, award ceremonies, parties, and other social events, in flamboyant clothes and silk headgears which sometimes reminded people of the Bollywood star Rekha. Ghosh, an ardent fan of the legendary actor who had gradually emerged as a style icon, in fact asked his friends whether he looked like Rekha and was the happiest when they agreed. He even walked the ramp for the young fashion designer Abhishek Dutta, after undergoing abdominoplasty and cosmetic surgery, which gave him a very petite, feminine appearance. Dutta told us that he had actually replaced a Bollywood actor with Ghosh, when she failed to turn up for the show, and Ghosh surprised him by 'rocking the ramp like a pro'.[14]

After coming out, Ghosh was seen experimenting with his attire even more: sometimes he combined a Japanese top with a Burmese *lungi*; sometimes other kinds of wrap-around lowers with tops that were tied, rather than buttoned. Yet, he did not strictly cross-dress. He believed in inhabiting a liminality in his choice of clothes. He told Bakshi in the same interview as quoted above:

> I know many of my viewers apprehend that I might start wearing the sari any day. Let me tell you, I shall never wear a sari. I remember someone asking me whether I shall ever wear the *dhoti-kurta*? My answer was I wouldn't. I'll not wear any gender-determining attire ... neither sari nor *dhoti-kurta* ... I shall always go for something in-between. That's the best way of celebrating gender fluidity.
>
> (Bakshi 2013: 7)

In *Chitrangada: A Crowning Wish*, Rudra, the queer choreographer seeking sex reassignment surgery echoes this: 'I want to be a woman just on technical grounds ... I am neither going to wear a sari nor am I wearing a *ghagra*' (Ghosh 2012). While he became a symbol of sexual liberation for many, many queer men also followed him in their choice of clothes and accessories. Dutta thinks that Ghosh was a fashion icon in many aspects. He told us:

> In India queer fashion is very new; so it hasn't yet got its distinctive look. But Rituparno himself started a trend with the kind of clothes he wore more on neutrals but draped or easy fits. By and large, queer fashion in India is quite subdued: interesting cuts, textures

Figure 3.3 Rituparno with actress Deepti Naval in *Memories in March* (2012). Image courtesy of Shri Venkatesh Films.

and anti-fits defines it all. Definitely, Rituparno influenced my line since I was more into structure clothing; his presence in that fashion show helped me create a distinctive line target towards queer fashion.

Sayak Manna, a Kolkata based gay environmentalist in his mid-twenties, echoes Dutta to an extent:

Rituparno's style had a great influence on the queer crowd of Bengal, mostly the 'effeminate' men. The right choice of makeup, earthen/bold coloured ethnic attires, the choice of jewelleries, draping of shawls, *dupattas*, exhibiting exuberant individuality, femininity and the list goes on.

Darshan Shah, the Founder Trustee of the Weavers' Studio Centre for the Arts, and a close friend of Ghosh corroborates this view. Shah who often supplied clothes, shawls, quilts, etc. for Ghosh's films from her studio and sometimes helped style him for award functions, told us that she had observed how young 'gay' men, nowadays, effortlessly don slightly feminine cuts, wear *dupattas*, and carry designer bags, following Ghosh.[15] It was Ghosh's stardom and his social visibility in these kinds of clothes that attributed to this existing template of fashion as a label of sexual dissidence and queer non-conformity.[16] In fact, those who even slightly emulated his style ran the risk of inviting derogatory comments on the streets. As Amoha Das, a 25-year-old Kolkata-based fashion stylist notes:

> As far as Rituparno's influence on the queer fashion scene, his style was very unique and therefore, trendsetting. However at the same time, it was heavily feminine and flamboyant, and therefore not very practical on a daily basis for the closeted or even the openly flaming homosexual man, on the go, in the city. So rather than gay men emulating his style, what I feel it did for the common masses was that it created a culture of queer membership that could for the first time be expressed solely through clothing.

Das's observation is quite important. On one hand, whilst we argue that Ghosh was instrumental in creating a discourse on queer fashion amongst the Bengali youth, it cannot be denied that his clothes and style were a signature of class status which not everyone identified with, as Das explained.

CODA: THE DEFIANT BODY

Rituparno Ghosh was not the first 'queer' body to trouble the gender binary of Bengal. There are countless others such as Chapal Bhaduri, also known as Chapal Rani (Chapal the Queen), Tista Das, Manabi Bandopadhyay (the first transgender to have assumed the post of a Principal of a suburban college in West Bengal) and so on but it was Ghosh who we could not ignore. His flamboyant queer style, bright and colourful churidars were a powerful and defiant voice for the queer youth in Kolkata, India. Ghosh was not a queer activist and neither was he proactively involved with the neoliberal queer politics of the city, yet his defiant style stood him out and registered as a visual marker of dissidence (Dasgupta, 2014). Ghosh's transnational influence which went beyond Kolkata to Dhaka, London, and North America cemented his position as a Bengali cultural icon. His gender performance and rejection of socially sanctioned gender binary clothes appeared at a time when Bengali society was still coming to terms with queerness.

Ghosh's queer style echoes Tarlo's (1995) thesis of clothes instigating change in India and the visible defiant queer body. Ghosh contributed to the visibility politics at a time when mainstream media had only just started to acknowledge queer identities beyond the pathological narrative. Whilst we would not go so far as to call Ghosh's style subcultural; in similar ways Ghosh was recontextualising and repositioning female commodities by subverting their conventional use of being a female adornment/garment (as discussed in Vanita, 2014). In this sense Ghosh's style asserts Althusser's (1968) 'false obviousness of everyday practice' (Althusser cited in Hebdige, 1979: 102) opening up his sartorial style to new and covertly oppositional readings. Even in his death Ghosh's queer body and style remains active motivating a new generation of queer youth.

NOTES

1. The authors would like to thank Sumit Dey for his various creative inputs to this chapter. Some sections of this chapter have appeared in a different form as 'Opening Closets, Dividing Audiences' in *South Asian Popular Culture* (2018). The authors also dedicate this chapter to the the late South Asian film and cultural studies scholar, K Moti Gokulsing and the legacy of Rituparno Ghosh, who was an icon, friend and inspiration.
2. Ghosh played the role of the protagonist and was also the creative consultant for this film, having sufficient inputs into the screenplay.
3. *Ghosh & Company*, Episode 10, Star Jalsa India, 16 November 2008, https://www.youtube.com/watch?v=TkKTM2skj9U (accessed on 10 August 2014).
4. For people like British educated, Jawaharlal Nehru, the first Prime Minister of India, the Indian dress was also a site for nationalist struggle. Whilst he settled for the *kurta*, pyjama with a *sherwani* (now called the famous Gandhi jacket), he kept all components of the suit, only using the *khadi* or homespun cloth for the fabric (Tarlo 1996).
5. For example, see *Purab Aur Paschim*/East and West (Manoj Kumar, 1970), *Biwi No. 1*/Wife No. 1 (David Dhawan 1999). Also see Dwyer 2000 and Banerjee and Miller 2003.
6. Dutta designed clothes for Ghosh as well as other cultural icons such as the musician Ustad Amjad Ali Khan, sports personality Kapil Dev and painter M.F. Hussain.
7. For instance, the image of Amjad Khan (who is generally remembered as one of the stereotypical villain characters of Bombay cinema) as the dandy ruler of

Awadh, Wajid Ali Shah in Satyajit Ray's *Satranj ki Khiladi*, flaunting *chowbandhis*, *chowrah* pyjamas, designer cloaks, jewellery, danglers and kohl-lined eyes, or for that matter the ethnic costume of a male Kathak danseuse like Pandit Birju Maharaj. Such sartorial practices are familiar as androgynous, and are not necessarily identified as exclusively female attire. Of course one could accuse us of conflating attires related to performance and everyday life. But if the person concerned is Rituparno Ghosh, who considers himself to be a constant performer then such accusations would not hold ground.

8. This was his last completed feature film.
9. Chapal Bhaduri, who plays a ficto-historical character in the film, is a famous female impersonator of Bengali folk theatre who had his heyday in mid twentieth century. Bhaduri, also known as Chapal Rani, returned to public memory and began receiving serious attention from academicians, filmmakers and urban playwrights, once he chose to pronounce his sexual preferences in the much acclaimed documentary *Performing the Goddess* by Naveen Kishore.
10. We are grateful to Abhishek Dutta, Darshan Shah, Anindya Hazra, Amoha Das and Sayak Manna for taking the time out to talk to us. We are especially grateful to Abhishek Dutta for providing us with images of Rituparno Ghosh walking the ramp in his fashion show.
11. Tollygunje is a place in South Kolkata, West Bengal, where the main studios are located. Although newer studios have come up in other places over the past few years, Tollygunje metonymically represents the Bengali film industry. Recently, the term Tollywood has also come into vogue in the print and visual media.
12. By 'change', Das means his abandonment of T-shirts and jeans, his staple wear on his sets so far, and his shift into more androgynous clothing.
13. Later, when we began frequenting Ghosh's house, we noticed that the kind of clothes he wore at home were more radical than the ones in which he appeared in public. This was important; for the activism Ghosh engaged in publicly as regards to clothes was not abandoned once he was away from the public gaze.
14. Dutta explained this in an email interview with the authors.
15. However, Ghosh's style was primarily his own making. As Shah told us, he barely ever asked for advice and purchased clothes and accessories which caught his fancy at her store. In fact, Ghosh did not have a regular designer, and the ensemble of clothes, accessories, headgear and jewellery he donned was usually his own choice.
16. We also interviewed several cis gendered heterosexual women on their views about Rituparno. We received a fairly mixed response. Whilst none were particularly repulsed by his clothing choice and the queerness he embodied, there was some ambivalency. He was called a 'trailblazer' and a 'voice for the women'. The heterosexual men we interviewed were much more polarised in their views calling him 'rituporno' in reference to the erotic nature of some of his films. This was a fairly small sample group of audiences. Also see Dasgupta, Datta and Bakshi (2016) and Bakshi and Dasgupta (2017) on Bengali film audiences and their views on feminism and queerness.

REFERENCES

Allen, R. (2016) 'Closeted Desires and Open Secrets: Raincoat and Noukadubi', in S. Datta, K. Bakshi and R.K. Dasgupta (eds), *Rituparno Ghosh: Cinema, Gender and Art*, London: Routledge, pp. 153–169.

Bakshi, K. (2014) '*Arekti Premer Golpo*: The Yesteryear Female Impersonator, the Post-Liberalization Transvestite, and a "Queer" Stereotype', *Gay Subcultures and Literatures: The Indian Projections*, Sukhbir Singh (ed.), Shimla: IIAS.

―――― (2013) '"My city can neither handle me nor ignore me": Rituparno Ghosh in Conversation with Bakshi, K.', *Silhouette: A Discourse of Cinema* 10(3): 1–12.

Bakshi, K and Dasgupta, R.K. (2017) 'From Teen Kanya to Arshinagar: Feminist Politics, Bengali High Culture and the Stardom of Aparna Sen', *South Asian History and Culture*. Online First. Available from http://dx.doi.org/10.1080/19472498.2017.1304084 (accessed 10 September 2017).

Banerjee, M. and Miller, D. (2003) *The Sari*, Oxford: Berg.

Begum, L. (2012) 'Lingerie Brand Advertising in India: Through Saidian Logic', in R. Lifter (ed.), *Working Papers in Fashion Studies 2*, London: University of the Arts London, pp. 33–39.

Begum, L. and Dasgupta, R.K. (2015) 'Contemporary South Asian Youth Cultures and the Fashion Landscape', *International Journal of Fashion Studies* 2(1).

Das, S. (2013) 'Diva Unfolded', *Prothoma Ekhon* 1(1), 15 July: 51–54.

Dasgupta, R.K. (2014) 'Articulating Dissident Citizenship, Belonging and Queerness on Cyberspace,' *South Asian Review* 35(3): 203–223.

―――― (2017) *Digital Queer Cultures in India: Politics, Intimacies and Belonging*, London: Routledge.

Dasgupta, R.K. and Banerjee, T. (2016) 'Exploitation, Victimhood and Gendered Performance in Rituparno Ghosh's Bariwali', *Film Quarterly* 69(4): 35–46.

Dasgupta, R.K. and Gokulsing, K.M. (eds) (2014) *Masculinity and its Challenges in India*, Jefferson: Mcfarland.

Dasgupta, R.K., Datta, S. and Bakshi, K. (2016) 'The World of Rituparno Ghosh: An Introduction', in S. Datta, K. Bakshi and R.K. Dasgupta (eds), *Rituparno Ghosh: Cinema, Gender and Art*, London: Routledge, pp. 1–26.

Dey, N. (1998) 'Purush Ebar Notun Saje', *Patrika*, Kolkata: Ananda Bazar Patrika, 18 April 1998, p. 3.

Dissanayake, W. (2016) 'Rituparno Ghosh and the Pursuit of Freedom', in S. Datta, K. Bakshi, and R.K. Dasgupta (eds), *Rituparno Ghosh: Cinema, Gender and Art*, London: Routledge, pp. 49–62.

Dwyer, R. (2000) 'The Erotics of the Wet Sari in Hindi Films', *South Asia: Journal of South Asian Studies* 23(2): 143–159.

Dyer, R. (1979) *Stars*, London: British Film Institute.

―――― (2002) 'Dressing the Part', in R. Dyer, *The Culture of the Queers*, London and New York: Routledge, pp. 63–64.

Garber, M. (1992) 'Introduction', in M. Garber, *Vested Interests: Cross Dressing and Cultural Anxiety*, New York and London: Routledge, pp. 1–19.

Ghosh, R. (2008) 'Interview with Mir', *Ghosh & Company*, Episode 10, Star Jalsa India. 16 November 2008. Translated and transcribed by the authors. Available at https://www.youtube.com/watch?v=TkKTM2skj9U (accessed on 10 August 2014).

―――― (2013) 'First Person', *Robbar*, 9 June 2013, p. 3.

Gokulsing, K.M. and Dissanayake, W. (eds) (2013) *Handbook of Indian Cinemas*, London: Routledge.
Gopinath, G. (2005). *Impossible Desires: Queer Diasporas and South Asian Public Cultures*, Durham: Duke University Press.
Hazra, A. (2011) 'Amra Rituparnora' (We, the Rituparnos), *Prakashye: Prosongo Jounota*. Translated by K. Bakshi, pp. 4–6.
Hebidge, D. (1979) *Subculture: The Meaning of Style*, London: Routledge.
Holliday, R. (2001) 'Fashioning the Queer Self', in J. Entwistle and E. Wilson (eds), *Body Dressing*, Oxford: Berg, pp. 215–232.
Roychowdhury, S. (2011) 'Two Decades in Design', *Times of India*, 20 January 2011, p. 4.
Sengupta, R. (2010) '"I Don't Want to Become a Woman": Rituparno Ghosh [interview]', T2 *The Telegraph*, 22 December 2010: 2.
Shahni, P. (2010) 'The Fabulousness of the Indian Male', *VerveOnline*, 18(10). Available at http://www.verveonline.com/90/spotlight/parmesh.shtml (accessed on 7 July 2012).
Shukla, P. (2008). *The Grace of Four Moons: Dress, Adornment, and the Art of the Body in Modern India*. Indianapolis: Indiana University Press.
Tarlo, E. (1996) *Clothing Matters: Dress and Identity in India*, London: Hurst and Co.
Vanita, R. (2014) 'Foreword', in R.K. Dasgupta and K.M. Gokulsing (eds), *Masculinity and its Challenges in India*, Jefferson: Mcfarland, pp. 1–3.
Vanita, R. and Kidwai, S. (2000) *Same Sex Love in India: Readings From Literature and History*, New York: Palgrave Macmillan.

4

IN/VISIBLE SPACE

Reflections on the Realm of Dimensional Affect, Space and the Queer Racialised Self

Raisa Kabir in conversation with Lipi Begum and Rohit K. Dasgupta

In/visible Space is a series of photographic essays documenting the use of dress and self-created queer spaces of six young South Asian Lesbian, Bisexual, Transgender and Queer[1] (LBTQ) self-identified women and Transgender, non-binary[2] persons in Britain, and the transformative healing processes it produced, experienced as spatial affect. It explores how South Asian LBTQ persons assert their queer and diasporic identities, either in public or private spaces, using cross-cultural dress markers to subvert normative standards of western dress. The project questions how South Asian LBTQ youth, specifically women and minority genders, construct their identities through dress in their lives at home, and aims to counteract the dominant landscape of whiteness, prevalent in mainstream LGBT and queer culture in the UK.[3] Lipi Begum and Rohit K. Dasgupta met up with the artist Raisa S. Kabir to discuss her practice and motivations for this project. The conversation has been lightly edited for clarity.

Lipi and Rohit: Can you tell us a little bit about this project and your motivation for it.

Raisa: It came out of my need for community and South Asian queerness. I was 22 and was experiencing isolation whilst finishing my BA in Textiles at Chelsea College of Art. I felt that specific kinds of queer South Asian identities at the time were really not very visible in contemporary art practice – I didn't see images of trans, queer, lesbian, bisexual transgendered non-binary people that didn't focus on gay men. Through my art practice I began to question what does a multidimensional queer South Asian identity mean. I felt the world that I was seeing and feeling at the time was not being reflected, and this project was a way for me to engage with my own trauma of being in a predominantly white art institution, being of Bangladeshi South Asian diaspora, with a disability and identifying as a queer femme.

The project was initially started as part of my final show. The project was embedded within a multifaceted textile piece that was a juncture between sound, textiles and photographic images. I was interested in components that are laced together and how they speak to each other. The project started as a particular self-reflection piece, a montage, of myself, looking through a mirror, at a time when I was thinking about reflections, mirrors. I first sent a call out to community groups in London that focused on South Asian lesbian and queer women. The project asked South Asian queer women and transgender non-binary persons if there was a space that they could see themselves as South Asian and LBTQ simultaneously, and if this space was real and existed or was imagined. We worked together to collate the details of this space and if it could be recreated. And the photo shoots were very firmly designed by how they, the participants, wished to be represented or reflected through their own eyes. I arranged the images into the narrative photo essays myself, although some of the participants did also consult on the arrangement. The photo shoots themselves became a vehicle for them to also reinterpret their own gaze and question how they embody chosen spaces; an attempt to reverse this gaze of invisibility, of being seen and yet unseen. The use of differing cross-cultural dress in relation to the various spaces was crucial in constructing the narratives seen in the photo essays.

Lipi and Rohit: Can you tell us a little bit about what the process involved and how you managed to put the show together for Rich Mix, the community art centre in East London?

Raisa: The process of putting the show together at the Rich Mix involved meeting with participants over several months and conducting interviews. I established a certain level of trust through multiple conversations about the concept and by exploring what participants wished to achieve through this collaborative project. I saw myself very much as an artist who was facilitating each participant's ideas around their own sense of self and identity in a creative and collaborative way. My early work included four photo essays, two of which are seen here, *Ungendering Prayer* and *Sita*. As a result of wanting to develop the work further, I put together a proposal for Rich Mix to run a show a year later. I went on to explore more participants. It was important for me to question and find visibility beyond my initial ideas and my own reflections and agency of gaze. Through the second phase to reach out further, I mainly found participants through word of mouth as I had become more involved in South Asian queer women's networks.

I quickly realised, I wanted to work with more people and expand my understanding of the relationship between space and South Asian queer identities, and how this was reflected in dress choices. I was interested in the differences between choosing what to wear at home, in public, in private, between themselves and their parents. I also wished to explore how dress choices contributed to a sense of comfort or dissonance in particular spaces, especially heterosexual, non-South Asian white gentrified spaces. Did the South Asian queers that I was working with feel visible, invisible, how did they negotiate and navigate and mediate their multifaceted identities through dress?

Lipi and Rohit: You mention dress and youth; did you come across any difficulties, limitations, opportunities, and possibilities with working with this age group of South Asian queer identities?

Raisa: Whilst living in Britain, white hetero-public space often dominates the terrain we navigate and there is often visible discomfort in being a brown body in white space, or a queer body in hetero-public space. I realised that nobody had ever asked them what it feels like to be young, South Asian and queer. Dress was a way to dig deeper and unpack these feelings. The conversations created possibilities to share and exchange stories, build mutual trust; the project became a safe space to vocalise experiences and things that had hurt and shaped them.

For example Y who is 19, having grown up in the predominantly working-class Bangladeshi lower south end of Brick Lane found that she became invisible/was rendered invisible when she passed into the upper north Shoreditch end of the street – an area that had become gentrified beyond the markers of the Bangladeshi migrants who had settled there in the 1950s and 1970s. As elsewhere, this process of gentrification displaced working-class and minority ethnic, and religious communities, installing a middle-class white cultural norm that was, in this instance, mixed with an 'edgy' art/fashion vibe and small business scene. Although Y became invisible, her invisibility also gave her a sense of freedom and made her less self-conscious of the Bangladeshi community. You can see this in her dress; she is in the invisiblising space of the upper Shoreditch end of Brick Lane wearing a *hijab*, but holds onto markers of her hybrid visibility by wearing a Ramones punk T-shirt, jeans and Converse sneakers navigating less-gentrified and personalised corners of Brick Lane with art and graffiti. These images show a younger generation of South Asian women and queer identified persons fluently curating their dress identity in confident ways to deconstruct predetermined ideas of what is traditionally expected of them; reassessing both South Asian gender conformity and culturally queer normativities with their dress politics.

Lipi and Rohit: There is a rich intertextuality in not only your subjects' identity but the variation of montages you present; how do your pictures depict different South Asian queer perspectives? Your participants come from different backgrounds, does that influence some of their choices?

Raisa: Say, if we look at Y, we get a strong sense of self-policing of appearance. In real life, the *hijab* wasn't a fixed garment for Y; she would sometimes take it off and then put it on. She is mediating her very religious family and her own individual queerness. Her hybrid dress choices are partly based on feelings of self-consciousness of the rules and norms of dressing expected by her community, and from not being out; and partly her own feelings of both wanting to negotiate cultural expectations and white dissonance. Y identifies as bisexual, and still lives with her family around the lower Whitechapel end of Brick Lane as part of the Bangladeshi community in East London. The nearby district of

Shoreditch became a place where she could be herself, almost anonymous amongst the vibrant graffiti art that she loves, rather than the nearby district of Whitechapel where she felt consciously hyper visible as a Muslim woman within a racialised public space. In the White hetero-public space of Brick Lane, previously a majority Bangladeshi area, now heavily whitened and gentrified, she felt relief being able to be invisible among the crowds. She mentioned feeling out of place in mainstream queer spaces, where the racism and Islamophobia meant that as a hijabi queer woman she is visible as Muslim, yet made invisible as bisexual. The concept of the private space of her friend's car became a safe place to be with other queer South Asian women to smoke or have a can of beer and not be made to feel conscious for being Muslim and queer.

This is different to Maryam. Maryam's essay and photo shoot was based a lot more in performing protest. She is publicly queer, and an active feminist, and less self-policing and more challenging of dress choices. You see this in her choice to wear a beanie hat in place of a *topi*, a Muslim prayer hat traditionally worn by men, instead of *hijab*. She mixes South Asian *kurtas* with western jeans and regularly wears a very queer lesbian aesthetic of street-style beanie hats and hoodies with denim jackets. Religion is a huge part of her identity; this is why she wanted to be photographed in the mosque as a feminist protest of public prayer. We chose the first mosque ever to be built in the UK, the Shah Jahan Mosque in Woking, Surrey – which is a mosque situated within and frequented mainly by its local Pakistani community. She wanted to see what would happen if we turned up to the mosque as queer muslim women, and experienced how it would feel to be in the centre of a predominantly masculine space of this mosque. Usually in Islam many women are culturally expected to pray at home, and the act of public prayer can be a limited option, especially within smaller community mosques such as this. On this occasion, we found the women's prayer area full of men when we arrived during *Jumma* (Friday prayers) to do the photo-shoot and had to wait until it was empty. More inclusively open and larger mosques that aren't affiliated with an ethnic community are known to be more accessible to women for prayer, and there are more Muslim women that are taking action to take up space in mosques and religious spaces, which are still so dominated by men.

Whilst Y found comfort in performing invisibility, Maryam found comfort in asserting her visibility. Exploring what it means to be young and straddling these identities is predicated around the need or desire to question preconceived ideas, and to continually challenge presumptions that you must perform your gender and ethnicity in traditional binary patterns of dress. Many people have become adept at tailoring their dress and expressing their identities in ways that permit them to navigate multifaceted terrains, whilst subtly subverting expectations of how their gender and race fit into certain spaces. It is through this altering of their dress with nuanced codes to draw queer cultural visibility, or to move within and beyond binary parameters, that new cultural formations and use of space are forged. They are creating *brown* ways of being queer through their dress. Their use of dress in this way speaks volumes and demonstrates the flexibility in the languages of queerness that it creates.

Lipi and Rohit: We're interested in the points you make about brown ways of being. Do you think the diaspora has had a specific influence on how young queer South Asians dress and how this might be different from their parents or grandparents when they came as first generation migrants? I guess we are trying to find out if the diaspora had a specific role in how some of your participants dressed on top of queer aesthetics and individualism?[4]

Raisa: Although you could say subjects are choosing to dress differently from parental and community expectations of dress, these images depict a certain freedom of choice and are carefully constructed. The outfits they chose were significant to each of them both in terms of how they wanted to be seen and how they wanted to navigate these spaces. In some images, such as *Ungendering Prayer*, both the clothing and the spaces are 'fictional', chosen and/or constructed for the purpose of the photo shoot rather than being an accurate reflection of how my participant actually dressed in particular spaces. This provided an opportunity to comment on and temporarily bypass or rework religious and cultural regulations about gender, dress, space and the body. This gave the process of planning and taking the photos a personal charge for both of us – a chance, albeit momentary, to restore the queer and non-gender binary body to the spaces of South Asian religiosity. This sitter, who came from a conservative Muslim Indian background, didn't feel safe in a mosque; they missed and longed for the memories they held of visiting the mosque as a child with their father, and wearing looser, less gendered clothing to pray in when they were younger. They wanted to recreate a space to experience that sense of belonging. They felt the act of public prayer in a religious space was restricted for them as a non-binary gendered person because of the segregation of sexes in Islam and mandatory gendering in Islamic dress with the *hijab*.[5] They didn't feel comfortable entering a mosque because they were unable to personally draw together their gender presentation, queer and Muslim identities in such a way that was authentic to themselves. We chose to create a private queer Muslim fictional space where they could be comfortable with various parts of their identity at once – by not wearing a *hijab* and praying in a non-male dominated space. A space where they felt free of gender policing, free from the constraints of dress conformity and the expectation that they had to be heterosexual. This project allowed them to immerse within prayer whilst being a visibly queer non-binary Muslim in safety. Wearing male South Asian Islamic clothing was a new healing and restorative process. The project allowed us to document the moment and the conversations that took place.

Many of the subjects were influenced by their parents' understanding of moral codes of religious and cultural dressing; yet they also questioned their parents' ideals of dressing, coming to regard them as partly the result of diaspora experiences that naturalised regional and cultural dress conventions as religious practices. Maryam lives with her mum and comes from a Pakistani background in Nottingham, in the Midlands, England. Growing up she noticed and absorbed how male members dominated the cultural Pakistani community; it was only through her own journey into feminism and establishing her queer identity that she routinely began to question male authority, and began to see herself and identify as Muslim first rather than Pakistani. Like many other second, third and fourth generation young South Asians in the UK, she felt that dress norms in the Pakistani diaspora community were linked to culture and not religion. Maryam chose not to wear the flowery gendered garments or pretty shoes often imposed for attending community weddings. She chose to navigate her Pakistani and diasporic identity through the wearing of modest *shalwar kameez*, Converse sneakers, leather jackets and darker colours, which she calls 'q-wearing' – a term we often talked about together under the hashtag #queeringsouthasiandress in terms of playing with hetero gendering of clothing and mixing particular garments

Lipi and Rohit: You say your images are fictional, but the stories have a sense of realness to them; and like gender binaries, fiction and reality seem to be blurred. Can you say more about this?

Raisa: Yes. Take Sita, for example. They chose to be photographed at their local barbers. Sita has been going there for over five years while living nearby the barbershop. Unlike *Ungendering Prayer*, Sita chose to perform their identity within a non-fictional setting. As a South Asian masculine-of-centre-identifying lesbian, getting a buzz-cut at a heterosexual, Pakistani, male-dominated space, gave Sita a sense of familiarity and 'brown' solidarity. It was a documentary shot, as she had her haircut in real time whilst I was taking all of the photographs during that time, but we chose a place that Sita had a prior relationship with, where they didn't feel like an outsider – something not out of the ordinary. The heterosexual male geography adds power to the image; Sita is safer in the heterosexual brown male barbershop than in white queer spaces. What comes through is the shared solidarity and acceptance of being brown, but also dispels the notion that Sita being visibly queer in a Pakistani Muslim barber's shop wouldn't be able to take place, and that there would implicitly be a homophobic interaction, which of course there simply was not.

Nikita, is Gujarati Indian, bisexual femme and openly a sex worker. The photographs explore the process of Nikita becoming and undoing the performance of Kiki, the alter ego she uses for work. Kiki is often a performance of a heterosexual woman acting out fantasies of the 'sexually repressed Asian housewife' for male clients. Here Nikita uses dress to explore her queer and South Asian femme[6] identity, without being fetishised by the white heterosexual male gaze, as is with Kiki, or erased by the white queer gaze, as is with often whitewashed queer spaces. Here the private space of her bedroom is at the intersection of race, sexuality and gender, where she can be who she is.

We also see this with Raju at their local Indian South Asian supermarket in Stoke Newington, London. Raju chose to reproduce their

Sikh, queer femme identity through creating an assemblage of turban, draping, shawls, nail varnish, and earrings. They wanted to locate their trans feminine East African/Indian/Punjabi Sikh identity, but within the public and racialised setting of their local South Asian supermarket. Like Sita, there was a sense of solidarity from the familiarity of being a frequent customer and of sharing a common South Asian identity. Through Raju and Sita, we see how predominantly heterosexual spaces like the South Asian supermarket are not spaces of violence, but spaces where two very visible non-conforming identities can come together. This disrupts any assumptions that South Asian heterosexual spaces are spaces of violence for South Asian queers. There is camaraderie with Raju and the shopkeepers and a bridging of South Asianness. And this is something that runs through my images, of a larger South Asianness and mixing of specific ethnicities. Many South Asian queer people, tend to use the term South Asian as a political stance to resist the ways we have been divided by ethnicity and religion within colonial violence, although it is of course important to acknowledge our distinct cultures, languages and communities, it is also felt imperative to forge political solidarity through the term South Asian. In this way we can actively resist the tensions that come with being Diasporic South Asians and our respective differing ethnic communities, where perhaps our parents might have pit each community against an other. Instead, younger South Asian queer people finding each other can be like creating new families, where there is a desire to celebrate the crossovers of our cultures rather than the divisions, because that community is so small to begin with.

NOTES

1. Queer, is sometimes used as a catch all of LGBT, but also used as a political identity that is affiliated with left wing, radical, anti-mainstream commercialisation of LGBT groups. Queer is also used to mean (and especially in this context) to be attracted to different genders including your own but a sexual attraction that is not fixed to binary gendered sexualities, such as Lesbian or Gay, Women or Men but could include those identities. Queer is also an academic term that takes the premise of not being fixed in a binary way, such as attraction, but is used in different academic applications to create or illustrate a multiplicity of theoretical outcomes, by bringing disparate ideas, objects and subjects together in a way that queers them. Also see Ahmed 2006; Jagose 1996.

2. The gender binary gives options of female or male, to be feminine or masculine, to present as a woman or man. Non-binary is a gender identity that cannot be coded in these binary ways and as a result there are many different genders, and no single gender presentation as an example.
3. For a good discussion on this see Kawale 2003 and Puwar 2004.
4. For example Gayatri Gopinath (2005) argues a queer diasporic framework challenges the hierarchical construction of nation and diaspora in which the nation is often seen as superior, and the diaspora is often constructed as an inadequate recreation or copy.
5. Hijab, the practice of covering the hair with a head scarf or cloth worn by Muslim women. Also see Lewis 2014.
6. Femme, different from feminine, is used to describe a political feminine/effeminate presentation of gender and energy associated with queer women, men and non-binary persons.

REFERENCES

Ahmed, S. (2006) *Queer Phenomenology: Orientations, Objects, Others*, Durham: Duke University Press.

Gopinath, G. (2005) *Queer Diasporas and South Asian Public Cultures*, Durham: Duke University Press.

Jagose, A. (1996) *Queer Theory: An Introduction* (Reprint edn), New York: New York University Press.

Kawale, R. (2003) 'A Kiss is Just a Kiss ... Or Is It? South Asian Lesbian and Bisexual Women and the Construction of Space', in N. Puwar and P. Raghuram (eds), *South Asian Women in the Diaspora*, Oxford: Berg.

Lewis, R. (2015) *Muslim Fashion: Contemporary Style Cultures*, Durham: Duke University Press.

Puwar, N. (2004) *Space Invaders: Race, Gender and Bodies Out of Place*, Oxford: Berg.

PLATES

5
FACES OF SUBVERSION

Queer Looks of India

Sunil Gupta and Charan Singh

From classical traditions in western and Indian art to the covers of contemporary fashion magazines, the accessories and style of clothing depicted in a portrait provide great insight into the time, space and culture of a person. This essay is a dialogue between two artists Sunil Gupta (**SG**) and Charan Singh (**CS**) discussing their contrasting approaches towards the photographic depiction of same-sex desire in India. The term 'queer' in India is understood by urban English-speaking people as anybody who makes non-conforming sexual choices. Indigenous terms are still in use by non-English speaking people. Both artists are from urban India and are English-speaking. Here they use photography to illustrate how queer youth in urban India use Indian popular culture to codify their appearance.

Mr Malhotra's Party by Sunil Gupta (2007–2012) is a topographical survey of mostly young middle-class educated queer people in Delhi, depicting the parts of the city where they study, live and work. This set of portraits has been constructed to confront the viewer; whilst other people in the frame are in motion, the portrait subjects are mostly standing still, gazing directly at the viewer. This is in contrast to an earlier generation who would have looked away. This moment, after India's economic liberalisation in 1994, depicts a sense of gender and sexual fluidity reflected in global unisex and androgynous styles. Kothis, Hijras, Giriyas and Others by Charan Singh (2013–2014) is a series of studio portraits of vulnerable groups including: lower-class effeminate male youth who take on female gender roles in same-sex relationships (*Kothis*), and transsexual/transwomen (*Hijras*). The sitters report that they feel vulnerable in public places, because they are a recognisable subculture in the street. In these portraits sitters were asked to reflect on their unrequited desires and their gender identities by dressing and posing like their favourite fictional female characters from Bollywood and TV serials.

CS: Your photographic series 'Christopher Street', (1976–1977) and *Mr Malhotra's Party* (2007–2012), have recently been exhibited together in New York. Both series are almost a generation apart. Why is it that you have continued making street portraits of young queer men?

SG: I have always made portraits of gay/queer men. With 'Christopher Street', I was witness to the aftermath of a defining moment in and around the bar Stonewall Inn in New York, 1976, where the modern gay liberation movement was born. This was a place where there was an overwhelming public display of young gay men. Here they could safely and freely walk and mingle, dress in the way that they liked, and publicly express their desires for each other. In terms of the history of photography, it's also a time when the street photograph had been solidly validated as art by the museum world. The ethos of the time was to go out and shoot on the street, especially in New York, where the far reaching influence of the 'New Documents Show' had been originated at the Museum of Modern Art in 1967 with work by Arbus, Winogrand and Freidlander. So it was something I was doing intuitively without a lot of thought. *Mr Malhotra's Party*, on the other hand, was a very slow, deliberate art exercise. I wanted to update my work *Exiles* (1986) and present portraits of out queers in their own city in public spaces. However, there is no equivalent in India to a public queer street like Christopher Street, so it was a case of organising each picture one at a time. It developed in directions more in tune with contemporary times, as immediately there were women in it and later trans men and the dress styles reflected this. In both scenarios people dressed as they wanted. It was an attempt to present the private queer as more public in India. A break from the past.

SG: With *Kothis, Hijras, Giriyas and Others* what were you trying to show and why did you get them to pose like that with lighting and studio backdrops? Are the poses meaningful?

CS: The ideas for these portraits I can trace back to 2009 when I met you and had seen your work along with that of other gay/queer photographers including Claude Cahun and George Platt Lynes, whose work influenced my interest in making posed studies in the photographic studio. When I looked at the history of Indian photography, I realised that only the upper-classes, with the exception of some urban working class, which are not those living in slums or the rural poor living in bonded labour conditions had the means to commission studio portraits of themselves. When I came to making photographs, I not only wanted to make something queer but also challenge nineteenth- and early twentieth-century stereotypes about studio photography from India. The main stereotype is the upper middle-class patriarch and his family in a heteronormative pose and dress, a trope that came to India from European painting. Any creative challenges by unmarried youth were not possible due to the cumbersome process of photography and the expense involved. The situation only changed due to the proliferation of cheaper high street studios in the mid twentieth century. However, these remained unaffordable to the underclass. Many of my models have not had a studio portrait made in their lifetime. Therefore I attempted to create a studio where people could feel comfortable enough to create their own styles and poses. The poses and postures they came up with derive from popular movies and TV serials, as that is the most widely accessible cultural discourse that we have in India. The young models have chosen to dress and style themselves with clothes and accessories and imitate poses of their favourite movie characters in their most treasured movie moments. For example, *Untitled* 6, the gesture and henna painted hands in the picture is a common bridal pose inspired by posters of several movies and TV stars in India.

CS: I see *Mr Malhotra's Party* as an anthology of fashion and how queer people dress, it's almost like a version of the *Gay Semiotics*[1] (Fischer 1977) in an Indian context. Do you think so?

SG: That's interesting that you should think that. On the whole with *Mr Malhotra's Party* I let people represent themselves so they were free to wear any markers they liked. However, I couldn't discern too many indicators of sexual role playing preferences as were outlined in the Hal Fischer study you are referring to. Over and above a more generalised leaning towards the more masculine or feminine in dress styles, they were not wearing any indicators of actual sexual role choices regardless of their gender identification.

SG: In your work, I am interested to know what kind of characters from TV and cinema are being referred to in each pose and each costume. And why that appeals to the youth you photographed and what they might say about desire and their lives in general?

CS: That's right! The people I was working with are greatly influenced by Hindi cinema and TV, which is perhaps because they are primarily Hindi speaking people and their main source of visual reference is cinema and TV. Art galleries and museums in India are not welcoming to young people who are not from the middle and upper middle class and are consequently not frequented by *kothis*[2] and *hijras*.[3] Many had styled themselves on popular vamps from TV serials. It shows in the way they use broad eyeliner and *Sindoor* (red colour powder, a mark of a married woman in Hinduism) in their hair partition. Others posed the way famous courtesan characters did in classic Bollywood films like *Pakeezah* (Amrohi 1972) and *Umrao Jaan* (Ali 1981) in the 1970s and 1980s. They are attracted to how these fictional female characters are never allowed to obtain the object of their desire, they exist in a continuous state of tragic un-fulfilment and it is this un-fulfilment which I reflected in the lives of the people in my series *Kothis, Hijras, Giriya* ... I heard them quoting a famous line from a song in Umrao Jaan '*Justzu Jiski Thi Usko To Na Paya Humne*' (I did not attain whom I desired). And so their relation with cinema and the TV goes a long way. In other words, it is part of their daily lives. In the 1980s and 1990s growing and colouring one's thumb nail was the limit of subversive and ambivalent style amongst 'regular' men in South Asia. See the young boy is wearing embroidered flowery shorts, which is quite a brave fashion statement for the Indian street, but then this type of look inspired the metrosexual millennium Bollywood look, which is based on stereotypical styles of femininity where male stars appeared in bathtubs with beauty soap and rose petals.

CS: Sunil, would you say your work (maybe unconsciously) gives a variety of queer looks? From queer feminists, students, corporate workers to new age hipsters, you show interest in a wide range of people and their looks.

SG: That may well be so. Initially when I first started the series I was working with a very particular group of people who I came to know though my membership of the cultural activist organisation, Nigah. One of the things I did, was run a photo workshop around self-portraiture over a number of weekly sessions. I used individuals from this group whom I had come to know quite well to pose for the new series, Mr Malhotra's Party. The participants of this group, were of course, mostly under thirty years old, English speaking and had completed at least one degree. The group originally emerged from Jawaharlal Nehru University, New Delhi, so you could say, they did have a lefty, intellectual student look about them. The portrait of Anusha, JNU is fairly typical. Though as the group went in search of a non-student membership, into the city and outside the campus, a broader range of people joined. Still young and usually educated in English, but I suppose the budget and the dress codes shifted to a more urban activist look, a more up-market and trendy city look. Therefore not the hippy kurtas[4] and jholas[5] of an earlier lefty activist NGO look, although some persisted, but unisex T-shirts and skinny jeans were making inroads for a streamlined look. As dress became more unisex, it was harder to distinguish what kind of people and what codes of desire were operating. I don't know, perhaps masculine/feminine desire has more purposefully shifted onto the internet? I believe what the urban educated young are showing with their dress codes today is the fluidity between their gender and sexual identities.

SG: My last question for you, then, is whether your subjects, by appropriating gender specific codes from popular culture, are using their dress to exhibit very specific women's traits (mostly tragic fallen women) as trans men and are therefore perhaps less fluid or more fixed in their gender and sexuality choices?

CS: I think, there is much more complexity to their gender identities than it appears at first glance. It is true that they embrace the 'fallen women' (See Untitled 2) etiquettes to lure their lovers and potential sexual partners, which may limit their gender choices. But in actuality, gender performances including the attire they are wearing does not necessarily comply with their sexual role, it is a fantasy of how they want others to look at them, or which actress they fantasise to become like. From Hindu mythology to Bollywood films, gender is so spectacular and performed in a variety of ways in a variety of scenes in India. It is okay to cross-dress in one song scene but then play a macho hero in a leather jacket and denim for the rest of the film. I am still trying to understand the many ways, how in South Asia, the notions of masculinity/femininity are suggested by clothes and mannerisms? I am not sure what it means when they say, 'act like a man'? Perhaps they mean, 'dress like a man'.

Sunil Gupta and Charan Singh have produced a photo book investigating how the human rights of LGBTQ lives in India and are affected by recent changes – Delhi: Communities of Belonging, The New Press, New York 2016. They also curated the exhibition, 'Dissent and Desire', at the Contemporary Arts Museum, Houston 2018.

NOTES

1. *Gay Semiotics: A Photographic Study of Visual Coding Among Homosexual Men* by Hal Fischer 1977, Cherry and Martin.
2. *Kothi*, in the culture of the Indian subcontinent, is an effeminate man or boy who takes on a female gender role in same-sex relationships.
3. *Hijra* is a term used in South Asia – in particular, in India – to refer to an individual who is transsexual or transwomen.
4. *Kurta* is a traditional loose shirt falling either just above or somewhere below the knees of the wearer.
5. *Jhola* is a cloth bag often carried by writers and activists in India.

REFERENCES

Ali, M. (1981) *Umrao Jaan*. Integrated Films: India.
Amrohi, K. (1972) *Pakeezah*. Mahal Pictures Pvt Ltd: India.

6

DESIGNING FOR 'ZIPPIES' AND THE MADNESS OF *BHOOTSAVAAR*

On Commercially Inflected Artistic Nationalism and Branded 'Subcultures'

Tereza Kuldova

Luxury Indian fashion, or Indian haute couture, has for more than a decade revelled in tradition and heritage, capitalising on the skills and creativity of India's craftspeople. Leading designers, including JJ Valaya, Tarun Tahiliani, Rohit Bal, Sabyasachi Mukherjee, Ritu Kumar, have embraced an aesthetics that I have labelled 'royal chic' (Kuldova 2013; Kuldova 2016b). This is an aesthetics that invokes the opulent lifestyles of the maharajas, princely elites, or Mughals, with all their excesses, indulgences and taste for refinement and grandeur. Royal chic also invokes the ideal of a composite culture and (pseudo)-secularism so often celebrated in the nationalist and patriotic discourses, while projecting these onto the canvas of contemporary and future India and its cosmopolitan albeit firmly 'Indian' elite. Royal chic delivers an aesthetic of distinction to the contemporary elite 'rulers' served on a plate of cultural pride, crafting a special elitist space vis-à-vis other imaginary global and transnational elites. In other words, elitist Indian fashion has embraced a very visible and unmistakable form of 'artistic nationalism' (Ciotti 2012) that revels in heritage luxury and materialises the *doxa* of Indianness. Within this aesthetic the craftspeople embroidering and weaving the lavish attires are at once celebrated as the very embodiment of India's tradition and greatness, while at the same time playing the role of 'subjects' to the elites that benevolently patronise them through the designers, an act that typically reproduces their subjected and impoverished position of social exclusion rather than elevating it (Kuldova 2016b). At play here seems to be a logic that amounts to a social rule, namely, that that which is socially marginal and excluded becomes symbolically central for any given culture (Stallybrass and White 1986).

JJ Valaya's *Azrak* show at the 'Wills Lifestyle India Fashion Week' of 2012 succinctly materialised this logic. For the show, Valaya decorated the fashion ramp with fake impoverished street sellers, craftsmen and embroiderers impersonated by theatre students, while the models walked the ramp impersonating the phantasmatic neo-royalty. Reproduction of elitist nationalism with a hint of neo-feudalism is visibly at stake in the production of India's top designers. But what about the quirky youth fashions inspired for instance by steampunk and other western trends that often appear on the very same ramps following such opulent neo-aristocratic splendour? Youth brands like to portray themselves precisely as offering an alternative both to the elitist visions of prestige and to restrictive middle-class moralities. But are they not merely commodifying an image of a spontaneous lifestyle and capitalising on claiming to present an alternative and thus selling a symbol of an alternative rather than an actual alternative? Are they not in reality, despite their countercultural appearance, the true symbol of ideological co-option (Heath and Potter 2005)?

In the following, I will try to show that even if the designers of youth fashion try to convince the general populace in India of both its subcultural and cosmopolitan feel, still the 'production of the "global" occurs through nationalist imagination', as Leela Fernandes has argued in her work on media and the middle-class India (Fernandes 2000: 611). 'Branded subcultures' tend to correspond to a particular socio-economic position (urban/metropolitan aspiring middle class and upper middle class) that is mobilised by and mobilises a nationalist narrative, albeit one that places the emphasis elsewhere than the elitist nationalism of the very top 0.1 per cent. Rather than indulging in the celebration of cultural heritage as an anchor for a neo-feudal cosmopolitan identity, youth fashion dreams of the immense potential of the creative youth plugged into global networks, a youth that bears a promise of a bright future for India. While in imagination this youth encompasses hundreds of millions, in reality we may be talking of the top 2–4 per cent of the urban youth (Banaji 2012). The majority of India's youth remains impoverished and underprivileged, no matter how much the nationalist ideologues and media exaggerate the proportions, capacities and impact of the urban educated youngsters (De 2008; Das 2000; Mehta 2003; Banaji 2012). A similar situation can be discerned in other places across South Asia, such as Sri Lanka (Hewamanne in this volume). What is marginal in terms of numbers (here, cosmopolitan youth with considerable spending power), becomes symbolically central. These privileged youngsters are idealised not only because of their presumed creativity, openness to the world and cultural capital, but also because they are the perfect image of consumer-citizens, of citizens who have replaced politics with consumption that collapses, often becomes one, with their inward-looking individual identity projects (Banaji and Buckingham 2009). Turning individual consumption into a political tool is an act only the very privileged can afford. This might be a reason why consumer citizens (Scammel 2000) become the good model citizens for contemporary nationalist ideologues – due to their belief in the power of consumer choice they tend to give up on the idea of 'politics as purposive, collective action concerned with altering the distributional values of social institutions' (Hoare 2007) and hence pose little threat to the ruling political and business elites. In order to shed some light on the quirky fashion for these privileged youngsters, who might be socially marginal but symbolically dominant in the nationalist discourses centring on India's great future (Kuldova 2014), let us now investigate Nitin Bal Chauhan's brand *Bhootsavaar* ('Possessed'), while also considering the 'strategies of capture' (Lordon 2014) deployed by the brand to acquire young and loyal followers and produce obedient consumer-citizens.

DESIGNED 'PASSIONATE MADNESS': BE AUTHENTIC, BUT ONLY THE WAY I TELL YOU TO

Those few designers creating the Indian 'Gen-X market' cater largely to the upper middle-class urban youth that likes to perceive itself as rebellious (being privileged enough to break the social rules), creative and ambitious. Opinions differ about how to refer to this privileged urban class of Indian youngsters and about who should be included in the first place. Nitin Bal Chauhan labels this group the Indian Gen X ('x' here stands simply for next) and counts himself as its member. Some go with the western notion of the Gen Z, which they Indianise ('zippies') (Lukose 2009). Others still reject such labels altogether as misleading (Banaji 2012). Like all labels, the meaning of these classifications is situational and relational. The boundaries of those labelled as zippies tend to expand and contract, exclude and include, depending on the social, commercial or political purpose. So, for instance, brands like *Bhootsavaar* may systematically cultivate the illusion of vast numbers of youngsters who can potentially aspire to or belong to the urban creative class (they might even sell them aspirational printed T-shirts for 500INR). So too, the nationalist ideologues systematically overestimate the power and the social and economic capital of this imagined grouping. However, in reality, only few with the right cultural capital can really belong to the *Bhootsavaar* 'family', as Nitin calls it (by definition, family is about exclusion and not inclusion), and thus also can wear the custom-made dresses. Overall, however, all these labels tend to refer to those now between 15–30, those who are educated, English-speaking, digitally connected, have a considerable disposable income, cultural capital consisting of the knowledge of largely western media and diverse subcultural trends in addition to Indian pop and sub-cultural productions, those who are fashionable and who are the exemplary consumer citizens (and now also increasingly so called ethical/conscious consumers), eager to buy and display their status. As such, the urban zippies are the 'liberalisation's children' (Lukose 2009) and grand-children, those who are ambitious and aspiring, those who demonstrate an 'attitude', like the models on fashion ramps who belong to the same generation and class. Typically, they are portrayed as rebellious taboo-breakers, free-spirited individuals refusing to be constrained by tradition and so on. Brands like *Bhootsavaar* cater precisely to this desire of the privileged youth for *appearing* rebellious, unique, creative and special, for belonging to the privileged creative class.

We should not be misled here by their frequent insistence on and invocation of their own 'precarity', especially in light of workers who are truly living lives of precarity and declassify themselves through aesthetics precisely as a form of resistance against middle-class moralities (Hewamanne in this volume). Those in a real precarious position are the artisans, garment workers and craftspeople across the country, young and old. It is again telling that as opposed to these educated creative youngsters, the young craftspeople are not deemed 'creative' in the same way. Their creativity is represented as backward, as a mere repetition of tradition that is dragging the country down; they are a social nuisance rather than hope for the future, even if it is precisely their craft, art and skill that is celebrated as 'national heritage' and creates the value of the elitist royal chic (Kuldova 2016a; Kuldova 2016b).

The creativity of the youth that is celebrated by the national ideologues is very much dependent on the class position and social, economic and cultural capital (Bourdieu 1984) of the bearers of this 'creativity' rather than on the creativity as such. This youth marked by an accumulation of cultural capital has inspired and is meant to emulate Bollywood movies such as *Zindegi Na Milegi Dobara* (You won't get this life again; Akhtar 2011) or *Yeh Jawaani hai Deewani* (This youth is crazy; Mukerji 2013). Both movies portray these relatively wealthy, and on one hand carefree, while on the other also typically mentally and privately troubled youngsters (privilege has its own set of psychological troubles). While the privileged 'zippies', or those who buy into *Bhootsavaar*, might dismiss and mock these movies, there is little doubt that no matter what they say, in their material practices they tend to emulate the heroes of these movies – and when it comes to ideology, it is precisely primarily material practice that matters (Althusser 1971; Pfaller 2015). Possibly, the more they mock these movies, the more they actually embrace them and mimic their characters.

Recently, *Bhootsavaar*, sponsored by the whisky brand *Cutty Sark* hired Kalki Koechin to be its showstopper and the face of the brand. Not accidently, Kalki is the lead actress in both aforementioned youth movies,

Figure 6.1 Kalki Koechlin for *Hello India*, 27 May 2015. Image courtesy of *Hello India*.

a known 'socially aware activist' often hailed for her creativity, talent and for her slightly 'subversive voice' in the cinema. This goes well together with the brand's own claims to ethical production and sustainability that feed the imaginary of a 'conscious and aware consumer'. In this sense, she is the perfect face of the brand.

To reiterate, movies and brands like *Bhootsavaar* are intentionally quirky and ooze a distinct vision of creativity, while providing the young customers with both ready-made aesthetics of subversion, ethicality and a feeling of belonging to the new generation of 'cosmopolitan consumers' (Mazzarella 2006). They also perpetuate a particular version of the neoliberal mythology and a belief in the future super powerdom of 'Brand India' (Kapur 2012; Kuldova 2014) and proliferate 'discourses that proclaim India to no longer be struggling at the bottom of the modernization ladder' (Lukose 2009: 3). In these narratives, the nation is re-imagined and the 'producer patriot' (Deshpande 2003), the ideal of the Nehru's era, is replaced by the consumer citizen. Consumption is then closely tied to citizenship (Lukose 2009) and consumption is increasingly becoming the only (permissible) way to become political. This means that those who are unable to consume are expelled across the internal borders of 'society' (Sassen 2014), expelled from the 'India Shining' (Deshpande 1993). This goes for the vast majority of young people in India who are burdened by traditional roles, poverty, aspirational pressures, feelings of lack and inadequacy, structural violence and so on. Those with real holes in their trousers, and not branded *Bhootsavaar* holes, are pushed into invisibility and 'expelled' (Sassen 2014) from the new India of shopping malls, IT industry and utopian multi-crore projects of futuristic smart cities. (Indeed, sometimes they are included but only as the victims of the system, who need to be uplifted for instance through ethical fashion that provides them with a 'fair wage' and the buyer with a pleasurable feeling of good conscience.)

Good citizens are no longer those who produce, but those who consume. As the cliché about the 'zippies' goes, compared to the generation of their parents often concerned with saving money and with secure governmental jobs, the youngsters are rendered as great wastrels, defined by their insatiable consumption habits, big dreams and rising debt – which, in the eyes of the neoliberal ideologues is not such a bad thing. Popular brands such as *Bhootsavaar* not only encourage and normalise wasting – of yourself, your money and so on, but also instil the idea of the 'consumer-citizen' with all its inherent de-politicisation and privatisation of the public sphere, in the habitus and practice of the youth. Moreover, they directly feed into the neoliberal nationalist narratives of 'Brand India' by creating a distinct aesthetic of a whole new class of privileged young creatives, the aesthetic of the face of the 'new' India from which social problems and inequalities are erased or only mentioned at charity galas. Of course, this is a matter of analysis, and not something that would be openly endorsed. When asked about the ideological underpinnings of his brand, Nitin answered:

> *Bhootsavaar* follows a simple ideology of following your heart. To do that comes from within you. It is about acknowledging something that comes naturally to you or something that you are drawn to and aspire to do. Everyone is mad about something and that feeling and compulsion that comes from within to do that thing is the spark that one needs to acknowledge and respect. (...) It is so much about lifestyle than anything else. You become one with yourself and the picture you imagine to be. Time is fleeting and so is our life. Spontaneity is a key word, you go with the flow and take whatever comes your way simply because you chose that path to tread on. It is about making your choices and sticking by them.
>
> (Chauhan 2014)

No matter the talk of spontaneity and following one's heart, these brands reveal their own ambition to artificially create something akin to 'subcultures' (at least in an aesthetic form). In this case, the designer becomes the prime leader of this subcultural cult; he himself is the aspiration for the others and defines the terms of the game.

Being 36 and extremely cool, youthful and accomplished, Nitin is positioned just a bit above his most devoted consumers and hence presents a style that they can comfortably embrace, while embracing their aspiration as well. While we often see designers on the stage, who resemble in nothing the models on the ramp and who are often very simply dressed, here we encounter a designer who dresses himself in his over-the-top creations and is the face of the brand and an inspiration to others; he is both the producer and exemplary consumer. The case of *Bhootsavaar* with its desire to create a *Bhootsavaar* family reveals more pressingly the ultimate master-desire of the fashion designers, namely their fantasy of making others identical to themselves. When asked about their ambitions, designers typically respond by saying that their true desire is to

Figure 6.2   Nitin Bal Chauhan, New Delhi, 2012. Image courtesy of Arash Taheri.

'create their own world'. We should take this statement literally here, and not be deceived by its metaphorical lure. The desire to build a powerful fashion brand is driven by nothing less than a desire to create a world of one's own, where the designer's subjects passionately and obediently follow and buy into the dream (indeed, this is a more general dynamics discernible within fashion industries across the globe). In this sense, the desire is very similar to that of political ideologues keen to produce obedient and passionate subjects that embrace their vision of the world, whatever that may be. As often as the designers speak of creating their own worlds, or even empires, so often they dream of 'loyal followers' who are 'passionate about the brand', who embrace the lifestyle and emotionally invest themselves in the products. If we did not know that they were speaking of a fashion brand, we might have thought that the talk is of a religious cult or even an election campaign. Indeed, collective consumption with the attached branded rituals effectively caters to the universal desire for collective action, belonging and participation in the social at large; this is the underlying logic of branded 'postmodern neo-tribes' that according to Maffesoli operate 'without the rigidity of forms of organization with which we are familiar' and refer 'to a certain ambience, a state of mind, and is preferably to be expressed through lifestyles that favour appearance and form' (Maffesoli 1996: 98). Neo-tribes typically inhabit a shared imaginary territory and create an imagined social collectivity through shared aesthetic, symbols, rituals but often also ethics. This is how Nitin described his initial motivation for creating his brand:

> Bhootsavaar was born out of my desire to cater to the younger lot of our country. I had taken a 2-year sabbatical to extensively paint in public spaces especially in cafes which were frequented by people from all walks of life and especially the youth. I realised there was not a single designer label from our fashion industry that was designing for the younger lot. I made up my mind to create an edgy and affordable brand, which would address the GEN X of our country. This was also a good way of channelizing my street art skills to graphic designs for T-shirts and other merchandise. (...) The face of global India and Delhi is a witness to the change that they [Gen X] are creating. This eclectic mix of professionals lives by their own rules and never forgets to party hard. They are the generation behind huge turnouts at the music festivals and an ever-growing night life in the city. They are the reason why more and more youngsters can imagine taking a more challenging path to lead their life. Lot of Bhootsavaar is also bought by teenagers and college students who aspire to strike a different chord with the world around them.
>
> (Chauhan 2014)

Nitin's desire to create a movement, a loyal following consisting of creative young people that live according to their passions (but on his aesthetic premises), means that he has to find answers to the question of how to seduce the youngsters to actually buy his brand, or else *how to align their desire with his master-desire* (Lordon 2014)? The question is – how to mobilise the affects of the youth and push them in the direction of the brand? This is indeed the same question that is posed by politicians across the world. In this sense also, capitalising on already available and powerful political myths about the role of the creative youngsters for India's future is a viable strategy of capture, even if not one that is ever rendered explicitly. When it comes to loyal following, the underlying injunction here is: 'Be authentic, be spontaneous and desire it yourself, *but only the way I tell you to*' – a shared aesthetics of so called authenticity is at stake here. Any social movement consists of people who *move together* – but the question here is, to quote Yves Citton, who has provided some remarks on the matter in relation to populism, 'What makes them move together' (Citton 2010: 63)? Affects understood as unbound energy or intensity can push us to act, but the question is in what direction are they pushing us.

IDEOLOGY, AMBIENCE AND RITUAL

Staged rituals are among the most powerful tools of mobilising affects and directing passions. Theatrical fashion shows, be they during fashion weeks or staged in nightclubs, are exactly such powerful rituals. Nitin is an expert at staging such ritualistic shows that make the audience cheer and desire. However, arousing passions is one thing, another is directing them and – in the market – capitalising on them. As Citton argues, affects can become effective only when integrated into a narrative structure or a story line that can make sense of our experiences and structure our future paths of action – 'we feel in and through stories' (Citton 2010: 64). Here the implicit nationalist narrative about the exceptionality of the Indian youth and of the creative class comes to the fore as it is embraced through the *material practices* during such events. Ideology is first and foremost a matter of practice and everyday rituals rather than a matter of discourse (Althusser 1971). Here it takes the form of branded rituals, in which people passionately participate. As such, the brand offers the young customers venues that enable them to participate in this ideology and reproduce it – often even against, or precisely because of, their better knowledge (Pfaller 2005). The youth might be cynical about their consumption, about the whole notion of them being the future of the nation and so on, they might even mock the whole idea of them being somehow special – but what matters here are precisely the material practices in which, no matter what they say, they embrace this ideology. Branded rituals are exceptionally powerful. As Durkheim pointed out in his *Elementary Forms of Religious Life*, ritual is essential in the making and remaking of society as it exercises profound force and influence over its participants (Durkheim 1965). Lovemarks, a term introduced by Kevin Roberts, the CEO of Saatchi & Saatchi

(Roberts 2004), might be more appropriate than a brand here, as lovemarks mobilise emotions and passionate commitment of consumers. Lovemarks, like Nitin's *Bhootsavaar*, desire a passionate loyal following and capitalise on the Durkheimian insight that social knowledge and belonging are born and strengthened in the collective effervescence of ritual enactments (Durkheim 1965). Fashion brands often attempt to create ritual venues and provide ready-made myths that can serve as an attractor for action, or mobilisation both within and outside of a ritual ambient space. Therefore, vast amounts of social labour go into (1) developing ambient atmospheres, especially theatrical stage sets for the shows or stores, (2) creating a mythical narrative framing these environments and (3) developing ritual practices that take place in these ambient spaces.

Bhootsavaar, as we shall see, clearly capitalises on the prevailing nationalist framing narrative that places its hopes for a bright future onto the creative young 'zippies'. After all, nationalist narratives have a great track record of making people move together and passionately sacrifice themselves or – in the case of the market, passionately throw themselves into debt (just a different form of sacrifice suitable for the consumer citizens). In our case, collective representations are repetitively strengthened and recharged precisely through ritualised fashion events performed within 'sacred' ambient locations, where these collective representations are enacted and given material meaning. The brand mythology of *Bhootsavaar* that is materialised in such events matches the larger narratives of transformation in globalised India and the youth as its driving force, while giving an aesthetic form both to the myths and to the very notions of youth, creativity and passion. As Nitin says, he creates for people

> who constantly push themselves outside their comfort zone, [...] from various walks of life – musicians, DJs, artists, graffiti artists, social entrepreneurs, graphic designers, tattoo artists, architects, dancers, theatre artists, PR and communication professionals, advertising professionals, photographers, stylists, models etc.
> (Chauhan 2014)

Nitin is skilled in associating the right brands and collaborating with the right people. He uses several strategies to make the youth embrace his brand: (1) engaging audiences through affective ambient environments

(Anderson 2009; Babin and Attaway 2000) (2) directing these affects through carefully framed narratives about a distinct emergent class of young creatives and (3) engaging the audiences in ritualised fashion events.

In order to achieve maximum impact and in order for his products to appear as *spontaneously* embraced, as a true grass-root desire rather than a brand imposition, he employs 'regular' people to walk the ramp for him, or appear in creative fashion presentations staged in clubs and bars, documented and disseminated by bloggers, print media and so on, and shared on social media. The selected individuals that he chooses belong to the same segment to which he caters, or create the image to which certain youngsters aspire, they are often his friends and are recruited from the same creative circles, within fashion, art, photography, and music; people who meet in the same nightclubs. In this sense, the designer with his small team author these shows. As Nitin says,

> when common people who have style or are achievers walk the ramp, I think it creates an aspiration value inside the audience. The ramp no longer belongs to the well-built and beautiful. In fact, the ramp becomes a place for the real, unabashed and talented people. It becomes fashionable to be gifted, passionate and endowed with abilities to believe in oneself and one's expression. This is the future of fashion and this is the way *Bhootsavaar* is trying to build a community around it. Due to this reason even our shows at the fashion weeks follow the same format. (...) Collaborating with creative people is core to *Bhootsavaar* and it is an on-going process. These people are the true brand ambassadors and through their work and lifestyle they constantly inspire us to create and reach out to a larger number of people. We want to tell their stories to the common man [note: he refers to the designer and his core team]. The *Bhootsavaar* family keeps growing as we speak! (...) We have tie-ups with popular clubs and cafes where we invite people to come and be a part of our presentations. There is a theme for each night and that could be either the concept of our fresh collection that we would launch that night or else it is based upon another event in history. Popular dates like Halloween, Friday the 13th, Valentine's Day are

DESIGNING FOR 'ZIPPIES' 115

Figure 6.3 Rishi Raj, a stylist, *Bhootsaavar*, 2013, Crescent Mall. Image courtesy of Nitin Bal Chauhan.

always good to work around the event. A regular night would have a fashion presentation, choreographed in an unusual way, photo booths would be set-up for people to come and interact with, live bands and electronic music along with dancers who sporadically lighten up the evening with impromptu acts. We also set up make-up booths and provide different props to people to add to the vibe. As mentioned above *Bhootsavaar* attracts people from different walks of life. Most of the people who come are a talented lot and expect to meet like-minded individuals at these events.

(Chauhan)

The 'zippies' are as much driven by desire for distinction and class belonging as the elite. The only difference lies in the aesthetics, mythology and economic status of this distinction and belonging. Much like the elite spaces, so the spaces for the 'zippies' are gated (Brosius 2009) and carefully separated from the outside world of the not so privileged youth on the streets. It is also worth noting here that the marketing strategies are discernibly 'global', events like this can be found today across the world's high-end fashion industries. They have their origin in American and European fashion marketing, which is systematically taught at fashion institutes across India – it is also precisely this form of marketing that often clearly distinguishes vernacular markets from 'globalised' markets within the same market so to speak. Another notable matter here is the systematic appropriation of the hip and cool western 'traditions', from Valentine's to Halloween, accompanied by disregard for local festivals, which are normally the time to shop for new clothes and so on. This embracing of the western 'traditions' thus serves to distinguish their clientele from that of the bazaar or vernacular economy on the one hand, which is also centred around festivals, only this time they are Diwali, Holi, the wedding season, Eid and so on, and on the other hand, from the very elitist high fashion, which again is also centred around the Indian festivals. In this sense, the selection of western events and tastes, often slightly indigenised, adding additional cool without turning into ethnic spectacle, becomes a form of class-cum-generational (and thus often temporal and transitory) separation from both those lower and those above (typically when older, the once young and cool become co-opted into the logic of the very high-end fashion outlined at the beginning of this chapter). The question is again one of who is included and who is excluded from belonging. Nitin collaborates actively with a whole army of taste and style makers, from designers, artists to musicians, and with party and event venues such as the bar *Turquoise Cottage* in Vasant Vihar, known for its underground and yet elitist invite-only parties. As Nitin says, the '*Bhootsavaar* family keeps growing' – as of today, it comprises brand endorsers such as music bands like *Menwhopause, Reggae Rajahs, Indigo Children, Featherheads, Drop, Minute of Decay, Fuzz Culture, Mob Marley, Totara Jack, Kern Dalton Collective, Tritha Sinha* and *Pink Noise, Eshaan Chabra, Jazz Bastards, Advaita, Crystal Vision, Shantanu,* DJ Augustine Shimray and so on, as well as break dancers and hip hoppers from the Brooklyn Academy of Dance & Arts (BADA) in New Delhi, or the graffiti artist Harsh Raman Paul,

Figure 6.4 Ritika Singh, a singer, *Bhootsavaar*, 2013, Crescent Mall. Image courtesy of Nitin Bal Chauhan.

photographer Rahul Lal, or textile designer Shruti Raj Kirti. Furthermore, Nitin makes almost weekly interviews to circulate online with 'Bhootsavaars', i.e. passionate youngsters working in creative industries, who share their life stories enhancing the larger brand narrative about the rise of contemporary hip, young and wild creative class that lives on its own terms, unburdened by tradition – to reiterate, again the very same narrative that is so often taken for granted and reproduced both in media and pop-academic production on the rise of the globalised India to superpower (Das 2000; Kamdar 2007). Within the echo-chamber of the *Bhootsavaar* family or the hip and cool 'zippies', the youth desperately wants to be what they are told by the ideologues that they already are. The populist right wing political myths are smoothly incorporated into the 'simple brand ideologies', feeding of each other and enforcing each other. They effectively direct affects of large segments of society, while planting dreams in the rest, capturing in the process the hearts and guts of all, and with it also their power to act. It is precisely here that we see ideology operating at the level of enjoyment that leads to passionate participation, driven by collective libidinal investment. Perhaps not even paradoxically, there is a great emphasis placed on the appearance of authenticity and spontaneity of such a collective movement.

Bhootsavaar's strategies such as using the 'common people' are grounded in a drive towards deliberate authentication, one that outsources the promotional/brand message to creatively disinterested individuals, 'anti-establishment' or alternative settings, and 'democratically viral' customer-generated content. The goal is to convince the customer that their desire is authentic and spontaneous, that the desire was there before the brand rather than the other way round.

GOOD CONSUMER CITIZENS PASSIONATELY EMBRACE THE INJUNCTION: 'WASTE!'

To conclude, *Bhootsavaar* is just one case among many in the world of contemporary fashion brands that indulges in a form of artistic and commercially inflected nationalism while attempting to create a clearly distinct 'aesthetic subculture' (one that cares more for form than for content), or a niche defined by a distinct aesthetics. And yet, we should not let ourselves be deceived here by the particularity of this case pertaining to a very specific segment of Indian urban youth. Beyond the particular and the local, such as the capitalisation on the celebration of Indian creative youth in nationalistic discourses, there is another message, inherent to worldwide consumer capitalism (for the global privileged classes) that is very visibly – and materially reproduced here. Namely, the core injunction of consumer citizenship – 'waste!' Or more precisely, 'waste, while believing that your wasting can be politically effective and change the world into a better place'. While the position endorsed increasingly by contemporary business elites might be summed up as: 'greed is good and our corporate greed will save the world through our philanthropy and benevolence', or else a position of philanthrocapitalism (Bishop and Green 2008; Kuldova 2014; McGoey 2012; Kuldova 2017), the good consumer-citizens are similarly meant to perceive their wasting as beneficial to economy and society at large. Morality is being re-inserted into the market here, and as it appears increasingly only those with enough economic and cultural capital can, within the hegemonic capitalist discourses, claim the moral high-ground and at the same time seek redemption from the baneful capitalist system (Žižek 2009; Nickel and Eikenberry 2009). Even *Bhootsavaar* occasionally produces in villages in Himachal Pradesh, and claims to empower local workers, thus creating an added ethical value to its products. Those critical of the capitalist system and neoliberal ideology have been long pointing out that 'ethical capitalism' or 'moral capitalism' is practically an impossibility, and that there is no amount of reform of the current system that could effectively turn around the widespread human suffering and environmental destruction (Harvey 2000; Harvey 2001; Harvey 2003; Harvey 2016; Graeber 2012).

Being young and being a consumer-citizen in the Indian context is, as we have seen, a matter of privilege, as is belonging to a 'generation of global youth'. The majority of global youngsters are excluded from participation. Purchasing material symbols of rebellion, subversion, and creativity is increasingly also a matter of privilege on the one hand and on the other, for those who can see through the staged rebellion, a sign of co-option within the ruling system. Those who might be truly subversive and really using aesthetics to challenge middle-class moralities (Hewamanne in this volume) are nowhere as cool as their up-cycled fashion versions that sublimate the real dirty and ripped jeans, or prostitute-like bold fashions into a temporary fashion statement. Gated fashion events and parties in the Indian urban metropolises are to a large degree spaces where such privilege is reproduced together with all the relevant cultural capital (in case of the upper middle class and aspiring middle class for instance the knowledge of western and Indian punk or retro-futuristic fashion trends and so on). The aesthetic of subversion and creativity that brands like *Bhootsavaar* sell is clearly not aimed at *being* subversive; rather, precisely through appearing subversive it most effectively reproduces the status quo. Hence, the enclosed spaces of fashion events for privileged urban youth are also spaces where first-rate citizens, the good model consumer-citizens, are shaped. This is also where political or rather apolitical subjects are brought into being – subjects who prefer to buy ethical fashion to change the world (a discourse that increasingly permeates the fashion industry with all its 'sustainability', 'best practice', 'ethical business' and CSR (corporate social responsibility) campaigns aimed at creating added value), rather than to take collective political action.

Commercial rituals are the most effective tools for embedding such messages into material practices and ambient environments. Only events like these are capable of creating those most desired 'loyal followers'. 'Ambient governance', that Michael Serazio conceptualised as a kind of Foucauldian mode of power (Serazio 2013) is at work in most of these fashion events and ritual spectacles. One of its crucial features is the deliberate self-effacement of its own persuasive intent. The message is implicit everywhere, but nowhere is it stated explicitly. Moreover, it capitalises on the agency of consumers and exploits the power of seemingly 'disinterested' cultural spaces and 'authenticated' individuals. Ambient governance that attempts to induce and direct affects and thus capture the collective power to act has become the currently hegemonic paradigm for harnessing social power and profit.

When combined with the nationalist mythology of the good consumer citizen, something more is inscribed into the ambient environments – namely the neoliberal injunction to waste and to indebt one's future self. All of these spaces are marked by shared allusions to waste. Fashion events often resemble an excessive potlatch, where enormous amounts of labour and investment go into preparation and then are wasted in a matter of a few hours. The repetitive symbolism of death and waste (sculls, blood, Kali etc.) and (creative) destruction in Nitin's fashion is not coincidental. If money is to be wasted, it seems, it should be wasted on waste (or at least its symbols) (Crosthwaite 2011). The fashion environments thus seem to capitalise on a deep-seated desire for sheer annihilation of capital, while the ambiences keep at the same time screaming 'waste!' The parents of the 'zippies' might have a point after all, when they call their sons and daughters 'great wastrels' that passionately and joyfully fall into debt while purchasing clothes that are themselves symbolic of that very annihilation. The good consumer-citizens are precisely such great wastrels that keep the economy as well as the imaginary of achievement and enjoyment running. Fashion events not only interpellate us to waste, but are in themselves collective rituals of purification. This effect seems to be maximised when money is wasted on things that themselves represent waste. Fashion drives the desire of people for their own dispossession and annihilation, and thus perfectly co-opts them into a system built precisely upon these premises. In short, there is nothing revolutionary, rebellious or ethical about these wasteful excesses, the opposite is the case. Buying symbols of rebellion is the very opposite of actually acting out rebellion (Heath and Potter 2005). Buying those Marx teacups, Occupy Wall Street caps and '<3 Nasty Woman' T-shirts just won't cut it.

REFERENCES

Akhtar, Z. (2011) 'Zindagi Na Milegi Dobara' (You don't get another life). 153 min. India, Hindi.
Althusser, L. (1971) 'Ideology and Ideological State Apparatuses', in B. Brewster (ed.) *Lenin and Philosophy, and Other Essays*, London: New Left Books, pp. 127–188.
Anderson, B. (2009) 'Affective Atmospheres', *Emotion, Space, Society* 2: 77–81.
Babin, B.J. and Attaway, J.S. (2000) 'Atmospheric Affect as a Tool for Creating Value and Gaining Share of Customer', *Journal of Business Research* 49: 91–99.
Banaji, S. (2012) 'A Tale of Three Worlds: Young People, Media and Class in India', in C. Henseler (ed.) *Generation X Goes Global: Mapping a Youth Culture in Motion*, New York: Routledge, pp. 33–50.
Banaji, S. and Buckingham, D. (2009) 'The Civic Sell', *Information, Communication & Society*, 1–27. DOI: 10.1080/13691180802687621.

Bishop, M. and Green, M. (2008) *Philanthrocapitalism: How the Rich Can Save the World and Why We Should Let Them*, London: A & C Black.

Bourdieu, P. (1984) *Distinction: A Social Critique of the Judgement of Taste*, London: Routledge & Kegan Paul.

Brosius, C. (2009) 'The Gated Romance of "India Shining": Visualizing Urban Lifestyle in Advertisement of Residential Housing Development', in K.M. Gokulsing and W. Dissanayake (eds), *Popular Culture in Globalized India*, London: Routledge, pp. 174–191.

Chauhan, Nitin Bal. Personal interview. 1–5 September, 2014.

Ciotti, M. (2012) 'Post-colonial Renaissance: "Indianness", Contemporary Art and the Market in the Age of Neoliberal Capital', *Third World Quarterly*, 33(4): 637–655.

Citton, Y. (2010) 'Populism and the Empowering Circulation of Myths', *Open* 20: 60–69.

Crosthwaite, P. (2011) 'What a Waste of Money: Expenditure, the Death Drive, and the Contemporary Art Market', *New Formations* 72: 80–93.

Das, G. (2000) *India Unbound*. New Delhi: Viking.

De, S. (2008) *Superstar India: From Incredible to Unstoppable*, New Delhi: Penguin Books.

Deshpande, S. (1993) 'Imagined Economies: Styles of Nation-building in 20th Century India', *Journal of Arts and Ideas* 25/26: 5–35.

——— (2003) *Contemporary India: A Sociological View*, London: Penguin Books.

Durkheim, É. (1965) *The Elementary Forms of the Religious Life*, New York: The Free Press.

Fernandes, L. (2000) 'Nationalizing "the Global": Media Images, Cultural Politics and the Middle Class in India', *Media, Culture and Society* 22(5): 611–628.

Graeber, D. (2012) *Debt: The First 5000 Years*, London: Penguin Books.

Harvey, D. (2000) *Spaces of Hope*, Edinburgh: Edinburgh University Press.

——— (2001) *Spaces of Capital: Towards a Critical Geography*, London: Routledge.

——— (2003) 'The Right to the City', *International Journal of Urban and Regional Research* 27(4): 939–941.

——— (2016) 'Neoliberalism is a Political Project', *Jacobin*, 23 July. Available at https://www.jacobinmag.com/2016/07/david-harvey-neoliberalism-capitalism-labor-crisis-resistance/ (accessed 10 October 2017).

Heath, J. and Potter, A. (2005) *The Rebel Sell: How the Counterculture became Consumer Culture*, West Sussex: Capstone Publishing.

Hoare, G. (2007) 'Will Ethical Shopping Save the World?' *Battle of Ideas by the Institute of Ideas.* Available at http://www.battleofideas.org.uk/index.php/site/battles/834/ (accessed 3 July 2015).

Kamdar, M. (2007) *Planet India: How the Fastest Growing Democracy is Transforming America and the World*. New York: Scribner.

Kapur, J. (2014) *The Politics of Time and Youth in Brand India: Bargaining with Capital*, London: Anthem Press.

Kuldova, T. (2013) '"The Maharaja Style": Royal Chic, Heritage Luxury and the Nomadic Elites', in T. Kuldova (ed.) *Fashion India: Spectacular Capitalism*, Oslo: Akademika Publishing, pp. 51–70.

——— (2014) 'Designing an Illusion of India's Future Superpowerdom: Of the Rise of Neo-Aristocracy, Hindutva and Philanthrocapitalism', *The Unfamiliar: An Anthropological Journal* 4(1): 15–22.

——— (2016a) 'Heads Against Hands and Hierarchies of Creativity: Indian Luxury Embroidery between Craft, Fashion Design and Art', in M. Svašek and B. Meyer

(eds), *Creativity in Transition: Politics and Aesthetics of Circulating Images*, Oxford, New York: Berghahn Books.
—— (2016b) *Luxury Indian Fashion: A Social Critique*, London: Bloomsbury.
—— (2017) 'Forcing "Good" and the Legitimization of Informal Power: Philanthrocapitalism and Artistic Nationalism among the Indian Business Elite', *Asienforum: International Quarterly for Asian Studies* 49(1–2): 1–12.
Lordon, F. (2014) *Willing Slaves of Capital: Spinoza & Marx on Desire*, London: Verso.
Lukose, R.A. (2009) *Liberalization's Children: Gender, Youth, and Consumer Citizenship in Globalizing India*, Durham: Duke University Press.
Maffesoli, M. (1996) *The Time of the Tribes: The Decline of Individualism in Mass Society*, London: SAGE.
Mazzarella, W. (2006) *Shoveling Smoke: Advertising and Globalization in Contemporary India*, Durham: Duke University Press.
McGoey, L. (2012) 'Philanthrocapitalism and its Critics', *Poetics* 40: 185–199.
Mehta, S. (2003) 'India Reloaded', *Verve* 11(4).
Mukerji, A. (2013) 'Yeh Jawaani hai Deewani' (The Youth is Crazy), 161 min. India, Hindi.
Nickel, P.M. and Eikenberry, A.M. (2009) 'A Critique of the Discourse of Marketized Philanthropy', *American Behavioral Scientist* 52(7): 974–989.
Parveen, S. (2006) 'Embroidered Quilt: Nakshi Katha or Kaantha'. Available at http://sos-arsenic.net/english/womens_culture/index.html# (accessed 9 December 2014).
Paul, T.K. (2009) 'Textile/Handicraft Industry Today'. Available at http://www.textiletoday.com.bd/demo/magazine/print/6 (accessed 8 December 2014).
Pfaller, R. (2005) 'Where is Your Hamster? The Concept of Ideology in Slavoj Zizek's Cultural Theory', in G. Boucher, J. Glynos and M. Sharpe (eds), *Traversing the Fantasy: Critical Responses to Slavoj Zizek*, London: Ashgate.
—— (2015) '"How is it that we all function without having our own personal police officer at our butts?" The Efficiency of Ideology and the Possibilities of Art: An Althusserian Account.'
Roberts, K. (2004) *Lovemarks: The Future Beyond Brands*, New York: Murdoch Books Pty Limited.
Sassen, S. (2014) *Expulsions: Brutality and Complexity in the Global Economy*, Cambridge: Harvard University Press.
Scammel, M. (2000) 'The Internet and Civic Engagement: The Age of the Citizen-Consumer', *Political Communication* 17(4): 351–355.
Serazio, M. (2013) *Your Ad Here: The Cool Sell of Guerrilla Marketing*, New York: New York University Press.
Stallybrass, P. and White, A. (1986) *The Politics and Poetics of Transgression*, London: Methuen.
Žižek, S. (2009) *First as Tragedy, Then as Farce*, London: Verso.

7

TROUSER WEARING WOMEN

Changing Landscape of Fashion among Free Trade Zone Factory Workers and Contemporary Political Tensions in Sri Lanka

Sandya Hewamanne

Enduring the catcalls men directed at me was one of the most difficult experiences I faced when I began doing fieldwork around the Katunayake Free Trade Zone (FTZ) workers' boarding houses, bazaar and night market in 2000. Most of the catcalling was directed at my wearing jeans and trousers. Typical calls included, 'Is your elder brother home?' (suggesting I was wearing his trousers), 'Hello, how are you, gentleman?', or 'Have you come from England?' The catcallers were working-class men, three-wheeler drivers, stall keepers or market vendors, and unemployed youth. Apparently, at least among these working-class youth, trousers still remained mostly a man's dress that aroused anxieties about insidious westernisation when worn by a woman. The fact that very few FTZ women garment factory workers wore trousers indicated the strength of the social ostracisation.

I was usually with groups of garment workers and as they dealt with catcalls with good humour and clever ripostes I survived my initial days around the FTZ without incident. The first time I had to pass the market area alone and was subjected to the same catcalls, I made a rookie fieldworker mistake by confronting some of the catcallers. I passed the last stall, turned around, went over to the catcallers who were preparing their trading table and said: 'However much you ridicule women you will not be able to stop them wearing trousers.' Several others came near the table and pacified me saying, 'They are just joking, so don't mind them miss.' Yet as soon as I started on my way, most of the men who heard my protestation started hooting, with some using obscenities, in what appeared to be a unified male punishment for a 'trouser wearing' woman who probably was devoid of any 'shame-fear'. This connection of trouser wearing to losing shame-fear (*lajja-baya*) is a crucial point that signifies some of the anxieties associated with rural young women migrating to urban FTZs for work. Shame-fear – being ashamed to break internalised social behavioural norms and fearing the social ridicule that results in breaking such norms – is considered a vital characteristic of good Sinhala Buddhist rural women (Obeyesekere 1984; Hewamanne 2016). Although mid-length dresses that are considered acceptable are also not indigenous to Sri Lanka, trousers, when worn by particular groups of women and in certain areas, are a trigger point because they symbolise women's westernisation, which is considered the major cause for 'authentic' Sinhala values and customs being undermined. Therefore, it was not surprising that there was resistance to women wearing trousers, and deviating from what is considered to be 'respectable' attire for young women.

I use the term trousers as a direct translation for the Sinhala word *kalisan*. The word also refers to jeans, but in 2000 it was extremely rare for a woman FTZ worker to wear jeans. Thus when used at the time it referred to cotton or khaki trousers and cropped pants that were much looser fitting than jeans. By 2014 people were using the word *kalisan* as a catch-all to refer to jeans, trousers and cropped pants. The word almost never referred to *salwar kameez*, which was considered a modest and an appropriate dress for young women. People in 2000 noted that the *sari* was the best dress for women but said it was completely fine for FTZ workers to wear modest knee length dresses with full or half sleeves or *salwar kameez*.

As noted above, in 2000 very few FTZ workers, who are generally between 17–24 in age, wore trousers even when they were engaging in leisure time activities. In 2014, however, many workers wore jeans to work and in their everyday lives. This chapter focuses on this changing landscape of working-class fashion in the context of the contemporary political climate and its implications on subaltern identity politics by analysing fashions among global assembly line workers at Sri Lanka's Katunayake FTZ. The chapter starts with a discussion on how Sri Lanka's global factory workers use clothes and styles to negotiate an identity as a group of migrant industrial workers who are different from non-migrant workers, men and middle-class women. This is an important aspect of community building and developing a working-class consciousness that leads toward transformative politics. Although this engagement with fashion as an expressive practice entraps them in the new consumer culture created around the FTZ, it allows them to transgress norms of middle-class 'respectability' as part of their attempt to create a differential identity. Dress and styles also have a significant role in how workers play with the multiple cultural discourses they straddle as both unmarried daughters of patriarchal villages and industrial wageworkers. The chapter demonstrates how they perform transgressions as well as social conformity via fashion and the lack thereof and how this play is significant in opening up limited social, economic and political spaces for former FTZ workers. The chapter ends by discussing recent concerns among Sinhalese Buddhists over Muslim women increasingly wearing the *abaya* and how such feelings rooted in Islamophobia appear to have, paradoxically, contributed towards a more relaxed attitude towards Sinhalese Buddhist women wearing trousers. The irony here lies in how the island's contemporary ethno-religious tensions appear to have magnified anxiety over the conservative yet alien *abaya* while minimising concerns over FTZ workers getting westernised and corrupted due to western fashions. This discussion and analysis is based on long-term ethnographic research conducted from 2000 to 2018.

THIRD CLASS IS MY CLASS

'They say our fashions are third class. Well, third class is my class and that is just fine with me.'

A FTZ factory worker, Niluka, declared the above while explaining how difficult it is for women like her to achieve middle-class respectability even if they tried. Many Sri Lankans use the term 'third class' (in English) when referring to working-class tastes and in general try to dissociate themselves from such tastes in public. As a group, FTZ workers celebrated this stigmatised identity by unhesitatingly claiming stigmatised tastes and engaging in counter hegemonic cultural practices. Women were keenly aware of their subordination along class lines and consequently developed their own tastes, cultural practices and spaces to contest such subordination. These new tastes, practices and spaces contained many elements of what middle-class people consider disrespectable (Hewamanne 2003, 2008).

As Willis (1993: 206) states, the symbolic creativity of young people in endowing their immediate life spaces and social practices with meaning and their selective use of subcultural styles are crucial to creating and sustaining individual and group identities. FTZ women workers collectively expressed their difference from the dominant classes and males and articulated their identities as a gendered group of migrant industrial workers by cultivating new tastes with regard to clothes, make-up, accessories and hair styles. By performing subcultural styles that are subversive critiques of dominant values in public spaces, they posed a conscious challenge to the continued economic, social and cultural domination they endured. The conscious oppositional character of the workers' emergent class and cultural contestatory narrative became evident in the journal notes they wrote about me. In several journal entries they criticised my tastes in clothing and termed my preferences middle-class (i.e., hi-fi (upper class), western). In their boarding house conversations they also attempted to construct a difference between their own styles and those of urban working-class youth by pointing to the latter's desire to follow middle-class trends when they could afford to do so. The workers frequently pointed out that their bright coloured party dresses are more expensive than the pastel coloured, simple dresses that were considered more respectable and said they just did not want to follow the fashion rules of 'arrogant, big people' who would not respect them even if they wore 'respectable' dresses. Not all workers I talked to were able to recognise or articulate the critical potential of their choices. Yet, a significant number, in various ways, made clear that their preferences when it came to dress and style were mediated through and against middle-class expectations. It is this critique that allows me to assert that their creation of subcultural styles is a challenge to the continued economic, social and cultural domination they endure.

My focus on unique styles also situates their dress styles as gender critiques in that the workers refused to perform the ideals of respectability sanctioned for women by middle-class men. In claiming that FTZ workers' performances of their recently developed preferences in the realm of aesthetics was central to creating both working-class and gendered identities, my argument resonates with Dorinne Kondo's notion that 'the world of aesthetics is a site of struggle, where identities are created, where subjects are interpellated, where hegemonies can be challenged' (1997: 4). Kondo's study is one among several works that demonstrate the role played by dress and style in constituting identity (Tarlo 1996; Hansen 2004; Bahl 2005; Archer et al. 2007).

My earlier research among internally displaced Muslim women showed how middle-class Muslim women used a more strict form of veiling to express an identity that is in keeping with the local NGO understanding of Muslim women as oppressed and backward so that they could benefit from NGO financial and supportive services (Hewamanne 2010 and 2015). Both Krishnan (this volume) and Motsemme (2003) note how urban young women (in India and the USA, respectively) develop new dress styles to resist and critique oppressive social forces. Likewise, in a fascinating study of women's burial societies in Botswana, Ngwenya (2002) highlighted how women adapted a particular dress code (enrobing), to assign more meaning and dramatic edge to social action in AIDS related deaths which also allowed them to redefine gender relations and ritual practices.

Several scholars have noted how global assembly line workers use clothing to negotiate male-dominated work cultures and leisure activities. Amin (2006) and Lindquist (2008) demonstrate how women used the veil to create better work environments within the factories for themselves. According to Ong (1987), Malay FTZ workers used veiling together with an ascetic Islamic persona to counter the extant image of FTZ workers being westernised and pleasure seeking (186). Several other studies show how global assembly line workers change their dress and styles as part of becoming modern women and how that was an integral part of their changing senses of selves (Freeman 2000; Pun 2005; Lynch 2007; Hewamanne 2008).

Krishnan's work on female college students in Chennai (this volume) proposes a thesis similar to Lukose's work on male youth in Kerala (2009). They both note that these young people seek social power by 'faking it' or inscribing global culture on their bodies through consumption of counterfeit global brands. Sri Lankan FTZ workers did not aspire to such global cultural identities as their middle-class South Asian counterparts, and in fact were somewhat divorced from global flows (especially in 2000) given their extreme lack of access to technology. What they instead created and performed in the FTZ area was a combination of rural, urban and Indian traditional fashion; one that is not rural or urban and definitely not middle-class. FTZ workers' insistence on such unique tastes and their play with established categories of style subverted middle-class values and tastes and enabled them to register distinctive identities as migrant working women who are different to non-migrant industrial workers, men and middle-class women. This was a more empowering form of identity politics that critiqued the oppressive dominant cultural demands that were superimposed on their lives.

BODY ADORNMENT AND 'GARMENT GIRL TASTES'

Kathy Peiss, writing about working-class women of turn of the century New York, notes that 'dress was a particularly potent way to display and play with notions of respectability, allure, independence, and status and to assert a distinctive identity and presence' (1986: 63). Similarly, the colourful dresses and other accessories FTZ workers habitually chose to wear on special occasions registered for them a distinctive identity as garment factory workers. They wore bright coloured *shalwars* and *gagra cholis* that were embroidered with gold or silver beads, in combination with dark red lipstick, nail polish, and heavy make-up. They also wore high heels (even when on trips to beaches) and frequently wore multi coloured dots (*pottu*) on their foreheads. Such choices loudly proclaimed a difference from other women and made it easier for people to recognise them even if they were hundreds of miles away from the FTZ

(Hewamanne 2006, 2008). Their dresses could be loosely divided into two types: work clothes and party clothes. Their everyday work clothes were of different styles because they wore their old party dresses to work. This habit also ensured that they were easily recognised no matter where they went. These dresses included a flowing skirt (called a flared skirt), with puffed sleeves and round necklines, and skirts and blouses in several different lengths and patterns. Most of their work clothes suggested popular urban fashions, modified with elements from favoured rural fashions. Their party dresses, however, were a combination of several Indian-inspired, middle-class fashions and their own colour preferences. Haney writes that the creation of a hybrid style called fantasia by female performers in Mexican American tent shows asserted Mexican American identity while marking the performers' entry into 'newly public female roles' (1999: 437). The hybrid styles among the FTZ workers similarly marked their newly acquired public role as urban factory workers who are different from middle-class or rural women as well as other urban factory workers.

In 2000, while hanging out at several boarding houses, I often observed workers bringing their newly made work dresses from the nearby seamstresses. One by one they acquired so-called 'Titanic dresses', a long dress with a cross-laced back and tight waist, which was inspired by the period dresses the female lead wore in the film Titanic and which quickly turned into a fashion craze among them. While in the film the dresses were made of light colours, the FTZ workers preferred bright and dark colours. They especially favoured yellow, maroon, magenta, dark green, purple and black. This choice of colours was especially significant when considering that Anagarika Dharmapala, a writer and nationalist who campaigned for reviving Sinhalese Buddhist culture, considered the white saree the optimal dress for respectable ladies, since this signalled their chastity and purity (De Alwis 1997: 98–99). Incidentally, many FTZ workers liked to match black skirts with bright yellow or bright pink blouses even though middle-class people associated such colour combinations with sex workers. The workers' choice to sport these stigmatised colours as well as other marked fashions could not be attributed simply to an ignorance of middle-class dos and don'ts since they watched TV and read fashion pages of magazines. As noted above, these colourful dresses were sometimes more expensive than 'simple, accepted fashions', ruling out affordability as the only reason. This play with the sex worker image seems a particular mediation of culture and style by women who have found themselves in between the categories of 'respectable' and 'promiscuous'. This play pushed them further towards the 'whore' category, but workers as a group did not seem particularly concerned about it. However, they did care about the effects on their individual reputations, leading them to assume different styles when they visited their villages.

Neighbours as well as factory officials talked about workers wearing excessive gold jewellery to work. Some women wore up to four rings to work and sported thick gold chains with pendants. During my research in 2000 many women wore a plastic hair band that featured letters from the English alphabet, which was not in vogue in 2014. Their favourite hairstyles necessitated the use of braids, bands and pins and the workers experimented by combining different coloured or patterned hair accessories. There were other accessories like cheap handbags, sandals and fake brand name watches that they bought at the FTZ bazaar that also contributed to their visual group identity.

FTZ workers could easily buy or make pastel coloured dresses of the kind that were fashionable among female students attending Colombo's higher educational institutions. By doing so they could have passed for belonging among those who congregated at 'respectable public spaces', but they showed no interest in this. When I visited some seamstresses near Saman's boarding house, where I stayed with several women during my initial research at the FTZ, I noticed that they mainly made 'Titanic dresses' and a two-piece dress that most urban women tried to stay away from due to its association with FTZ workers.

I attended four parties at different factories and attended several wedding receptions at workers' homes. On these special occasions women proudly displayed FTZ party clothes and jewellery. They also wore make-up, perfume, bright lipstick and nail polish. They took many photographs at these parties in all their finery, especially while posing with their superiors. Women showed photographs from past annual parties, and it was easy to see that their fascination with brightly decorated *shalwar* and *gagra choli* as a party dress had been present for at least five years. In photos taken in 2014 too, the same kind of dresses, which now go by the name *lenga*, dominated, showing the workers' continuing fascination with Indian-inspired party dresses. Those photographs presented an ongoing story whereby a workers' clothes evolved over the years from pink and blue 'flower girl dresses' (bigger version of poufy dresses worn by flower girls at weddings) to colourful *shalwars*, *cholis* or *lengas*, and the gradual addition of other accessories, including gold jewellery. This material change coincided with another transformation – wide-eyed young girls to self-assured, lively women posing for photographs holding beer cans while seated on men's laps.

FTZ workers used make-up when they went out on trips or attended special functions. Refusing to follow the barrage of middle-class advice about beauty they were subjected to in the media, they almost always chose bright red lipstick. Although they never acknowledged it, the workers also craved fairer skin through ways that made sense to them. While this preoccupation with fairness is partly rooted in racist British colonial-era ideologies, it is elitist to condemn this obsession on senseless prejudices alone. As Kondo (1997: 15) writes, it is only the dominant and unmarked sections of society that can afford to be unconcerned about appearance. She also warns that it is a mistake to think that being unconcerned about appearance is a politically innocent position since this apparent lack of concern itself is a preoccupation with appearance. Interestingly, FTZ workers who wrote journal entries about me opined that my own relatively unconcerned attitude towards appearance was the very mechanism through which I registered my difference from them.

New workers who came directly from their villages learned the appropriate attire, fashions, and behaviour within the FTZ through an intense socialisation process at the factories as well as in their boarding houses. After a few months of FTZ life, workers acquired dresses and accessories that conveyed their membership in the community. Many workers confided that they were determined to uphold their ruralness when they first came to the FTZ. But they reported that the strength and happiness derived from following other workers and the gentle prodding from senior workers soon made them change their minds. According to Lynch, village garment factory workers spoke disparagingly of the way rural workers first came to work with 'dirt dripping from their clothes'

(2000: 234) and celebrated the newcomers' gradual transformation in hygiene levels and style as a mark of modernity. Marking the difference between the two groups, FTZ workers did not talk disparagingly about new workers or the way they slowly acquired the styles and habits of the FTZ. They all came to the FTZ as rural women and had to collectively suffer the stigma of being 'backward, ignorant and tasteless rural women'. This instilled an 'us' against 'them' mentality that focused on whether a woman wanted to be identified as a FTZ worker, as opposed to what her appearance or conduct was when she first arrived in the FTZ.

COMMUNITY BUILDING

The clothing, make-up and accessories that workers chose to wear indicated their willingness to be identified and treated as a FTZ garment worker. This identification sometimes resulted in painful experiences, such as snide remarks and even virulent outbursts about being 'whores' who have forgotten where they came from. Still when they were in a group, women workers seemed to derive pleasure from this group identity. Especially in the context of the FTZ where unionisation is prohibited, such seemingly minor ways of belonging to a group of workers bode well for working-class politics. The importance of fashion as a way of building a community and a signifier of belonging was emphasised by how workers created systems of vigilance, critique and punishments for those who did not follow the 'proper' dress and styles unique to FTZ workers.

Once on a trip to Unawatuna beach, Suishin factory workers sent a strong message to Amila, their colleague from the assembly line C, who kept refusing to embrace FTZ fashions. It was close to noon when we got to the beach and the gold and silver beads on the women's *shalwars* and *gagra cholis* glittered in the sunlight. The purple, orange and green silk material swished upward in the strong sea breeze giving way to fits of loud laughter as women struggled to balance themselves on high-heeled sandals. Holding hands in groups of three to four we walked to the far corner of the popular beach passing men in swimming gear and women in shorts and T-shirts. While men laughed and catcalled, the middle-class women curled their lips in disapproval.

Amila liked to insist that she worked only because she was bored at home and this combined with her eschewing FTZ fashion made clear that she wanted to be considered different from the rest of the workers. By constantly pointing out that she came to work from her family home, which was located close to the FTZ, she also emphasised the fact that she was not a migrant worker from a rural area. For the trip to the beach, Amila wore tight black jeans with a black checked shirt and little jewellery. She used make-up sparingly and applied a soft pink lipstick; in stark contrast to the bright shades of reds the others wore. Perhaps the biggest difference in attire was her simple pair of beach sandals, which were popular among Colombo youth. But with many workers wearing bright coloured party dresses, we attracted much interest from the numerous male vacationers present at the beach. The indirect, group flirtations between men and the workers climaxed when a group of men surrounded the women and dragged them to the sea in all their finery. As women ran back from the sea, men tossed sand on their wet clothes.

When the men started to drag the women to the sea, Amila, myself and two other women managed to run away and hide. After about half an hour of play the group prepared for picnic lunches on the beach. When we finally joined them, the other women had taken showers and were opening their lunch packets. When Amila sat down with her lunch, a conspiratorial air enveloped the excited group. Sanka and Nuwan (Line C supervisor and quality controller), who accompanied us on this trip, grabbed Amila by her arms and dragged her to the sea. With all her clothes soaked with salty water, Amila came out cursing everybody only to be dragged back to the ocean. After dipping her three times, the men allowed her to pay Rs.10 and take a shower. As soon as she finished the shower they again dragged her to the sea. The workers, obviously enjoying the scene, encouraged the men by clapping and whistling. They looked on with glee while commenting how they had all gone through the forced drenching and that Amila ought to suffer the same experience. But I was puzzled as to their focus on Amila, since there were at least three other women who managed to escape the drenching.

'Look, my nice blouse has shrunk in size because of the sea water', Amila loudly complained when she came back to eat. Ever ready with a combative rejoinder, Mangala answered, 'Our clothes are nice clothes too.' Although she motioned to Mangala not to aggravate Amila further, Vasanthi whispered, 'whatever we wear we all are garment workers'.

The punishment meted out to Amila for refusing to identify with her fellow FTZ workers demonstrated the workers' sense of collective identity and the role clothing and style play in expressing this identity. The incident showed that workers consider adopting FTZ fashion to be a necessary step in community identification and solidarity. The abuse that Amila was subjected to was directly connected to her refusal to identify with the workers' narratives and their clothing and fashions. The choice of clothing not only signalled a woman's willingness to be identified as a FTZ worker but also signalled her membership in a stigmatised women's group that led to 'humiliating' incidents at the hands of men. Workers, however, refused to acknowledge the incident as humiliating or as an act of violence against them, opting instead to recognise it as a mutually pleasurable game. In this way they not only refused to be victims but embraced the consequences of being identified as FTZ workers – in other words, as women who transgressed.

SAMPLE GARMENTS AND HOME CLOTHES: VILLAGE PERFORMANCES

Furthermore, women workers loved to go out in groups wearing the same colour or same patterned dresses that got sold from their own factories to the bazaar because they were slightly damaged. When they went out in those garments and proudly displayed allegiance to their group, men in bus stops and shops called after them saying, 'Ah, sample, where are you going?' Women expressed pride in being recognised as garment workers – the garments they produced being a 'sample' of who they were. However, when they visited their villages they left behind these 'slightly damaged' garments in their boarding houses and put on clothes they typically wore in their villages.

If expressing group identity via fashionable clothing was important, so was reverting to home styles once back in their villages. I once visited my factory friends Mala and Karuna's village home in Pollonnaruwa on a four-day vacation. Although we had much fun with returning soldiers on the night train, Mala and Karuna quite abruptly changed their clothes and behaviour no sooner than we approached their village. They put on what they called 'home clothes,' which were old, faded, knee length dresses in pastel colours, and also put their hair up in knots or plated into braids. Without any make-up and in this village-friendly attire they transformed themselves into looking like any other young woman in the village. At the same time, they seemed to put me on display as a counterpoint that magnified their performed rural sensibilities.

In deference to rural sentiments, I had brought long skirts and tops to wear in the village, instead of my usual jeans and T-shirts. Mala and Karuna were not happy with this and earnestly asked me not to wear skirts when going around the village. Feeling pressured, I wore the same pair of jeans I started out with for most of my stay in Polonnaruwa. Both of them, however, chose to wear long faded skirts. Walking with them among the paddy fields and small houses I felt considerably ill at ease in my jeans. It aroused much interest among the villagers and Mala and Karuna explained in different ways that I was an important person at the factory and that I was a 'miss from America'. My presence contributed to a positive identity in the village for Mala and Karuna; for not only were they associating with a 'miss' who came from America, they also managed to maintain their 'ruralness' and village traditions in a space where they were constantly exposed to 'dangerous' people such as the 'miss' from America. Their insistence on my wearing clothes associated with the western world sharpened the contrast they projected by wearing home clothes. The difference in clothes and mannerisms not only signified differences in taste but also other associated binaries such as westernised/traditional, urban/rural, bad/good women.

I have also seen workers busying themselves by covering up their glittery FTZ clothes with old shirts when village relatives visited boarding houses without giving prior notice. Why was it so important for workers to project an image that was quite different from what they had become through their FTZ experience? Occupying an awkward position, as temporary migrants, FTZ workers did not have the luxury of shaking off all that was associated with their village lives. They would be forced to leave their employment and retreat into the village sooner or later. It was in this context that their village performances took meaning and became an important process geared towards repairing the damaged identity brought about by associating with a stigmatised space.

I have since 2005 been visiting former FTZ workers in their homes to study how they renegotiate identities within more surveillance-oriented and patriarchally organised villages. Almost all of them exchanged their FTZ fashionable clothes and hair styles for acceptable village styles that symbolise innocence, purity, serenity and modesty. This was a crucial change for many who wanted to get into arranged marriages. Even within love marriages it was important for former workers to perform the non-corrupted, industrious former worker role by changing clothes, styles and mannerisms. The first few years among affinal kin is a test for many newly married Sri Lankan rural women who move to their husband's villages. For former FTZ workers, who have spent a number of years at a stigmatised, urban space, this trial period is even more intense. Almost all former workers I visited continued to wear pastel coloured, modest village dresses while performing extreme forms of social conformity by suppressing many aspects of the new selves they developed during their FTZ stint. Although I found this bemusing in the beginning, as my field work seasons continued I realised that most of these former workers engage in this show of social conformity as a conscious way to build a supportive female network within the community so as to facilitate their entry into entrepreneurship and village social leadership (Hewamanne Forthcoming). Thus most former FTZ workers are engaged in a process of changing existing gender norms with regard to what young married women and mothers can do in local public domains. The nuanced situational play with fashions is important for former workers to manage the stigma of FTZ work; just as it is important for current former workers to transgress some forms of patriarchal control through dress and style. Both are about communicating with their immediate communities, and form part of their repertoire of tools with which they embody protest, critique and conformity.

TROUSER WEARING WOMEN AND *ABAYA* WEARING WOMEN

I earlier noted that, in 2000, only a few workers dared to wear trousers or jeans, and those who did so were subjected to ridicule. I also noted how Mala and Karuna used the jeans-wearing miss from America (myself) as a way to enhance their reputations within the village as 'good girls' who had not changed and become 'mod' like the miss from America. Fast-forward to 2014 and one sees many current FTZ workers wearing jeans to work, to the store, on pleasure trips and other journeys. Only senior workers remembered the days when men shouted, 'Is your elder brother home?' to ridicule those wearing trousers. Many workers said that jeans/ trousers are freely and cheaply available in Katunayake shops and no one ridiculed them for wearing trousers. As an eight-year veteran worker, Nelum, noted: 'women kept wearing trousers despite catcalls and men got tired of trying to dissuade us'. It appears that my prediction at the marketplace has come true.

I first began noticing this change from around 2010 and the trend seems to follow a general pattern of change in acceptable womanly attire within Colombo and its suburbs. An explosion of ready-made garment outlets in these areas also contributed to a form of homogenisation across class boundaries. Although catcalls on Katunayake streets persisted, none seemed to be aimed at women wearing trousers. This prompted me to interview working-class men around the FTZ area and explore their thoughts on this particular clothing issue. My very first focus group discussion at the three-wheeler parking stand of the Averiwatthe junction was revelatory. I was talking to four young men and an elderly man about the changing attitude toward women wearing trousers. The first man to speak, Chaminda, set the tone of the discussion by agitatedly saying, 'With what is happening to the Sinhala people these days, girls wearing jeans is nothing. Haven't you seen the *goni billo* (a Sinhala term usually used to refer to a bogeyman with a sack and in this case used derogatorily towards Muslim women wearing the *abaya*) in Colombo. Okay miss, you yourself tell me how many you saw in 2005 and how many you are seeing this time.' All four joined the conversation echoing Chaminda's anxieties about Muslim women's attire. According to another man, 'Most of those women are Sinhalese who have been converted to Muslim religion (Islam). They are forced to wear the *goni billa* suit so that their families cannot find them. Otherwise, why this sudden increase in *goni billo*.' This comment led to more accusations about how rich Muslim traders forcibly convert their female Sinhalese employees. The trick, according to these men, was to hire only Muslim men and only Sinhala women and then let the inevitable love relationships and marriages happen. These anxiety-filled tirades against Muslim men echo the fears of love jihad expressed in India and the UK (Gupta 2009; Mallet 2014; Naqvi 2014). The accusations made against Muslims here echo those made by the extremist Buddhist group *Bodu Bala Sena* (Buddhist Power Force), which beginning in mid 2012 began resorting to anti-Muslim agitprop and is mostly responsible for fanning Islamophobia in the island (DeVotta 2016a, 2016b; Silva 2016).

When, during the same focus group meeting, I mentioned that there is a turn toward a rigid interpretation of Islam and that Muslim women, accordingly, may be expressing their new religious fervour, several angrily noted that it had nothing to do with religiosity, but had to do with attempts to change the demographics of the country by getting Sinhala women to have Muslim children. Deciding to not pursue the clear connotations of how nations are built and fought over women's bodies, I brought the conversation back to fashions and asked whether they catcalled the women in *abayas* as they did women who wore trousers. This question took them by surprise, leading to hesitation and some joking about how they would not dare catcall as they are not sure whether it is a woman or a man 'inside that thing', and how they could not have fun by catcalling women who look like fat mothers (*ammandiyo*) due to 'that black sack'.

I have had three more focus group discussions, including one with six army soldiers, and conducted ten in-depth interviews with men who worked at bag centres, record bars, jewellery shops and at the market, together with three FTZ factory executives. Not surprisingly, perhaps, the most reserved of them all were the six soldiers who claimed they have never ridiculed women for wearing trousers and they would protect *abaya*-wearing women if anyone harassed them. The others, at varying intensity, expressed deep anxieties about a Muslim takeover of the country and how Sinhala women are the unwitting catalyst in this political agenda. This revealed prevailing patriarchal ideas of how women were unwilling victims of men's agendas and how love and sexual desire are not emotions that women experience but are imposed upon them by men. Many have noted how trousers are a modest dress that cover more than they reveal and that just because a woman is wearing trousers does not mean that she has forgotten her culture or is trying to be like men. Three young men in fact noted that trousers are more modest than *saris*, as long as the top is long and loose.

During these times, I mentioned that the *abaya* that they now reviled is also a very modest dress that covered the entire body. While all agreed that it is modest, they, in varied ways, expressed their fear of the 'unknown' – the blackness of the dress, the hidden identity of the person wearing the robe, etc. Showing how ethnic, religious and gender concerns intersect in interesting ways, some of the discussants and interviewees noted that it pained them to see women so restricted, uncomfortable and unfree. Lila Abu-Lughod's classic work asks a vital question 'Do Muslim Women Need Saving?' (2013). Similar to simplistic western discourses on 'saving Muslim women', that led to Abu-Lughod's response, these men's concerns about women's lack of choice were expressed as a justification for Islamaphobia.

The January 2015 defeat of President Mahinda Rajapaksa, whose brother supported the extremist *Bodhu Bala Sena*, regenerated hopes of peace and good governance. Yet, my interviews in the FTZ area evidenced that the distrust has hardly waned. While working-class men I talked to in July 2015 agreed that communal violence was not the way to respond, they reiterated their uneasiness with *abaya*-wearing women, claiming that they are being forced by rich Arabian countries to dress in an alien dress. Chaminda again asked me to consider the numerous shops that have recently cropped up exclusively selling black *abayas*. They highly praised the Muslim Council of Sri Lanka's initiative to exchange black *abayas* for coloured *abayas* to minimise the alienation from the majority community, noting that Muslim people in Sri Lanka are peace loving and it is the terrorists in the middle eastern countries who are trying to get good Muslim women to look like 'terrorists'. Nandana, the older three-wheeler driver, was adamant that he is not against good Sri Lankan Muslims. He brought up the names of Kabeer Hashim and his father, who were members of parliament and at times government ministers, and said, 'Those are the (good) people. They did not try to convert people. In fact, Mr Kabeer helped me get my first three-wheeler. People like Mr Kabeer are also mad about what Arabs are doing.' Such differentiation has not prevented rising anti-Muslim sentiments

(Stewart 2014; Sarjoon et al. 2016). Together with the fears fanned by *Bodu Bala Sena* and other new Sinhalese Buddhist extremist groups, nationalist anxieties have manifested once more over women's bodies; this time on too much covering of Muslim women's bodies.

While these new concerns with women's clothing rage together with anti-Muslim sentiments, working-class women in Katunayake now clearly get away with wearing trousers, which is a marked contrast to what their predecessors faced. Female trouser-wearing seems to have become normalised due to concerns over the rising number of Muslim women taking to the *abaya*. Of course, women's persistence, their deeper entrenchment in neoliberal regimes, and new local garment market patterns have all contributed to this normalisation at varying levels. It is also interesting to note that several ready-made garment outlet chains owned by Muslim businessmen were partly responsible for the deluge of easily affordable jeans in Sri Lanka. One of the rumours that contributed to Islamaphobia and attacks against the Aluthgama Muslim community in 2014 and in Kandy and Ampara in 2018, was that the underwear and jeans sold by these Muslim establishments were sprayed with an infertility-inducing chemical in an effort to reduce the population growth rate among the Sinhala community (DeVotta 2016b; Haniffa 2016; Taub and Fisher 2018).

While it is a welcome change that a woman can wear trousers or jeans in the FTZ area without being ridiculed, I doubt this represents a political victory. Building community identity through FTZ fashions has been a vital aspect of the subaltern political world that FTZ workers created around the Katunayake area (Hewamanne 2008). In this sense, dressing like any other middle-class young woman zaps the critical potential of creating her own fashions and tastes. Thankfully, the women workers still mark their bodies in other ways that conspicuously express their particular working-class identity: that of a gendered group of migrant industrial workers who are different from men, middle-class women and non-migrant workers.

CONCLUSION: SUBVERSIONS THAT MATTERED

Huisman and Hondagneu-Sotelo (2005) note that dress is a discursive daily practice of gender and that the hair, make-up and dress practices among Bosnian Muslim refugee women living in Vermont are rooted in relational processes that occur at the macrostructural level of history and nation, and at the micro world of social interaction. The FTZ workers gendered dress and style practices are also mediated through their macro and micro interactional worlds and are shaped within changing social, political, or economic processes.

I have explicated elsewhere that the FTZ workers are becoming neoliberal subjects and have adapted neoliberal ways of thinking, aspiring and self-investment (Hewamanne 2017). Other studies have also shown that global factory workers adopt new dress, style and make-up practices as part of claiming modernity (Mills 1997, 1999; Freeman 2000; Lynch 2007; Prentice 2015). However, unlike in most other such contexts Sri Lankan FTZ workers insisted that they did not want to follow the middle classes but expressed considerable pride in being able to follow fashions and tastes that were their own. They were happy in the knowledge that their clothes irked the middle classes. Their performances of FTZ garment worker identities at public places, through fashion deemed disrespectable, represented a critique of middle-class and male enforced cultural hegemony.

Eighteen years after I first carried out long term research in the FTZ, women workers still love colourful, glittery party clothes and combine unusual colours that the middle classes associate with sex workers. They still love gold jewellery, high heels and thick make-up. The prominent change from 2000, however, is the high number of workers who wear jeans without attracting much male attention. As explained in the last section, new ethnic and religious anxieties appear to have over-shadowed gendered concerns that were important a decade ago.

Having the freedom to wear jeans may threaten their unique identity, yet for the most part these workers retain other styles that still make them a part of a gendered working-class community. Although their contestatory practices contain levels of opposition and complicity, they still subvert dominant cultural norms. These subversions form an important part of their daily cultural struggles and have the potential to reconfigure the terms of dominant discourses. Yet, none of the workers I talked to in 2014 were able to connect the anxieties over *abaya*-wearing women to the ridicule their predecessors suffered for wearing trousers.

Evidencing how gendered concerns are dwarfed by the contemporary Sri Lankan ethno-religious milieu, many workers themselves expressed anxieties over *abaya*-wearing women by resorting to nationalist rhetoric that claimed foreign attire like the *abaya* were bound to infuse cultural changes unsuited for Sri Lanka.

In an interesting twist, the influx of Tamil workers from the formerly war torn North and Eastern provinces to the FTZ has provided another measuring tool for the eager audiences. Many young Sinhala men in the area, including some of the men who criticised *abaya*-wearing women, praised the new Tamil workers for dressing modestly in loose skirts and blouses with hair in plaits and pottu (traditional dot) on the forehead (Hewamanne 2016). Neoliberalism, modernity and global cultural flows aside, female dress and style practices are still measured, debated and responded to within nationalist and patriarchal contours. Add to that the global trend in Islamaphobia and women of marginalised communities still have little space to subvert. Therein lies the cruciality of the subversions in styles that FTZ factory workers develop and enact in the FTZ area against the agents and institutions that seek to make women conform.

REFERENCES

Abu-Lughod, L. (2013) *Do Muslim Women Need Saving?* Cambridge: Harvard University Press.

Amin, S. (2006) 'Implications of Trade Liberalization for Working Women's Marriage: Case Studies of Bangladesh, Egypt and Vietnam', in C. Brown, E. Braunstein and A. Malhotra (eds), *Trading Women's Health and Rights? Trade Liberalization and Reproductive Health in Developing Economies*, London: Zed.

Archer, L., Hollingworth, S. and Halsall, A. (2007) '"University's not for Me – I'm a Nike Person": Urban, Working-Class Young People's Negotiations of "Style", Identity and Educational Engagement', *Sociology* 41(2): 219–237.

Bahl, V. (2005) 'Shifting Boundaries of "Nativity" and "Modernity" in South Asian Women's Clothes', *Dialectical Anthropology* 29(1): 85–121.

De Alwis, M. (1997) 'The Production and Embodiment of Respectability: Gendered Demeanors in Colonial Ceylon', in M. Roberts (ed.), *Sri Lanka Collective Identities Revisited*, Colombo: Marga Institute.

DeVotta, N. (2016a) 'A Win For Democracy in Sri Lanka', *Journal of Democracy* 27(1):157.

——— (2016b) 'Engaging Sinhalese Buddhist Majoritarianism and Countering Religious Animus in Sri Lanka: Recommendations for the Incoming U.S. Administration', *The Review of Faith and International Affairs* 14(2): 76–85.

Freeman, C. (2000) *High Tech and High Heels in the Global Economy: Women, Work, and Pink-Collar Identities in the Caribbean*, Durham: Duke University Press.

Gupta, C. (2009) 'Hindu Women, Muslim Men: Love Jihad and Conversions', *Economic and Political Weekly* 44(51): 13–15.

Haney, P. (1999) 'Fantasia and Disobedient Daughters: Undistressing Genres and Reinventing Traditions in the Mexican American Carpa', *Journal of American Folklore* (112): 437–449.

Haniffa, F. (2016) 'Stories in the Aftermath of Aluthgama', in John Clifford Holt (ed.), *Buddhist Extremists and Muslim Minorities: Religious Conflict in Contemporary Sri Lanka*. New York: Oxford University Press, pp. 164–193.

Hansen, K. (2004) 'The World in Dress: Anthropological Perspectives on Clothing, Fashion, and Culture', *Annual Review of Anthropology* (33): 369–392.

Hewamanne, S. (2003) 'Performing Disrespectability: New Tastes, Cultural Practices and Identity Performances by Sri Lanka's Free Trade Zone Garment Factory Workers', *Cultural Dynamics* 15(1): 71–101.

——— (2006) 'Pornographic Voice: Critical Feminist Practices among Sri Lanka's Garment Factory Workers', *Feminist Studies* 32(1): 125–154.

——— (2008) *Stitching Identities in a Free Trade Zone: Gender and Politics in Sri Lanka*, Philadelphia: University of Pennsylvania Press.

——— (2008) '"City of Whores": Nationalism, Development and Global Garment Workers of Sri Lanka', *Social Text* 95–26(2): 35–59.

——— (2010) 'Gendering the Internally Displaced: Problem Bodies, Fluid Boundaries and Politics of Civil Society Participation in Sri Lanka', *International Journal of Women's Studies* 11(1): 157–172.

——— (2015) 'Complicated Belonging: Gendered Empowerment and Anxieties about "Returning" among Internally Displaced Muslim Women in Puttalam, Sri Lanka', in Huma Ahmed Ghosh (ed.), *Walking the Tight Rope: Gender and Islam in Asia*, Albany: State University of New York Press.

——— (2016) *Sri Lanka's Global Factory Workers: (Un)Disciplined Desires and Sexual Struggles in a Post-Colonial Society*, London: Routledge.

——— (2016) 'Neoliberalism's New Recruits: Tamil Workers, Human Rights Clashes and "Mundane" Politics in Post-War Sri Lanka'. Paper presented at the 5th Sri Lanka Round Table at University of Edinburgh UK, April 2016.

——— (Forthcoming) *Manipulating Capital: Former Free Trade Zone Factory Workers Negotiating Village Identities*, Philadelphia: University of Pennsylvania Press.

Huisman, K. and Hondagneu-Sotelo, P. (2005) 'Dress Matters: Change and Continuity in the Dress Practices of Bosnian Muslim Refugee Women', Gender and Society 19(1): 44–65.

Kondo, D. (1997) *About Face: Performing Race in Fashion and Theater*, New York: Routledge.

Lindquist, J. (2008) *The Anxieties of Mobility: Migration and Tourism in the Indonesian Borderlands*, Honolulu: University of Hawai'i Press.

Lukose, R. (2009) *Liberalization's Children: Gender, Youth, and Consumer Citizenship in Globalizing India*, Durham: Duke University Press.

Lynch, C. (2000) 'The Good Girls of Sri Lankan Modernity: Moral Orders of Nationalism, Gender and Globalization in Village Garment Factories'. Ph.D. dissertation. University of Chicago.

——— (2007) *Juki Girls, Good Girls: Gender and Cultural Politics in Sri Lanka's Global Garment Industry*, Ithaca: Cornel University Press.

Mallet, V. (2014) 'Hindu Right Fights Against "Love Jihad"', *Financial Times* (US Edition), 29–30 November, p. 7.
Mills, M.B. (1997) 'Contesting the Margins of Modernity: Women, Migration and Consumption in Thailand', *American Ethnologist* 24(1): 37–61.
——— (1999) *Thai Women in the Global Labor Force: Consuming Desires: Contested Selves*, New Brunswick: Rutgers University Press.
Motsemme, N. (2003) 'Distinguishing Beauty, Creating Distinctions: The Politics and Poetics of Dress among Young Black Women', *Agenda: Empowering Women for Gender Equity* 57: 12–19.
Naqvi, S. (2014) 'Needed, a Love Jihad for the Soul', *Outlook*, 14 September, pp. 32–33.
Ngwenya, B.N. (2002) 'Gender, Dress and Self-Empowerment: Women and Burial Societies in Botswana', *African Sociological Review* 6(2): 1–27.
Obeyesekere, G. (1984) *The Cult of the Goddess Pattini*, Chicago: The University of Chicago Press.
Ong, A. (1987) 'Spirits of Resistance and Capitalist Discipline: Factory Women in Malaysia', Albany: State University of New York Press.
Peiss, K. (1986) *Cheap Amusements: Working Women and Leisure in Turn of the Century New York*, Philadelphia: Temple University Press.
Prentice, R. (2015) *Thiefing a Chance: Factory Work, Illicit Labor, and Neoliberal Subjectivities in Trinidad*, Boulder: University Press of Colorado.
Pun, N. (2005) *Made in China: Women Factory Workers in a Global Workplace*, Durham: Duke University Press.
Sarjoon, A., Yusoff, M. and Hussin, N. (2016) 'Anti-Muslim Sentiments and Violence: A Major Threat to Ethnic Reconciliation and Ethnic Harmony in Post-War Sri Lanka', *Religions* 7(10): 125.
Silva, K.T. (2016) 'Gossip, Rumor, and Propaganda in Anti-Muslim Campaigns of the Bodu Bala Sena', in John Clifford Holt (ed.), *Buddhist Extremists and Muslim Minorities: Religious Conflict in Contemporary Sri Lanka*, New York: Oxford University Press, pp. 119–139.
Stewart, J. (2014) 'Muslim–Buddhist Conflict in Contemporary Sri Lanka', *South Asia Research* 34(3).
Tarlo, E. (1996) *Clothing Matters: Dress and Identity in India*, Chicago: The University of Chicago Press.
Taub, A. and Max, F. (2018) 'Where Countries are Tinderboxes and Facebook is a Match: Rumors set Buddhists Against Muslims in Sri Lanka'. *The New York Times*. Available at https://www.nytimes.com/2018/04/21/world/asia/facebook-sri-lanka-riots.html (accessed on 21 May 2018).
Willis, P. (1993) 'Symbolic Creativity', in A. Gray and J. McGuigan (eds), *Studying Culture: An Introductory Reader*, London: Edward Arnold.

8

CHANGING FASHIONS OF BHUTANESE YOUTH

Impacts on Cultural and Individual Identity

Paul Strickland

THE BHUTANESE NATIONAL ATTIRE

There has been very little available scholarship on Bhutanese style cultures and fashion even though Bhutan has a long history of textile production dating back four centuries (Adams 1984). Mythology dating back 2000 years (Kumar 2005; Little Bhutan 2014) is entrenched in Bhutanese historiography and is evident in its textile design as perceived through costumes depicting Buddhist mythological figures such as Garuda, the Snow-Lion, the Tiger, the Elephant and the Horse. This has become part of the attraction for international tourists (Pek-Dorji 2007). In this chapter, using a qualitative approach based on focus groups conducted with young people, I describe how Bhutanese youth relate to contemporary fashion and dress cultures.

Bhutan opened its borders to westerners in the 1970s, prior to which the kingdom limited the impact of other non-Bhutanese cultures for centuries (Singh 2010). As a response to this, a strict dress code was imposed in 1989, requiring all Bhutanese to wear the national dress of Bhutan; a *kira* for females and a *gho* for men at certain occasions, times of the day and in certain occupations (Ritchie 2008). Women wear the *kira*, a full-length dress, secured by a chain at the shoulder (*komo*) and a belt at the waist (kera). A blouse (wonju) is worn underneath the kira and a cropped jacket called a toego is worn over the top. The kira is usually made of bright coloured, fine woven fabric with traditional patterns (Strickland 2013). Men wear the gho, a long robe hoisted to the knee and held in place by a belt known as the 'kera' (Strickland 2013). The large pouch at the front is used as a carrying aid. Ceremonial kiras and ghos are hand woven in traditional patterns and are highly prized. In addition, scarves must be added by women as a mark of respect when entering Dzongs (fortresses) and monasteries (Ritchie 2008). There was a transition to a democratic constitutional monarchy in 2007, however traditional Bhutanese cultural codes were retained (Lo et al. 2016). This can be attributed to Driglam Namzha, the formal cultural code for Bhutan and its citizens outlining dress code and rules of etiquette (Kuensel 2015; Lo et al. 2016). Research suggests that Bhutanese people see their costume as an essence of their national identity and wear it with pride (Choden 2012). This, indeed, is reported by my respondents who find in national dress a sense of belonging. The encouragement of national dress in the making of national identities is also supported by a policy of supporting national songs and dance (Pek-Dorji 2007). However, like all regional, 'national', or ethnic dress cultures, in Bhutan this as Lo et al. demonstrate, 'it does not mean that these traditional garments have remained unchanged' (2016: 308). The introduction of television in 1994 followed closely by the proliferation of Internet and mobile technologies has seen a significant shift in attitudes towards clothing and fashion amongst Bhutanese youth. This increased exposure to global media influences and encourages favourable attitudes towards western fashion. One of the country's most popular blogs on Facebook and Instagram, the Bhutan Street Fashion Project (started in 2010) regularly showcases how contact with the outside world, combined with nostalgia for vintage looks, has created a hybrid street style. Begum and Dasgupta (2015), Kuldova (2013a) and Sandhu (2014) among others have highlighted that street style can be interpreted in a number of different ways and is not limited by dichotomous analysis such as East versus West or traditional versus modern in Asian countries. However, these street styles have also been met with some forms of resistance by some sections of the populace promoting traditional attire.

NON-BHUTANESE CLOTHING IN BHUTAN

The government has raised concerns that global cultural imperialism is threatening the national identity of Bhutanese nationals. Lo et al. (2016) argue that young people are discarding the traditional *gho* and *kira* and replacing them with western style jeans and T-shirts instead. Customs and protocols such as the *Driglam Namzha* are still referenced to combat these concerns of cultural imperialism. Another concern raised is with regard to affordability as Bhutanese traditional dress is expensive compared to western clothing (Strickland 2013). However ethnic minorities such as Chinese and Nepalese citizens maintaining Bhutanese roads are not expected to wear traditional Bhutanese clothing (see Figure 8.1).[1] This also applies to teachers, health workers, lawyers and aid-workers from foreign countries who are residing in Bhutan (Choden 2004). These workers have little impact on the homogeneity of traditional Bhutanese dress as foreign worker numbers are low (compared to the overall estimated population of Bhutan).

Figure 8.1   Foreign road workers in Bhutan, 2016. Image courtesy of Paul Strickland.

Since 2011, it was mandated that members of the national assembly, which includes about 30 per cent of the population, also wear the national dress during office hours (Tourism Council of Bhutan 2014). The adoption of national dress has received mixed response due to its impractical nature for some professions such as those working in agriculture (Aris 1994). There have been some forms of 'mix and match' for example; heavy western jackets worn for warmth in winter on top of traditional clothing such as the *kira* (see Figure 8.2).[2] These attitudes or depictions often appear in Bhutanese youth fashion blogs, where images are frequently posted of traditional dress worn with western fashion influences such as in *Bhutanese Youth and Fashion Magazine*.[3]

The resistance to national dress codes is indicative of the changes and influence of modernity in Bhutan. Karma Wangchuk, the founder of the Bhutanese Street Fashion Project, explains that Bhutanese youth take a balanced view of western fashion that is indicative of changing generational attitudes. Wangchuk explains that the leniency in dress codes has also helped Bhutanese youth realise the significance of traditional dress (Newbold 2016). Wangchuk, in an interview with the *Telegraph* explains that 'in a homogeneous world where we are all getting *McDonald-ised* by cheap, fast fashion; it's nice to stick to our roots and have an identity'. Wangchuk further notes that 'when our country is squashed between two giants, like India and China, it's so easy to lose our identity' (Newbold 2016). Wangchuk reinforces the view that modernisation, as a process, helps to maintain cultural difference; that cannot be reduced to unambiguous cultural homogenisation or equating it with western capitalism. The changing fashion in Bhutan by the youth is complicated and a contested process of disjuncture, creating both cultural similarities and difference that go beyond cultural imperialism and are capable of producing agency (Appadurai 1996). Royal weddings in Bhutan are a good example of this. The 2011 Royal wedding instigated an increase in local manufacturing of over fifty traditional clothing styles dating back to the nineteenth and twentieth centuries (Strickland 2013). Many Bhutanese nationals ordered traditional clothing from local companies to celebrate the wedding – as part of the celebration Bhutanese people

Figure 8.2 Western influence on youth fashion: dressed for going out at the weekend, 2016. Image courtesy of Paul Strickland.

lined the streets in their newly purchased traditional clothing as the royals walked past. According to Strickland (2013), it sensitised, inspired and inculcated a sense of pride, empathy and appreciation for Bhutanese textiles among the Bhutanese. It also highlighted emerging Bhutanese youth fashion trends that included a resurgence of national attire with an adoption of western and modern influence. This includes wearing American shoes and western underwear under the *gho* or a western jacket over the *kira*. The Duchess of Cambridge, Kate Middleton, on a visit to Bhutan in 2016 wore a traditional embroidered wool cape by French designer Paul & Joe with a *kira*-style skirt by an undisclosed designer but made from traditional local Bhutanese fabric that represented modern fashion blended with tradition (Spedding 2016). The global media attention to the Duchess's dress choice drew popular attention to the richness of traditional Bhutanese textiles, embedded within an emerging contemporary fashion context influenced by western fashion media.

MODERN AND WESTERN INFLUENCES ON ATTIRE

The first western influences in Bhutan date back to 1744 and before the appointment of the first king, the ruling spiritual leader signed a Treaty of Peace agreement with the British East India Company that effectively allowed trade with merchants of London. However, for the next century, boundary disputes, threats of foreign invasion and failed peace missions from Britain saw little real progress in trade including trade with textiles and fabrics. It was not until the instalment of the Wangchuck Dynasty in 1907 that these tensions began to cease and allowed Bhutan to be exposed to external influences and cultures including trade in textiles with Britain, India and China (Chakravarti 1979). A century later, the introduction of cheap western clothing and iconic American symbols such as Mickey Mouse and Levis Jeans manufactured from neighbouring countries (mainly India and Bangladesh) emerged and is currently available in local stores and clothing markets (Zelinsky 2004).

Since the mid 1970s, the impact of tourism has created a new industry aimed at foreign tourists shifting traditional occupations from agriculture to working in the tourism and hospitality sector mainly in the larger cities (Strickland 2012). This has also influenced the choice of clothing for these workers. Today, shops and clothing markets are able to supply items such as jeans, baseball caps and designer shoes although of a lesser quality. Since 1999, fashion items are now available to be purchased via the Internet (Giovannetti and Sigloch 2015). Tourists are also known to gift items of clothing to local Bhutanese youth when they leave the country. Even the King has succumbed to western style and is often fondly referred to by western media such as *Vanity Fair* as the 'Asian Elvis' because of his western hairstyle though he continues to dress in traditional attire (Harris 2011; France-Presse 2011). It should be noted that His Majesty continued his tertiary studies in America and England; that may also contribute to his international approach to fashion.

The government has tried hard to legislate that Bhutanese heritage and culture must be upheld. This includes legislation regarding religion, art, crafts, textiles, architecture, the natural environment and languages among others, but this has been difficult to monitor (Uddin et al. 2007). Unsurprisingly, Bhutan's youth have embraced the acceptance and

Figure 8.3 His Majesty Jigme Khesar Namgyel Wangchuck and Queen Jetsun Pema, 2011. Image Courtesy of *Yeewong* Magazine.

availability of foreign clothing, fabrics and jewellery and have inadvertently become more fashion focused (*Yeewong* 2014) which is similar to what is happening in other South Asian countries such as India (Kuldova 2013b). Decisions based on modesty are also considered especially by women, but generally limited to what is worn in public (Kuldova 2012).

CURRENT BHUTANESE YOUTH STATISTICS

It is very difficult to establish reliable statistics regarding the youth population of Bhutan for a variety of reasons. Firstly, prior to the 1960s, there was no actual data collected on the population. Secondly, Bhutan has many remote areas that are hard to access with many communities living in isolation and not frequenting larger towns and villages. Thirdly, education was poor and hard to access. Many people could not read or write and almost half the population still cannot (Index Mundi 2013). Statistics that the government provides suggest there is an even spread of men and women with the majority being between 25 and 54 years of age in Bhutan. As the life expectancy of Bhutanese nationals is currently 66, the number of people dramatically declines after this age. Therefore, for discussing youth in this chapter, the age range I have chosen is 15 to 24 years representing 27.8 per cent of the population, which equates to approximately 146,000 people (Tourism Council of Bhutan 2013).

In 1994, the average Bhutanese citizen earned US$330 annually, which is less than one dollar per day. A decade later, the average yearly income was US$1,160.70. In the last census (2012), the figure was US$2,449.15. In economic terms, this is a significant increase in individual income and wealth, which has had a profound effect on purchasing power. Spending money on fashionable clothes is one of those increasing trends as reported by the Bhutanese women's magazine *Yeewong* (2011). *Yeewong* is the only Bhutanese fashion magazine for women that states: 'This magazine is Bhutan's first and only women's magazine which celebrates every aspect of womanhood that makes us special and unique with a special focus on the women of Bhutan' (*Yeewong* 2014: 1). Additionally they say 'we celebrate the beauty and splendour of Bhutanese women in a whole new never-before-seen fashion' (*Yeewong* 2014: 2). Although the magazine is a women's magazine, images of Bhutanese men are often displayed in the three issues printed annually. Slogans used in the magazine include 'youth and sex', 'fill up your wardrobe with BURAY kiras this winter', 'they're stylish and affordable'. Some articles depict more traditional Bhutanese attire focusing on different colours and textile techniques whilst others highlight fashion from other cultures.

Textiles have always been a vital industry for Bhutan and more recently for tourism. For example, 67 per cent of international tourists named 'culture' as the number one reason for visiting Bhutan with 42.8 per cent of international tourists reporting they had visited textiles/weaving facilities (Tourism Council of Bhutan 2013). In the most recent royal wedding that was broadcast internationally, the world saw the image of a youthful King and Queen in traditional *gho* and *kira* attire. However, the media reported that some of the Queen's outfit was manufactured in New York and Hong Kong by well-established, internationally renowned designers (*Yeewong* 2011). The Queen is revered as an influential fashion icon amongst female youth in particular (Strickland 2013). The Queen Jetsun Pema was educated in a variety of schools in Bhutan and India then completed a degree in English and International Relations from the Regents College in London. This exposure to international culture and as a result fashions may assist in her choice of clothing that is capable of being internationally and locally reputed.

This 'mixing and matching' of modern and tradition can be further seen in women's beauty magazines and online fashion blogs. International magazines such as *Elle* and *Marie Claire* have undertaken fashion photo shoots in Bhutan and are increasingly using Bhutanese models.[4] This may have both positive and negative connotations; colourful native backgrounds are not always celebrated and this depends on the choice of models and their nationality or ethnic background (Cheang 2008). The *Bhutan Street Fashion Project* has also become a resource that communicates Bhutanese youth fashions through its Facebook and Instagram pages. This site describes itself as, 'the fashion on the street. We show you like it is, no pretensions, no wannabe Mother Teresa promises, no HIDDEN agenda, no moral policing. Everyday lifestyle and FASHION on the street' (Bhutan Street Fashion 2015). Volunteer photographers representing the project take photos of people that are on the streets of Bhutan, visually documenting what locals and visitors to Bhutan wear in public. Written comments include 'what a well-dressed street vendor', 'the beautiful ladies of Jaipur, elegant, traditional yet very urban' and 'spanish intern at a NGO in Jaipur, dressed for the place, comfort over style' accompany the photographs (Bhutan Street Fashion 2015). Webpages such as these suggest a changing attitude towards fashion but also celebrate traditional attire. As Misener (2011: 5) argues, 'interest in Bhutanese fashion is growing in a nation with a historically isolated culture'.

BHUTANESE YOUTHS' PERCEPTION OF FASHION

This study used focus groups representing Bhutanese youth to try to understand their perceptions of fashion. Representative comments from some groups included 'We are very proud of our heritage and culture',

'We have always worn the national clothing' and 'It is something that will always be with us'. It seemed apparent that collectively, the Bhutanese youth like their national dress. It 'makes us proud' said fifteen year old Sonam. Their statements also gave a sense of loyalty to their country. 'No other country has a dress code like ours', 'it makes everyone equal' and 'I know what to wear every day' were mentioned. After visiting Bhutan on many occasions, this positivity towards the Bhutanese culture and clothing became apparent among the many Bhutanese youth I interacted with.

When questioned about the monarchy and fashion, a surge of excitement seemed to take over all three focus groups. 'We love the royal family', 'The King and Queen look so good together' and 'The Queen is a fashion goddess' were three separate responses. The Queen in particular appears in many images that inspire younger women through the Internet and official portraits that are very popular amongst the youth. The admiration for the royal family by the Bhutanese youth is genuine. The succession of coronation, marriage and birth of their first child within a few years has cemented the affection of the people for the current royal family.

A discussion regarding the status of the royal family was initiated. The participants did not overtly communicate any concerns about the royal family or how high status Bhutanese officials have access to greater wealth and therefore are more likely to wear expensive clothing. It was presumed, as Dorji stated: 'They are respected and have high-level jobs. Of course they should be paid more and spend it on whatever they want.' A shy Penam commented 'There is a class system here and everyone knows their place. It is just how it is.' This emphasis on class demonstrates the complexity of social hierarchies often present within Asian cultures. Material wealth such as clothing often acts as symbolic means to communicating individual status. Except for highly regarded practising monks, for whom clothing can also symbolise wealth that is not material (Pye and Pye 2009). These perceptions of spirituality and of material status offered by the Bhutanese youth reinforce that hierarchies of class, occupation and status in Bhutan are complicated, non-binary and closely intertwined with spirituality, respect and collective thinking.

ASIAN INFLUENCES ON BHUTANESE FASHION

Participants were asked their thoughts regarding Asian fashion. The answers varied depending on the specific country. Some participants vocalised that Bhutan does not have a particular fashion sense. 'Most of our clothing manufactured here is traditional and not fashionable' remarked Norbu. Similarly, 'I wouldn't say Nepal has a fashion scene or India because of national dress, unless you have money', stated Sonam. China on the other hand received differing comments: 'China's clothes are amazing', 'We have to buy from somewhere cheap like China so that's why we follow their fashion', 'China's fashion sense is the best in Asia' and 'the Chinese in cities dress so much better that those in rural areas'. The fixation for Chinese fashion can be attributed to its relative newness and novelty factor in the marketplace, as clothing from India has been available in Bhutan for some time. Participants who placed importance on affordability of clothing said their actual level of choice was determined by the fact that purchasing Asian clothing is cheaper than purchasing western clothing in Bhutan (Gereffi 1999).

Practicality is also important for some Bhutanese youth. Asian countries that are perceived as too progressive or avant-garde were dismissed for being unpractical or for looking ridiculous. Hong Kong, Shanghai, Beijing and Japan were given as examples of fashionable locations that the participants did not aspire to wearing clothes from. Ruy articulated:

> Japan and large cities of China have a totally different fashion sense to other places. They take risks and sometimes look ridiculous. I don't think it's fashion when you look at what they are wearing and think, that looks terrible or I would never wear that or even worse, laugh. Those types of clothes don't last long, so I wouldn't wear them. To me, it's a fad, not fashion.

These comments were partly made in reference to Japan's Harajuku fashion (Slade 2009) and designer brands such as Daydream Nation (by Hong Kong designer Kay Jing Wong) and Rose Studio (by Beijing designer Guo Pei) (Peirson-Smith 2013) who are renowned for pushing the boundaries of fashion. However, not all responses echoed the same sentiments. The majority felt that Asian fashion is fun, exciting and trendy. Often Asian fashion is viewed as cutting edge and desirable; this supports Tsui's (2013) findings. Comments such as 'Asians know how to dress', 'We are Asian therefore the designs are for Asians, not westerners' and 'There is so much choice in new clothes from Asia that whatever you choose is fashionable' were said.

WESTERN INFLUENCES ON BHUTANESE FASHION

It appears that not knowing exactly where clothing was originally designed had a strong influence of what is considered western. For example, the majority of respondents stated that most of the jeans they purchased were manufactured in Asia and therefore considered Asian. Furthermore, Dorji mentioned 'Lots of people wear jeans and they are made everywhere. I don't think it is just trendy in western cultures anymore', highlighting the acceptance of jeans in Bhutan.

An interesting comment was made by Tshering: 'I see the images of foreigners [western females] in their clothes. If I don't have anything like it, I would say it is western. But it is most likely the colour of the skin [based on the image of a person] that I assume they are western and so are their clothes.' Identifying fashion through ethnicity, culture or skin colour is prevalent with all participants assuming that all Caucasians are westerners.

It can be said that Bhutanese youth mostly assume that western branded clothing is more expensive. Western clothes made by famous designers are perceived to be more resilient than locally manufactured clothes from Asia. Tashi stated that 'the clothes from India don't last long. This man [visiting tourist from Germany] gave me his sweatshirt and it has lasted for years'. He described the stitching was threaded closer with more cotton being used, indicating a greater quality and hence lasting longer. When asked if western clothing is more fashionable than Bhutanese clothing, the responses were overwhelmingly 'yes'. Pema articulated a common view by stating the following: 'Wearing our national dress is fairly restrictive. It must be a certain cut and worn a certain way. We really only have choice of colour and type of fabric.' Additionally, 'western clothes can be any cut, any style and any fashion. The choices available change all the time and you can wear almost any jewellery you want. You do not have to conform so it [western clothing] is definitely more fashionable'. Thinley's perspective was:

> I really like my *gho* and what our King is trying to achieve but it is not really fashionable. I see fashion as something that people look at and like, and then want to buy. Heaps of tourists visit Bhutan but very few actually buy our national dress. And if they did, would they wear in their own country? I can't see an American man wearing a *gho* in New York. So, it can't be fashionable if no-one but Bhutanese are going to wear it I think.

It is interesting to hear comments that Bhutanese national dress is not considered fashion if only Bhutanese wear the clothing. The female respondents appear to value national dress as fashionable if it has modern colours or is made by a well-known designer. The men's perceptions indicate that fashion is a current trend and not necessarily reflected by tradition. They tended to question the authenticity of fashion if only a certain ethnic group wear the clothing. These comments highlight some of the concerns and understanding of clothing and fashion cultures of Bhutanese youth.

FASHION IMPLICATIONS TO CONSIDER FOR BHUTANESE YOUTH

When discussing what the youth can actually wear, the Bhutanese people are in a situation that national dress must be worn at certain times, in certain areas and in specific occupations. The youth must wear national dress to school and also if they have a job working for the government, the monarchy, tourism enterprises, hospitality businesses, local shops, official monuments, festivals, *Dzongs* and other cultural sites among others. Monks are also restricted to red robes at all times in the monasteries and in public. This is to ensure the continuance of their textile, traditional and cultural heritage. This can be seen also in some countries like the United Arab Emirates and Turkey which strongly encourage traditional dress codes in schools and government, although this is not always compulsory (Schvaneveldt et al. 2005). Conversely, some countries often discourage 'non-citizens' from wearing certain clothing based mainly on religious grounds (Akou 2007).

These restrictions are not always practical. As Thinley states: 'I have on underwear because traditionally, nothing should be worn [under a *gho*]'. Penjor said whilst laughing, 'I wear a bra underneath and none of my mothers do' [includes grandmothers and aunts]. The choice of footwear has also been adapted to suit their current lifestyle. For example, more practical and comfortable shoes may be worn to and from school if long distances are required compared to traditional footwear. It was also noted that jackets and waterproof coats are acceptable in varying weather conditions which were previously not available. 'Winter gets so cold here and it can snow, so you need a jacket. My *gho* is too cold otherwise' a twenty-three year old male stated.

The word 'comfort' was also mentioned as a reason for choosing non-traditional clothing. Yebar says, 'I love feeling soft clothes'. Karma also says, 'Having comfortable clothes is important'. When asked: 'What are the most comfortable clothes?' and 'Where do they come from?' answers were specific: 'The most comfortable clothes are made from quality fabric' said Ugen who then proceeded to list America, France, Australia and Europe as places that produce quality fabric. 'I have really comfortable shoes from America' said Sonam. From these responses, it should be noted that all participants viewed western clothing as being of higher quality than Asian produced clothes. Elson (1994) commented that countries such as Japan produce some of the best quality textiles, but this is not representative of all Asian countries.

The male participants were conscious of 'looking good' but not as forthright as the female participants. 'I like being in comfortable clothes that are trendy but usually just wear the same stuff I have' remarked Tshewang, a male. Additionally, 'Guys don't share their clothes for fashion', said 20-year old Kinley. He continued 'We'd only wear each other's clothes if we were cold or something.' This differs for my female respondents who often swapped clothes on weekends, shown by statements such as 'We have dress-up parties where we go to a friend's house and try on all their clothes' and 'Girls share clothes all the time'.

The females justified sharing clothes between friends as 'something to do' and a way to wear different clothing without having to purchase new items. All participants showed a preference for western style clothing based on concerns of affordability, perceived quality, modesty and accessibility.

CONCLUSION

There are many considerations that need to be examined before an overall conclusion regarding Bhutanese youth and fashion can be drawn. As my respondents have demonstrated, sartorial identity is complicated and interconnected with power relations along the lines of national and colonial identity, regional and local identity, gender, as well as religious and social hierarchies. Bhutanese citizens are bound by the government's decision to enforce national dress. This restricts individual choice to dress in certain ways, but also attempts to inculcate pride in national attire. Currently, the Bhutanese textile industry is undergoing resurgence, especially with the most recent royal wedding, which reinforced the need for stability in heritage through national dress. The Queen was able to showcase the Bhutanese national dress to the world in a way that made a strong contemporary fashion statement. The Queen was viewed as a very modern monarch and extremely fashionable through the wearing of traditional clothes with a modern twist.

Alongside this resurgence of fashionable traditional textiles, the majority of the youth of Bhutan view westernised clothing as more fashionable than Asian clothing. The influence of western fashion in Bhutan is shaped by the imagery of cinema, television, Internet, visiting tourists and the wider dominance of western fashion. Although leading fashion blogs promote the mixing and matching of eastern and western styles, this interplay is a lot more complex and cannot be taken at surface value. Bhutanese youth showed favourability to western clothing over Asian clothing, demonstrating similar views by youth in other Asian countries such as India and Japan (Niessen et al. 2003; Sandhu 2014).

Additionally Buddhist values of sharing are very much instilled into the Bhutanese young people. Therefore it is not uncommon for friends to share and borrow clothing to overcome issues of affordability. The gap in what fashion Bhutanese youth have access to and what they desire, demonstrates the potential growth opportunity for youth fashion in Bhutan. With greater access and exposure to fashion media, technology and international tourists, Bhutanese youth are constantly engaging with various forms and influences of fashion. For young Bhutanese women, fashion is also perceived to be a legitimate reason to 'hang out' with friends outside of the domestic environment. This is similar to the argument made by Sneha Krishnan in this volume about style cultures of young women in South India.

The challenge for the Bhutanese youth as this study suggests is to strive for a balance between retaining a sense of pride for the national attire and the influence of western and other Asian style clothing. Scope exists for Bhutanese fashion designers to create strong designs for the youth that could be used to market the Bhutanese fashion sector on the world stage, thus allowing another side of Bhutan's creative industry to emerge.

NOTES

1. The mother is wearing a thick, wool, white headscarf with a yellow silk blouse and a check-patterned cotton dress secured with a traditional silver chain fastening across the shoulders and a fabric belt at the waist that covers cotton trousers and sturdy shoes made of leather. The father is wearing a branded grey knitted beanie hat, white cotton T-shirt, traditional patterned cotton overalls attached with orange straps and a western-style zipped jacket. Below the waist he has jeans and leather boots. The young boy in front is wearing a collared tennis T-shirt with a Buddhist prayer thread around his neck, which he wears with a western-style sportswear jacket, jeans and open sandals, resembling the clothes of the other young persons in the background.
2. On the left, the mother is wearing denim jeans and a light green western style knitted top over white undergarments. Her daughter is wearing western-style brown cotton T-shirt and a denim jacket with a fake-fur lining over a traditional *kira* dress with no shoes. The backdrop is a typical youth bedroom with a traditional Buddhist-inspired wall hanging, and bedding-styles in bright red, yellow and blue colours.
3. See https://www.facebook.com/bhutanyouth 2017; also see Chari 2014. Accessed 20th April 2018.
4. See https://www.marieclaire.com/fashion/advice/g209/fashionbhutan. Accessed 20th April 2018.

REFERENCES

Adams, B. (1984) *Traditional Bhutanese Textiles*, Bangkok: White Orchard Press.
Akou, H.M. (2007) 'Building a New "World Fashion": Islamic Dress in the Twenty-first Century', *Fashion Theory* 11(4): 403–421. DOI: 10.2752/175174107X250226.
Appadurai, A. (1996) *Modernity at Large: Cultural Dimensions of Globalization*, Minneapolis: University of Minnesota Press.
Aris, M. (1994) 'Textiles, Text and Content, The Cloth and Clothing of Bhutan in Historical Perspective', in D. Myers, and S. Bean, (eds), *The Land of the Thunder Dragon*, London: Serindia Publications, pp. 27–32.
Begum, L. and Dasgupta, R.K. (2015) 'Contemporary South Asian Youth Cultures and the Fashion Landscape', *International Journal of Fashion Studies* 2(1): 31–145, DOI: 10.1386/infs.2.1.131_7.
Bhutan Street Fashion (2015) *Bhutan Street Fashion Facebook Page*. Available at https://www.facebook.com/#!/BhutanStreetFashion/info (accessed on 9 April 2016).
Chakravarti, B. (1979) *Cultural History of Bhutan*, Vol. 1. Calcutta: Hilltop Publishers.
Chari, M. (2014) 'Bhutanese Street Fashion is Changing', 22 August 2014, *Bhutanese News Network*. Available at http://www.bhutannewsnetwork.com/2014/08/bhutanese-street-fashion-is-changing/ (accessed 2 March 2017).
Cheang, S. (2008) *Hair: Styling, Culture and Fashion*, Oxford: Berg.
Choden, K. (2012) 'Colours', *Colours Magazine*. Available at http://www.colorsmagazine.com/blog/article/dress-code (accessed on 15 February 2016).
Choden, T. (2004) 'Indo-Bhutan Relations Recent Trends', in K. Visweswaran (ed.), *Perspectives on Modern South Asia: A Reader in Culture, History, and Representation*, London: Wiley-Blackwell, pp. 298–302.
France-Presse (2011) 'Bhutan Counts down to a Royal Wedding', 11 October 2011.
Gereffi, G. (1999) 'International Trade and Industrial Upgrading in the Apparel Commodity Chain', *Journal of International Economics* 48(1): 37–70.
Giovannetti, E. and Sigloch, S. (2015) 'An Internet Periphery Study: Network Centrality and Clustering for Mobile Access in Bhutan', *Telecommunications Policy* 39(7): 608–622.
Harris, D. (2011) 'Bhutan Royal Wedding: A Commoner Becomes a Queen', Australian Broadcasting Commission, 13 October 2011. Available at http://abcnews.go.com/international/bhutan-royal-wedding-commoner-queen/story?id=14727724 (accessed on 3 April 2012).
Hellomagazine.com (2016) 'Bhutan's Baby Prince Looks Adorable in New Official Portrait', Hellomagazine.com, 31 May 2016. Available at http://www.hellomagazine.com/royalty/2016053131693/bhutanese-royals-official-portrait-baby-prince/ (accessed on 3 March 2017).
Index Mundi (2013) *Bhutan Demographics Profile* 2013. Available at http://www.indexmundi.com/bhutan/demographics_profile.html (accessed on 4 June 2014).
Kuensel Online (2015) 'Driglam Namzha: Bhutan's Code of Etiquette', 16 August 2015. Available at http://www.kuenselonline.com/driglam-namzha-bhutans-code-of-etiquette/ (accessed on 23 February 2016).
Kuldova, T. (2012) 'Fashionable Erotic Masquerades: Of Brides, Gods and Vamps in India', *Critical Studies in Fashion & Beauty* 3(1–2): 69–86.
——— (2013a) *Designing Elites: Fashion and Prestige in Urban North India*. Thesis submitted for the degree of PhD at anthropology department, University of Oslo, 2013.

―――― (2013b) '"The Maharaja Style": Royal Chic, Heritage Luxury and the Nomadic Elites', in T. Kuldova (ed.), *Fashion India: Spectacular Capitalism*, Olso: Akademika Publishing.

Kumar, R. (2005) *Costumes and Textiles of Royal India*, Antique Collectors Club Ltd.

Little Bhutan (2014) *The National Textile Museum*. Available at http://www.littlebhutan.com/attractions/the-national-textile-museum.html (accessed on 19 May 2014).

Lo, J., Macintyre, L. and Kalkreuter, B. (2016) 'Investigating Markers of Authenticity: The Weavers' Perspective: Insights from a Study on Bhutanese Hand-woven Kira Textiles', *Textile, Cloth and Cultures*, May 2016.

Misener, J. (2011) 'Jetsun Pema, Queen of Bhutan: A Newlywed Style Icon', *The Huffington Post*, 27 October 2011. Available at http://lharikhamba.blogspot.com.au/2011/10/bhutan-street-fashion-in-huffington.html (accessed on 7 May 2014).

Newbold, A. (2016) 'Bhutan Fashion: The Unique Street Style Scene in a Country with a National Dress Code', *Telegraph UK Online*. Available at http://www.telegraph.co.uk/fashion/style/bhutan-fashion-surveying-the-unusual-street-style-scene-in-a-cou/ (accessed on 2 March 2017).

Niessen, S.A., Leshkowich, A.M. and Jones, C. (eds) (2003) *Re-Orienting Fashion: The Globalization of Asian Dress*, Oxford, New York: Berg.

Peirson-Smith, A. (2013) 'Wishing on a Star: Promoting and Personifying Designer Collections and Fashion Brands', *Fashion Practice* 5(2): 171–201.

Pek-Dorji, S.S. (2007) *The Legacy of a King. The Fourth Druk Gyalpo Jogme Singye Wangchuck*, Thimpu, Bhutan: Department of Tourism, Royal Government of Bhutan.

Pye, M.W. and Pye, L.W. (2009) *Asian Power and Politics: The Cultural Dimensions of Authority*, New York: Harvard University Press.

Ritchie, M. (2008) 'Tourism in the Kingdom of Bhutan: A Unique Approach', in J. Cochrane (ed.), *Asian Tourism, Growth and Change*, Oxford: Elsevier.

Sandhu, A. (2014) *Indian Fashion: Tradition, Innovation, Style*, London; New York: Bloomsbury Academic.

Schvaneveldt, P., Kerpelman, J. and Schvaneveldt, J. (2005) 'Generational and Cultural Changes in Family Life in the United Arab Emirates: A Comparison of Mothers and Daughters', *Journal of Comparative Family Studies* 36(1): 77–91. Available at http://www.jstor.org/stable/41603981 (accessed on 1 March 2017).

Singh, D. (2010) 'Bhutan: Monarchy and Simulated Democracy in the Amphitheatre of Hills', in J. Benjamin (ed.), *Democratic Process, Foreign Policy and Human Rights in South Asia*, Gyan Publishing, pp. 109–119.

Slade, T. (2009) *Japanese Fashion: A Cultural History*, Oxford: Berg Publishers.

Spedding, E. (2016) 'Five People, 3 Months, £1,000: Behind the Workmanship that Went into the Duchess of Cambridge's Bhutanese skirt', *Telegraph UK Online*. Available at http://www.telegraph.co.uk/fashion/people/the-duchess-of-cambridge-wears-bhutans-national-dress/ (accessed on 1 June 2016).

Strickland, P. (2012) 'The Benefits of National Dress and Fashion Trends of a Royal Bhutanese Wedding', in K.M. Williams, J. Laing and W. Frost (eds), *Fashion, Design and Events*, London and New York: Routledge.

―――― (2013) 'National Dress and Fashion Trends of a Royal Bhutanese Wedding', in K.M. Williams, J. Laing and W. Frost, *Fashion, Design and Events*, Oxon, UK: Routledge, pp. 57–68.

Tourism Council of Bhutan (2011) *Bhutan Tourism Monitor: Annual Report*. Thimpu.

―――― (2013) *Bhutan Tourism Monitor: Annual Report*. Thimpu.

——— (2014) 'Thag Zo'. Available at http://www.tourism.gov.bt/about-bhutan/Thag-zo (accessed on 10 April 2014).
Tsui, C. (2013) 'From Symbols to Spirit: Changing Conceptions of National Identity in Chinese Fashion', *Fashion Theory* 17(5): 579–604.
Uddin, S.N., Taplin, R. and Yu, X. (2007) 'Energy, Environment and Development in Bhutan', *Renewable and Sustainable Energy Reviews* 11(9): 2083–2103.
Yeewong (2011) *Bringing Her Forward*. December 2011, Thimpu: Yeewong Design and Publishing Company.
——— (2014) Yeewong Facebook Page. Available at https://www.facebook.com/#!/pages/Yeewong/287096243266 (accessed 14 April 2014).
Zelinsky, W. (2004) 'Globalization Reconsidered: The Historical Geography of Modern Western Male Attire', *Journal of Cultural Geography* 22(1): 83–134.

9
MATCHING CLOTHES AND MATCHING COUPLES

The Role of Dress in Arranged Marriages in Kathmandu

Sarah Shepherd-Manandhar

Young women in Kathmandu, Nepal, find themselves on the cusp of several important life transitions. For many, their families are beginning to consider marriage proposals, signifying potential changes in young women's homes, family structure, mobility, independence and class status. In this context, clothing and adornment become important means by which young women can attempt to dictate and control their own futures.

Clothing tells us many things. It can tell us an individual's gender (Shukla 2008; Hopkins 2007; Lynch 1999), class (O'Dougherty 2002; Tarlo 1996), aspirations (Liechty 2003; Freeman 2000), professional associations (Costello 2004) and political leanings (Tarlo 1996; Cohn 1989). It can provide nuanced, material evidence of inter-personal relationships and even serve as a measure of day-to-day mood changes (Hansen 2004; Schneider & Weiner 1986; Schneider 1987). Clothing creates embodied identities, even as it inhibits and restricts us (Comaroff & Comaroff 1992; Keane 2005). Further, dress is used by youth to signal shifting membership in a range of subcultures, in addition to its use, as described here, as a site for intergenerational negotiation (Perullo 2012; Sweet 2010). Clothing does all of these things through its pliable nature.

Here, I discuss how dress is used as a means for power negotiations across generations in the context of family arranged marriages in Kathmandu, Nepal. I show how young women deploy locally defined 'modern' and 'traditional' garments (both terms in English) to gain access to their desired futures through arranged marriages. The information they convey through dress becomes crucial in forming familial alliances and making major life decisions. In this process, dress performance effectively determines and restricts young women's life chances. This chapter looks at the ways in which emerging fashion trends alongside traditional forms of dress and adornment are mobilised by young women, both to evaluate potential marriage partners and to make active claims to particular types of futures. I will explore the connections between the discourses of modernity and tradition, the use of clothing to signify acceptance or rejection of these discourses and the effects both discourses and dressing practices have on young women's 'possible lives', in Appadurai's sense (Appadurai 1996: 53).

This chapter is drawn from ethnographic fieldwork conducted from September 2008 to November 2010 in Kathmandu, with follow-up fieldwork conducted in the summers of 2011 and 2013. In addition, I conducted a series of interviews with ten young middle-class 19–25-year-old Nepali women. The participants were all unmarried at the time of our first interviews, but were in the process of having marriages arranged for them. By the time of my final field visit in 2013, all but two of the women had married. My informants all considered themselves to be middle-class. Finally, the young women's marriage outcomes spanned the full range of possibilities in Kathmandu; with one young woman living abroad with her new husband, one young woman having a love marriage, and two young women (including the young woman living abroad) living in small, nuclear family arrangements.

DRESS IN KATHMANDU

Following Nepal's entry into global markets in the late 1950s, clothing from all over the world has accompanied a wide range of consumer goods into Nepali markets and homes (Liechty 2003; Rankin 2004; Whelpton 2005). These goods, ranging from Japanese *saris* to German Shepherd puppies, have brought new moral economies and an increased emphasis on the importance of class. The middle class has grown significantly since this period as a result of increased labour migrations and a growing remittance economy (Seddon et al. 2002; Thieme & Wyss 2005). Dressing practices have also changed throughout this period, as styles originating all over the world have become increasingly common. For example, Hindman and Oppenheim (2014) have documented the increasing popularity of Korean fashions among Kathmandu youth. In their interviews, Nepalis explained that they find the 'Mongol look', a reference to Korean fashion trends, more suitable for Nepalis.

Though there has always been fashion in Nepal, Liechty documents the introduction of the word 'fashion' (in English) into Nepali middle-class discourse in the late 1990s with the emergence of a new aesthetic and consumptive regime (Liechty 2003). Within this regime, dress became a key signifier of class belonging and the associated moral economy of each class. Liechty found that many women enjoyed 'doing fashion' but at the same time experienced the expectation to be fashionable as an intense social pressure. For these women, 'fashion' was as much of a responsibility as it was an avenue of personal expression and they tied their performances of fashionability to familial notions of *ijat* (honour) (Liechty 2003). The literature regarding aesthetic and emotional labour, particularly in Entwistle's (2002; Entwistle and Wissinger 2006) work, has shown that both providing care and keeping up appearance, tasks often demanded of young women in Kathmandu by their families, entail a type of labour and represent an additional stress for many women. The labour involved in maintaining appearances and preserving family honour adds to the burdens that women face in their homes and posits fashion as an ambivalent social practice.

Finally, Bourdieu's notion of 'distinction' is useful here (Bourdieu 1998). Bourdieu's understanding of the way in which class marking behaviours shape, and are shaped by, the broader social milieu of the habitus is important for thinking through how young women understand and mobilise dress in daily life. Bourdieu refers to these specific behaviours as 'dispositions'; tendencies, preferences, and habits which appear to be individual idiosyncrasies, but which are generally reflective of each individual's complex social environment. These dispositions are not entirely socially determined, but they do reflect, with remarkable accuracy, an individual's upbringing, class belonging, education, gender, home location, and much more. Of the many dispositions that exist and could be considered, this paper focuses largely on dispositions that are communicative of class belonging, as they are most relevant to the Nepali dressing practices I observed.

In his analysis, Bourdieu's primary concern is with marking 'relational' categories such as class, education, or honour, but what is lost in this analysis is the communicative aspect of an individual's 'position taking' (Bourdieu 1998: 6). 'Position taking' in Bourdieu's sense, refers to actions individuals engage in to signal, claim, or substantiate their relative position within society. In the research described here, 'position taking' can be seen in the way that young people and their families actively seek to communicate (and effectively, create) their class belonging. When an individual or a family has successfully 'taken' a class position, they are then able to assert that their favoured marriage arrangement is socially acceptable, and the other family signals their acceptance of this fact by pursuing the match further. This kind of 'position taking' is well explored in literature that is concerned with performances, and Goffman's foundational work on the topic begins with this discussion (Goffman 1959). In this work, Goffman describes how many human characteristics are not only made evident by behaviour which displays or 'performs' particular ways of being, but that these characteristics are, in fact, brought into being by these actions. His work shows that behaving 'as if' one had a particular characteristic or trait transforms us in to being that way. Today, thanks to the insight of Judith Butler, the most well-known example of the power of performance to bring ways of being to life is Butler's discussion about how gender is not a biological fact, but a result of continuous gender performances that reflect, and recreate, the societal expectations of men, women, and increasingly, multiple other gender roles as well (Butler 1990a; Butler 1990b).

Performance literature has its own blind spot in that aspiration is noted, but rarely functionally described. Yet, understanding how aspiration results in attempts, both failed and successful, to use performance to realise one's aspirations is crucial to understanding how individuals behave when they find themselves in liminal positions, like the vital conjunctures, described by Johnson-Hanks (2002). Johnson-Hanks explains that there are points in each person's life that require a drastic re-envisioning of the self; moments where we come of age or are understood in a new way according to societally determined 'coming of age' events. This includes traditional rites of passage like the marriages in negotiation in my study. For young women in Kathmandu, marriage is a vital conjuncture, because it requires that young women use performative behaviours to make strong claims about who they are, who they hope to be, and who their future spouses and in-laws hope to shape them to be. Investigating this vital conjuncture elucidates the way that young women use dress to communicate their suitability for marriage into an upper-class family, and through successful claims, to effect significant material changes in their lives. The observations of Nepali dressing practices discussed here show how all three aspects – distinction in Bourdieu's sense, performativity, and aspiration – function to create class mobility for some young women. Through their choices of what to wear, young women, and to some extent young men, communicate with each other about the kind of future they hope to have and are thus able to make decisions that enable those hopes. Further, families are also able to use the specific dispositions of young women, as evidenced by their clothing choices, to make decisions about potential daughter-in-laws and the ability of these young women to behave in a way that re-enforces class divides, performs appropriate gender expectations, and, with the expected birth of children, quite literally reproduces the current class hierarchy.

Kathmandu's visual and moral landscape therefore, presents women with a wide variety of styles and moral demands. Shops that specialise in French *saris* neighbour ready-made garment shops selling T-shirts and jeans based on designs popular in Korea, the USA and India. Yet, the free mixing of garments in the marketplace is not mirrored in the fashions worn by many shoppers. Despite a general easing of the expectation that married women wear *saris* at all times, clothing remains a clear index to one's age, class, and position within one's family. The oldest generation of women continue to wear *saris* at all times. Younger, married women, often with children and more household responsibilities, reserve *saris* for parties, choosing to wear *kurta surawel* when out of the home. Young girls, attending primary school and below and when not in their school uniform are often seen in imported dresses with full skirts and an abundance of bows. Among these various styles, *saris* and *kurta surawel* are considered to be traditional garments, whereas T-shirts, jeans, skirts and blouses are described as modern garments. Yet despite the attribution of tradition and modernity to different types of dress, social expectations for young girls and older women allow few opportunities to choose between the two types of clothing. It is only in the short period between childhood and marriage, in a state of liminality, where young women can choose between modern and traditional dress.

Compared to other women, young unmarried women are given the most leniency, being free to choose between *saris*, *kurta surawel*, T-shirts, jeans, and skirts as it suits them. Leniency is given because these young women are still '*puchiharu*' (cute, little girls). As one informant put it, 'They are just children! No one cares if they look good', the implication being that young unmarried women are still below the age of serious censure. Her family members may be involved by providing shopping money, giving gifts or through comments they make about the acceptability (or lack thereof) of her dress, but by and large a young woman makes these decisions for herself. As many of the streets of Kathmandu have become home to a wide variety of garments shops, socialising with friends and the commute to and from school provide young women with ample time for shopping.

Parents are of course, concerned that their daughters should be modest and well behaved, but there is also a general sense that young women should be given as much freedom as possible in these last few years before their marriage. The understanding is that because they will sacrifice so much after marriage, unmarried women should be allowed to dress as they choose. This is not to say of course that dressing practices in Kathmandu are not guided by strict notions of appropriate dress, but rather that these norms are enforced by the community at large, even at the level of what is made available in stores.

There are additional external factors that are considered by young women when choosing what to wear. Attention to the ways in which particular types of dress restrict or enable movement plays an important role in young women's choices about what to wear. Motorcycles and scooters are another signifier of middle-class belonging and even young women without one will spend considerable time on the vehicles of their friends. The ease of travel provided by jeans and *kurta surawel*, make one of the two of these garments the primary choice of middle-class young women. Finally, all garments are not available at the same cost. Party *saris* are the most expensive garment that most young women will own, followed by jeans and finally by *kurta surawel* sets. For young women on the cusp of middle-class-ness who need to be cost conscious, *kurta surawel* are the most immediately affordable garment, though, as we will see, this choice entails hidden costs elsewhere.

DRESS AND GENDER ROLES IN KATHMANDU

In Nepal, as elsewhere, the increasing pace of globalisation and its assimilation of formerly isolated markets has produced conditions in which traditional gender roles are confronted by an influx of new modern conceptions of the self (Appadurai 1996; Breckenridge 1995; Crawford et al. 2008; Heiman et al. 2012; Liechty 2003; Rankin 2004). The newly imagined 'possible lives' available in Kathmandu are predicated on an influx of consumer goods which present new class dynamics and aspirations (Heiman et al. 2012; Schielke 2012) and the 'developmental goals' centred around the 'rights of women' that are voiced most forcefully by NGOs involved in Nepali political and civil life (Ahearn 2001; Colekessian 2009; Crawford et al. 2008; Shtrii Shakti 2010; Yami 2010). For young women in the liminal state between childhood and marriage, most of their attention is focused on imagining and pursuing the possible lives available to them via different marriage outcomes.

In current discourse, the terms modern and traditional signify a way of being and a set of normative gender expectations. To be clear, here I refer to the use of these English loan words by Nepali families in Kathmandu and not to the meaning that these terms hold for scholars. Traditional young women are expected to be self-sacrificing, hard-working and highly skilled in domestic tasks, whereas modern young women are thought to be more independent and more focused on personal fulfilment. These contrasting roles are both appealing and problematic as young Nepali women recognise both the opportunities inherent in and the difficulties of each role. Additionally, the discourses around each of these roles provide a template for how women should behave within their new families after marriage, as well as what treatment they should expect in return.

Within these discourses, the new economy of fashion has led to new sartorial knowledge practices. Prior to the recent flood of foreign clothing, clothing options reflected women's status within their family (married, unmarried, widowed) but were not believed to communicate about personality or preferences. Though dress has always been used as a marker of expendable income, the recent expansion of global markets means it is also considered a reliable witness to the character of the individual wearer (Liechty 2003). In the context of marriage arrangements, where it is vital to know who someone is, dress becomes a key piece of information. In this context, young women actively use fashions to support their claims to be modern or traditional and thus to entitlement to the lifestyles those positions entail.

The contrasting gender roles of modern and traditional are not only presented to young women as a choice they must express through their clothing, they also represent the choice that families looking for brides are considering. Because of the continued prevalence of joint family arrangements and arranged marriages, for most young women marriage is a rupture from their previous lives after which they embark on a new one within a new kin network. Marriage is not only a time of shifting from one family to another, but a particularly salient moment for self-making as the bride must define herself and her position within her husband's home and family. This makes marriage an opportune moment for giving shape to and expressing a host of aspirations and life goals.

LIFE BEFORE MARRIAGE

In their natal homes, most young women are accustomed to sharing in daily domestic labour, but the majority of such work falls upon their mothers and their sister-in-laws. In Kathmandu, where school attendance is relatively high for Nepal, even through college (Shtrii Shakti 2010), young women are also accustomed to spending time away from home, at classes or with friends. Their parents expect to know where their daughters are, who they are with and that they will be home before dark, but beyond these restrictions they are trusted to behave appropriately without additional supervision. Because Kathmandu has only a few major centralised shopping areas, combined with the expansive extent of Nepali kinship networks, it is highly likely that a young woman out in public would be seen by adults who could report back on her behaviour to her parents. Therefore, while parental supervision may be relatively thin outside of the home, young women are still mindful of the gaze of others and the potential consequences of unseemly behaviour.

While young women are out enjoying themselves, relatives of both families will be observing the young people around them with an eye to potential marriage arrangements. Before the subject of marriage has been broached with the parents of either the bride or the groom, other relatives may begin a series of inquiries and friendly visits to try to evaluate whether the couple could be a good match. These visits may at first be indistinguishable from any other social visit except to the match-making relative and it may be some time before more relatives and eventually the bride and groom themselves are made aware of what is already at work. In order to spare the feelings of their children and the families, early informal arranging is never acknowledged, so that a rejection of the match by either the bride or the groom causes as little damage to feelings and *ijat* (honour) as possible. Therefore, the bulk of the process of arranging a marriage is only separated from normal day-to-day social life in the past tense, after the marriage has been agreed formally. In this sense, young women between their late teens and early twenties are never really off the marriage market until their marriage has been formally arranged, and their dress and behaviour at all times is subject to scrutiny and evaluation. As mentioned above, young women are well aware of this fact, and it is in this context that their dress choices become so powerful.

ARRANGING MARRIAGES: TRANSACTIONS OF *IJAT*

Another layer of importance is added to this process when one considers the Nepali concept of *ijat*. The *ijat* economy described extensively by

Liechty (2003) and more recently commented on by Rankin (2004) serves as the defining structure within the arrangements of marriages. In the case of arranged marriages this concept takes on new dimensions as family honour and the future happiness of one's children become inextricably linked. Arranging a marriage is not simply about maintaining or enhancing the family honour but about leveraging *ijat* to secure the most desirable future life possible for one's children. It is key to recall that material wealth including dress and the class belonging it entails are made visible to other less well-known families in order to ensure that one's child continues to live within the same class, and continues to enjoy the material benefits of that class belonging (Kondos 1991). The family's *ijat* is therefore a primary resource that young women can draw on through their dress to further their own marriage goals. By dressing in a modern or traditional way and by wearing clothes that signal class belonging (through visible branding or higher quality fabrics), young women strategically present their natal family's *ijat* to potential matchmakers.

FROM NEIGHBOURLY VISITS TO WEDDING PREPARATIONS

Miller's description of the marriage arrangement process remains essentially accurate, despite a significant decrease in the use of *lami* (professional matchmakers) since her fieldwork (Miller 1992). The process of arranging a marriage rarely has a definitive starting point and usually begins with a few casual observances by family members that the young woman is old enough to be married. On the part of young women, these observations may not be acted upon at all until a young man's family has initiated marriage arrangements, though in some cases, either the young woman's own interest in marriage, or the marriage of a sibling may initiate more of an active search for a groom. In the marriages of my informants, however, there was only one case in which the young woman's side could really be said to have initiated the arrangements and this was in response to the initiation of serious marriage arrangements for her younger sister. In Nepal, the initiation of arranged marriages by the bride or groom remain rare, though love marriages and arranged love marriages are often the result of initiation on the part of the children but according to Netting (2010) and Sharangpani (2010) this seems to occur more often in India.

The importance of a young woman's choice in how to dress is often compounded by the fact that family may not be forthcoming about the reason for certain social visits. Miller (1992) discusses the need for this lack of transparency in match making as an important part of saving face. In some instances, the groom's family may choose to surprise the bride, showing up unannounced. The earliest visits are usually by extended kin who visit on other pretexts so that neither the bride nor her family can prepare. Finally, though private picture exchanges are increasingly less common, photos from a whole range of social events and social media may be used as information for both families.

As an example, in one potential match, the daily dressing practices of the groom, as portrayed by his Facebook page definitively foreclosed a possible marriage. One of my informants had been introduced to a man that her parents were eager to conclude a marriage with. After the meeting, the young woman was adamantly opposed to the match, but her parents were persistent. Within a few days, the young woman had reached out to other relatives for support. For her relatives, however, this produced a difficult situation. They wanted to support the young woman in her choice, but it was difficult without having met the man to marshal arguments against his suitability. Without any other means of evaluating the potential match, one of her relatives turned to Facebook. After a few minutes of scrolling through smiling photos of a young man surrounded by friends, the relative exclaimed, 'He doesn't ever wear jeans!' With that observation, the relative considered the matter settled, agreeing entirely with the young woman that this suitor was clearly too old fashioned and thus not a good match. This example highlights the fact that a young woman's day-to-day dressing practices, despite appearing to have little to do with the marriage arrangement process are instead the primary means by which young women make their desires and aspirations known to the families of potential grooms and martial evidence of their own modernity.

As Miller (1992) also noted, arranged marriages are a considerable risk for both families involved. Family members must balance a host of factors: their children's attraction to a potential spouse, how their child will fit in with a new family, the level of consumption their child is accustomed to, the amount of work a young bride will be expected to do in the married home and family honour, all in a single match. Families who are experiencing economic or labour insecurities tend to favour 'traditional' young women, who are believed to be self-sacrificing and willing to contribute domestic labour or unpaid labour in a family business. Yet these economic incentives come with the cost of an additional mouth to feed, an expensive wedding, and a small loss in a family's *ijat*, as their economic instability is made visible through their choice of a traditional bride. Alternatively, families who feel that their economic situation and their social standing are stable or improving tend to favour 'modern' young women, as such young women will increase the famly's *ijat* by allowing for a display of wealth at the wedding and increasing the household's consumption of goods and domestic services. A family's perception of their own social position, their beliefs about what will best ensure their son's happiness and their own preferences for gender roles all jointly determine whether a family will be looking for a modern or traditional daughter-in-law. Yet, knowing the qualities of a potential bride in the intense uncertainty that surrounds arranged marriages makes it difficult to know how a young woman will behave in her married home. It is here that dress begins to take on new importance.

DRESSING FOR THE FUTURE: WHAT IS AT STAKE IN WHAT TO WEAR

After marriage there is growing pressure on young women to embody the positive aspects of both modern and traditional gender roles, however families in search of a bride tend to conceive of their search as being for one type of young woman or the other. Each role is believed to offer both positive and negative characteristic traits to a woman's married family. But regardless of whether a family desires a modern or traditional bride, they must try to find a daughter-in-law who is willing to fulfil the role assigned to her, and it is in this respect that dress comes to play such a crucial role in marriage arrangements. Through their choice of dress, young women signal their desire or willingness to be construed in one way or the other and make claims to certain lifestyles after marriage.

For young women in Kathmandu, modernity often translates into the freedom (or expectation) to work outside the home after marriage, higher levels of consumption, immigration opportunities, and more flexibility about living within or apart from larger joint families. At the same time, the appearance of being too 'modern' can be construed as immodesty or selfishness in comparison to traditional young women (Liechty 2003). The perception of having these negative personality traits can cause strained relationships within joint families (Ahearn 2001; McHugh 2001). Additionally, young women who eschew appearing to be too traditional often sacrifice the support provided by living within larger joint families and experience more pressure to do the aesthetic labour of keeping up appearances outside of the home. The process of arranging a marriage, then, becomes a careful balancing act on the part of women's self-presentation.

Because marriage also serves to integrate the young women into a new family, another stake in the marriage arrangements is whether she will join her husband's joint family or live separately with her husband. It is often stated that modern young women will be better suited to surviving the isolation and struggles of living outside of Nepal and so embracing modernity can also be a path to migration as an accompanying spouse. For some young women, the idea of living with only their husband is enticing because it can mean greater freedom and less domestic labour to attend to. For other women, living outside of a joint family seems isolating and difficult, particularly if the young woman hopes to have children in the near future. For example, when another of my informants had finally decided to marry a young man that she was originally very unsure of, she explained, 'I have been friends with his sisters for a long time. It will be easy to live with them.' For her, the groom's family was one of his main attractive qualities and the comfort of living with women she already knew overshadowed any doubts she had about the groom himself. In other cases, the reputation of a family member can be an impediment to marriage, for example, if a woman has a reputation as being particularly harsh, it may be difficult to find a bride for her son.

Young women are acutely aware that they are being scrutinised as potential young brides at this stage in their lives, a point further brought home as more of their school friends and young relatives marry. Therefore, they are well aware of the importance of what they choose to wear at this particular time. For example, in response to family pressure to marry, one informant, Ritu, was engaged in a complicated exchange of seeing and being seen by prospective grooms. When I asked how the meetings were going, she replied, 'There was one boy I liked, but his mother and sisters were all wearing *saris* at home. Look at what I wear' she said, pointing to her jeans and sweater. 'I could never live in a traditional family like that.' Ritu was not only confident that she knew exactly what type of life she would live with this family, but her statement also definitively dismissed a potential arranged marriage that her family viewed as perfectly legitimate. In this example, both Ritu's dress and the dress of her potential spouse's kin were viewed not simply as aesthetic choices but as indicators of personal values and ways of life.

Though Ritu was more circumspect in her discussions, dress is also an important means of communicating expectations about consumption patterns. In another instance that I witnessed, after an arranged marriage, a young man was dismayed to find that the jeans and trendy clothing his fiancé had been wearing before their marriage were cheaper imitations of branded items. Now as husband and wife, he was frustrated that his spouse was not interested in the consumption patterns he felt were appropriate to their class standing. In this case, though happy with his wife in other respects, he felt betrayed and disappointed. More to the point, his mother and sister-in-laws who made up a large extended family were pleasantly surprised by the young bride. I learned that they had all worn *saris* and *kurta surawel* when first meeting the young woman and that she had taken their dress as a signal of the fact that maintaining modern fashionability would not be a requirement in her new home. This example is particularly interesting, because it echoes Liechty's (2003) findings that for many Nepali women the new consumption patterns are as much of a burden as they are an opportunity.

Interestingly, despite the apparent focus on clothing, this decision is often less about the particular garments at hand and more about the way such garments will be interpreted by other Nepalis, at home and out in public, and the extent to which they accurately express the aspirations of young women to these viewers. This was made particularly clear to me in one shopping trip when I examined several different T-shirt choices with one of my informants. I commented that the T-shirt she was examining was very pretty, but that I didn't like the large buttons attached to one side. My informant laughed and explained to me that details like the buttons were unimportant, what mattered was whether the shirt as a whole looked fashionable. Another familiar example of these kinds of choices can be seen in the continued popularity of T-shirts with misspelled or nonsensical English words on them. In Kathmandu, most middle-class young women have enough knowledge of English to recognise that what is written on the shirt has no meaning in English, but these are again classified as unimportant details. Rather than linguistically communicating, the English characters on these T-shirts more powerfully reiterate a connection between the T-shirt as a 'modern, western' garment, and its wearer as a 'modern, consuming individual'. Importantly, because of Nepal's close proximity to India and China: two places where inexpensive clothing production and export to Nepal is common, the English characters, as opposed to Hindi or Chinese characters, also signal some connection, tenuous though it may be, to imagined, western consumers. These imagined fellow consumers can be envisioned as consuming the same product, and perhaps, possessing similar dispositions. The irony, of course, is that the lack of linguistic meaning on the T-shirts is likely to prevent them from ever being exported to the West, because it is the linguistic content, and not just the indexicality of the characters, that will have meaning for the consumers there. The use of written words as design is a common phenomenon, but it only makes sense in this particular context if we understand that dress is being used indexically in a way that makes the garment's overall categorisation far more important than its specific design elements.

CONCLUSION

Weddings have always been a core topic in anthropology, but the 'vital conjuncture' presented to young people in the process of arranging marriages has received considerably less attention (Johnson-Hanks 2002).

Yet, this conjuncture is among the most crucial of young women's lives. It determines not only who they spend their lives with but where and how that life is lived as well. In Kathmandu, arranging marriages is considered a tenuous and stressful process, where both families take big risks involving their families' honour, social status, and for the bride and groom their whole lives. The proliferation of an incredible amount of styles and fashions has further complicated this liminal phase by introducing a variety of new gender roles, expectations and possible dispositions. Yet in Kathmandu, by reducing this diversity to a binary between modern and traditional, young women have been able to harness dress as a reliable medium for expressing their expectations and desires about the lives available to them after marriage. Young women contest, co-opt, and strategically adopt these dominant discourses by translating them into Bourdieuan dispositions, in part, through dress performances that materialise their personal preferences and their family's *ijat*. They do not passively accept the gender roles presented to them, instead they mobilise these roles by using their relative freedom from restrictions in what they wear. By choosing to wear *kurta surawel* or jeans in their daily lives, young women put their preferences on display to perform locally recognised ways of being, which signal to themselves, their families and their communities, their own expectations after marriage. Careful attention to these seemingly mundane decisions allows us to better understand the more subtle and relational ways by which young women bring their aspirations about class, consumption and a variety of 'possible lives' into being.

REFERENCES

Ahearn, L.M. (2001) *Invitations to Love: Literacy, Love Letters, and Social Change in Nepal*, Ann Arbor: University of Michigan Press.
Appadurai, A. (1996) *Modernity at Large: Cultural Dimensions of Globalization*, Minneapolis: University of Minnesota Press.
Bourdieu, P. (1998) *Practical Reason*, Stanford: Stanford University Press.
Breckenridge, C.A. (ed.) (1995) *Consuming Modernity: Public Culture in a South Asian World*, Minneapolis: University of Minnesota Press.
Butler, J. (1990a) *Gender Trouble: Feminism and the Subversion of Identity*, New York: Routledge.
Butler, J. (1990b) 'Performative Acts and Gender Constitution: An Essay in Phenomenology and Feminist Theory', in S.-E. Case (ed.), *Performing Feminisms:*

Feminist Critical Theory and Theatre, Baltimore: John Hopkins University Press, pp. 270–282.

Cohn, B. (1989) 'Cloth, Clothes, and Colonialism: India in the Nineteenth Century', in A.B. Weiner and J. Schneider (eds), *Cloth and Human Experience*, Washington: Smithsonian Institute Press, pp. 303–354.

Colekessian, A. (2009) *Reintegrating Gender: A Gendered Analysis of the Nepali Rehabilitation Process*, United Nations INSTRAW.

Comaroff, J. and Comaroff, J. (1992) 'Home-Made Hegemony: Modernity, Domesticity, and Colonialism in South Africa', in K.T. Hansen (ed.), *African Encounters with Domesticity*, New Brunswick, NJ: Rutgers University Press, pp. 37–74.

Costello, C.Y. (2004) 'Changing Clothes: Gender Inequality and Professional Socialization', *NWSA Journal* 16(2): 138–155.

Crawford, M. et al. (2008) 'Globalizing Beauty: Attitudes toward Beauty Pageants among Nepali Women', *Feminism & Psychology* 18(1): 61–86.

Entwistle, J. (2002) 'The Aesthetic Economy: The Production of Value in the Field of Fashion Modelling', *Journal of Consumer Culture* 2(3): 317–339.

Entwistle, J. and Wissinger, E. (2006) 'Keeping Up Appearances: Aesthetic Labour in the Fashion Modelling Industries of London and New York', *The Sociological Review* 54(4): 774–794.

Freeman, C. (2000) *High Tech and High Heels in the Global Economy: Women, Work, and Pink-Collar Identities in the Caribbean*, Durham: Duke University Press.

Goffman, E. (1959) *The Presentation of Self in Everyday Life*. Garden City: Doubleday.

Hansen, K.T. (2004) 'The World in Dress: Anthropological Perspectives on Clothing, Fashion, and Culture', *Annual Review of Anthropology* 33: 369–392.

Heiman, R., Freeman, C. and Liechty, M. (2012) *The Global Middle Classes: Theorizing Through Ethnography*, Santa Fe: SAR Press.

Hindman, H. and Oppenheim, R. (2014) 'Lines of Labor and Desire', *Anthropological Quarterly* 87(2): 465–465.

Hopkins, B.E. (2007) 'Western Cosmetics in the Gendered Development of Consumer Culture in China', *Feminist Economics* 13(3/4): 287–306.

Johnson-Hanks, J. (2002) 'On the Limits of Life Stages in Ethnography: Toward a Theory of Vital Conjunctures', *American Anthropologist* 104(3): 865–880.

Keane, W. (2005) 'The Hazards of New Clothes: What Signs Make Possible', in S. Kuchler and G. Were (eds), *The Art of Clothing: A Pacific Experience*, London: UCL Press, pp. 1–16.

Kondos, V. (1991) 'Subjection and the Ethics of Anguish: The Nepalese Parbatya Parent–Daughter Relationship', *Contributions to Indian Sociology* 25(1): 113–133.

Liechty, M. (2003) *Suitably Modern: Making Middle-Class Culture in a New Consumer Society*, Princeton: Princeton University Press.

Lynch, C. (1999) 'Good Girls or Juki Girls? Learning and Identity in Garment Factories', *Anthropology of Work Review* 19(3): 18–22.

McHugh, E.L. (2001) *Love and Honor in the Himalayas: Coming to Know Another Culture*, Philadelphia: University of Pennsylvania Press.

Miller, S. (1992) 'Twice-Born Tales From Kathmandu: Stories that Tell People'. PhD Dissertation. Cornell University.

Ministry of Health and Population (2012) *Nepal Demographic and Health Survey 2011*, Kathmandu, Nepal: Government of Nepal.

Netting, N.S. (2010) 'Marital Ideoscapes in 21st-century India: Creative Combinations of Love and Responsibility', *Journal of Family Issues* 31(6): 707–726.

O'Dougherty, M. (2002) *Consumption Intensified: The Politics of Middle-Class Daily Life in Brazil*, Durham: Duke University Press.

Perullo, A. (2012) 'Imitation and Innovation in the Music Dress and Camps of Tanzan', *English and Cultural Studies Book Publications*, Paper 11.

Puri, M., Tamang, J. and Shah, I. (2011) 'Suffering in Silence: Consequences of Sexual Violence within Marriage among Young Women in Nepal', BMC Public Health 11(1): 29.

Rankin, K.N. (2004) *The Cultural Politics of Markets Economic Liberalization and Social Change in Nepal*, London: Pluto Press.

Schielke, S. (2012) 'Living in the Future Tense: Aspiring for World and Class in Provencial Egypt', in R. Heiman, C. Freeman and M. Liechty (eds), *The Global Middle Classes: Theorizing Through Ethnography*, School for Advanced Research Advanced Seminar Series. Santa Fe: School for Advanced Research Press.

Schneider, J. (1987) 'The Anthropology of Cloth', *Annual Review of Anthropology* 16: 409–448.

Schneider, J. and Weiner, A.B. (1986) 'Cloth and the Organization of Human Experience', *Current Anthropology* 27(2): 178–184.

Seddon, D., Adhikari, J. and Gurung, G. (2002) 'Foreign Labor Migration and the Remittance Economy of Nepal', *Critical Asian Studies* 34(1): 19–40.

Sharangpani, M. (2010) 'Browsing for Bridegrooms: Matchmaking and Modernity in Mumbai', *Indian Journal of Gender Studies* 17(2): 249–276.

Shtrii Shakti (2010) *Revisiting the Status of Nepai Women (1981–2010)*, Kathmandu, Nepal: Shtrii Shakti.

Shukla, P. (2008) *The Grace of Four Moons: Dress, Adornment, and the Art of the Body in Modern India*, Bloomington, IN: Indiana University Press.

Sweet, E. (2010) '"If your shoes are raggedy you get talked about": Symbolic and Material Dimensions of Adolescent Social Status and Health', *Social Science & Medicine* 70(12): 2029–2035.

Tarlo, E. (1996) *Clothing Matters: Dress and Identity in India*, Chicago: The University of Chicago Press.

Thieme, S. and Wyss, S. (2005) 'Migration Patterns and Remittance Transfer in Nepal: A Case Study of Sainik Basti in Western Nepal', *International Migration* 43(5): 59–98.

Weiner, A.B. and Schneider, J. (1989) *Cloth and Human Experience*, Washington: Smithsonian Institution Press.

Whelpton, J. (2005) *A History of Nepal*, Cambridge; New York: Cambridge University Press.

Yami, H. (2010) 'Women's Role in the Nepalese Movement: Making a People's Constitution', MFzine.

Zhang, L. (2012) *In Search of Paradise: Middle-class Living in a Chinese Metropolis*, Ithaca: Cornell University Press.

10
'OF COURSE IT'S BEAUTIFUL, BUT I CAN'T WEAR IT!'

Constructions of Hindu Style among Young Hindustani Women in Amsterdam

Priya Swamy

INTRODUCTION

This chapter explores the ways in which fashion choices among young Hindustani women in Amsterdam are negotiated and constructed as embodiments of their Hindu identity. In the Dutch context, Hindustani colloquially refers to people identifying and identifed as descendants of British Indians who migrated to Suriname beginning in 1873 to work as plantation labourers. 'Hindustani' is therefore an ethnic marker that is used within the community itself, rather than a religious or class based identification. Religiously, the Hindustani community breaks down as 80 per cent Hindu, 15 per cent Muslim and 5 per cent Christian (Verstappen and Rutten 2007: 216). Hindustanis see themselves as culturally distinct from direct-migrant Indians because of their ancestors' migration to Suriname.[1] Throughout this paper, the Hindustanis whom I discuss are of a Hindu background.[2]

This chapter is based on ethnographic fieldwork[3] carried out between 2012–2013 in Amsterdam among Hindustani women between 18–40 years old. The first section briefly contextualises the history of Hindus in both Suriname and Amsterdam, highlighting the indentured labour experience and the postcolonial migration of Hindus into urban areas in the Netherlands. The second section provides a theoretical orientation, that focuses on three categories: diaspora, Hindu identity, and aesthetics. Rather than provide readers with a historical contextualisation of these terms, I focus on their current usages in the fields of diaspora studies, media and religious studies, and anthropology. By looking at diaspora as an identity that is mobilised and consciously constructed (Sökefeld 2006) through media, I argue that my respondents are agents of their diasporic identity and that their agency is well illustrated through their unique construction of embodied practices that they imbue with value (Mankekar 2002), such as styles of dress. The third section presents four fieldwork narratives. These narratives demonstrate how young Hindustani women in Amsterdam consciously construct their own Hindu identity from within their imaginings of what is 'Indian', imaginings that are not only heavily mediatised, but influenced by their position as diasporic subjects.

Hindustani forms of Hindu worship predominate in the Dutch public sphere. Although there is a steadily growing population of direct Indian middle-class migrants, temple spaces, cultural and religious organisations, and public festivals are most often organised and run by members of the Hindustani community. Throughout my fieldwork, direct migrant Indians who had settled in Amsterdam at around the same time that Hindustanis had begun to settle in large numbers in the Netherlands, said that they felt comfortable having Hindustanis run organisations and set up temples because they had strong Dutch language skills and more experience with navigating Dutch customs and manners.

For my female Hindustani respondents, embodied practices of dress and style play a central role in the construction of Hindu identities. While Indian fashion is considered beautiful, traditional, and an authenticating measure of Hindu identity, the young women I interviewed and observed are involved in dynamic processes of negotiating their own 'Indianised' style that expresses their experience as diasporic subjects: accessorising, home-made fan T-shirts, and even the rejection of popular Indian fashion trends and grooming they see in Bollywood films and Internet-based media, are all ways in which young women authenticate their own

Hindu identity. What is more, 'traditional Indian clothing' – the outfits they see in glossy magazines, on the Internet, and in Bollywood films, are ideals – young women rarely feel the need to emulate perfectly the styles they see in order to 'authentically' perform their Hindu identity through fashion choices.

Earlier scholarship has contested that the consumption of Bollywood films can be linked to the ways that young diasporic Hindus 'connect' with India, as 'India' is a mediatised construction of various images and ideas (Verstappen and Rutten 2007; Verstappen 2005). However, research has continued to perpetuate the idea that young Hindustanis use 'Bollywood culture' as a way to connect themselves to their Indian ancestry (Choenni 2011; Gowricharn 2009). I argue here that researchers should move beyond the framework of 'Bollywood culture' to ask how aesthetic practices, such as dress habits, operate not only within the framework of Bollywood but invert, reinvent and even reject what is presented to them in media through ways of dress. I suggest here that it may be more fruitful to speak of 'mediatised Indianised culture' as this lays emphasis on various forms of media, Bollywood and beyond. This includes images and styles circulating on Indian fashion websites, on the pages of glossy magazines, and in religiously themed television series.

HINDUS IN SURINAME

Suriname is a former Dutch colony in South America, bordering on Guyana, French Guiana, and Brazil. It became a major sugar plantation economy chiefly run by the labour of migrants from Java and India. In 1870, the British government signed a treaty with the Dutch government known as the 'Recruitment Treaty', and in 1872, under much duress, the British allowed the Dutch to recruit its first workers from British India (Choenni 2011: 5). This system of recruiting labour from British India lasted until 1916 (Choenni 2011; Hoefte 1998), with a period of brief suspension in 1877, eventually resuming in 1879.

Religious and cultural practices underwent significant changes as soon as labourers entered onto the boats at docks in Calcutta, awaiting their journey to Suriname. The rigid divisions of caste and *jati* (birth communities), embodied through dining and social interactions were impossible to uphold, resulting in greater contact not only between castes but also between people of different religious backgrounds. These communities were from different regions and performed their religion quite differently which meant that regional or highly parochial forms of Hindu practice were eventually replaced by a broader syncretic tradition that embraced the major gods and goddesses (Vertovec 1994: 130).

The years leading up to Suriname's independence in 1975 were politically tumultuous. Due to political unrest and an unstable economy, mass migration into the Netherlands began in the 1970s. Most Hindustanis have settled around the Hague, with significant populations also settling around cities like Amsterdam and Rotterdam. Major cities also have many speciality Indian and Hindustani shops, selling clothing, jewellery, ritual substances, iconography, food and media.

THE HINDU DIASPORA: CONSTRUCTIONS, MEDIATIONS, IMAGININGS

As Rogers Brubaker (2005) outlines, there are three general principles that most scholars of diaspora use to determine whether or not a community qualifies as a diaspora: dispersion into space, an orientation towards a homeland that holds authoritative value, and a maintenance of boundaries that are set up between a diaspora and their 'host' society (Brubaker 2005: 6). These three criteria have continued to frame the experiences of Hindustanis in the Netherlands, although the significance of these elements, along with the way they have been interpreted have shifted over time (Brubaker 2005: 6).

For my young female respondents, it is becoming increasingly important to establish an Indian cultural heritage. Many of my respondents feel that Suriname did not represent their culture, but the 'African [Creole] culture' of the majority population. Instead, India, especially because of its many temples and religious sites, is revered as a spiritual and cultural homeland (Vertovec 2000). Such a gendered response to 'Indianness' among second-generation Indo-Caribbean youth has been noted earlier (Warikoo 2005), where ideal womanhood according to Indo-Caribbean cultural norms that are policed by family members and perpetuated in the media are associated with embracing one's Indian roots. The connection between womanhood and Indianness, Warikoo argues, is strictly tied to ideas of maintaining and purveying tradition – an idea that has been widely observed across contexts, such as in Hindu-Trinidadian communities (Verma 2000; Khan 1995) and middle-class American Hindu families (Kurien 2007; Maira 2002).

For example, I spoke to two Hindustani women in their early thirties about their relationship to Suriname and to India. One respondent told me that: 'In India, temples are everywhere ... It's easier to be a Hindu there.' She lamented that the culture in Suriname was 'more of a party culture' and said that 'India was the place for spirituality'. As a spiritual person who took her religion seriously, she felt much more attached to India. Similarly, another woman told me that she felt Indians 'show more devotion' by 'falling at the feet' of gods and goddesses, while Hindustani people sit quietly in rows of chairs when they attend temples.

In turn, the young women I spoke to expressed shock and disappointment at seeing or hearing of young people (especially other women), 'acting modern' by dressing provocatively, eating meat, and drinking alcohol. It is clear that the India they refer to and relate to as a spiritual homeland is not a reified social fact (Appadurai 1996; Verstappen 2005), but a set of romantic and spiritual imaginings that are constructed. As Mankekar notes, 'India' in the diaspora is a construction of contested images, discourses and institutions (Mankekar 2002: 76), and these constructions take on an overwhelmingly spiritual focus among my young respondents. As India has become increasingly visible in popular culture and the international stage, Hindustani youth have been more vocal about their connection to India. This is especially relevant for Hindustanis who see India as the 'birthplace' of Hinduism (Vertovec 2000; Choenni 2015).

These sorts of romantic constructions have been previously linked to the consumption of Bollywood films. As Gowricharn (2009) has pointed out in the framework of mediascapes (Appadurai 1996), second generation Hindustani youth tend to exhibit a greater affinity for India than Suriname because of the ways in which Bollywood cinema acts as a 'commercial advertisement of Indian culture' (Gowricharn 2009: 1627). However, the India that is advertised is not 'real', but is a strategic representation of India as the centre of the world and its diaspora on the periphery (Verstappen and Rutten 2007: 214). Such an interest in Bollywood films does not necessarily mean my respondents are interested in the daily political or social life of India, much less its history. What is more, my respondents do not uncritically accept that what they see in films reflects what actually happens in India.

AGENCY AND REGIMES OF VALUE IN SURINAMESE HINDU DIASPORAS

In order to re-establish a position on a second generation diaspora community that places my young female respondents at the centre, I adopt Sökefeld's (2006) approach where diasporas are constructed through specific mobilisation strategies, actions, and institutionalisations (Sökefeld 2006: 267) that happen at group and individual levels. I focus on the strategic choices my respondents make through an engagement and selection of media beyond Bollywood films (particularly Indian television shows and Indian Hindu diaspora Internet sites) that are directly related to their style of dress. As I will demonstrate, it is not a simple case of borrowing styles from different films or even keeping up with the latest fashion: A Hindu way of dress is negotiated personally across various forms of media and reflects the aspects of Hindu life that my respondents think are relevant and appropriate in a given situation. Often, this means engaging with styles that are expressly 'Indian' (see below), but not necessarily popular, and looking at television, film, epic stories and soap operas to gain inspiration.

These independent constructions of Hindu identity through Internet based media involve shifting 'regimes of value' (Mankekar 2002: 76) that are placed upon various practices, styles, media and goods in the diaspora. As goods, styles and media come into the diaspora via transnational networks, my respondents attach value to them and set out to incorporate them into their daily lives. While regimes of value may change on the whole within a community, regimes of value among my respondents are largely self-constructed through their own sense of what is appropriate, beautiful and traditional from within their own imaginings of what it means to be a Hindu. As one of my respondents succinctly put it: 'Youtube is my Guru!', consulted when in need of information about weddings, funerals, specific fasts and celebrations. In turn, she found that she could discern style trends from the videos she watched, regardless of their subject matter.

INDIAN HINDU IDENTITY: RELIGION AS CULTURE AMONG HINDUSTANIS IN AMSTERDAM

My respondents use the term 'Hindu' to encompass a variety of cultural and religious practices. The emphasis on aesthetics among my respondents points to a conscious conflation of the two, where 'Indian' has become an ethnoreligious category.[4]

The Radha Krishna temple (RK temple) in Osdorp, Amsterdam sets itself apart from the other Hindu temples in the city by hosting days specifically aimed at youth. I attended 'Youth Day' in 2013 that dealt with the theme of marriage, where young people between the ages of 12–17 were broken into three groups and asked to examine a series of pictures related to the ritual of marriage and determine whether or not they were 'religious' or 'cultural'.

As a second-generation South Indian who had grown up in Canada, I was familiar with many (but not all) of the images that were presented. I had told the participants at Youth Day that my parents were born and raised in India, and that I had visited India many times throughout my life. After telling them this, I was struck by how often young people would turn to ask me whether or not I recognised a picture, and immediately assumed that if I did, based on my 'Indian' background, it must be something that is expressly 'religious' rather than cultural.

Young people also often asked amongst each other if they had seen the images in Indian films or on Indian television programmes before. If someone said they had recognised the image from Indian media, it was considered religious rather than cultural.

In particular, young people across all three groups opted to categorise images of traditional Indian[5] clothing, as opposed to Surinamese clothing, as religious rather than cultural. My observations echo David Pocock's 1976 article, where the Bochasan Shri Ashkar Purushottam Sanstha branch of the Swaminarayan movement in Britain venerates aspects of Gujarati culture, such as language, diet, and marriage networks as religious factors that contribute to the fulfilment of religious duty (Vertovec 2000: 15). Similarly, young Hindustanis are taking aspects of lifestyle that are Indian and imbuing them with religious value.

AESTHETICS: EMBODIED PRACTICE AND SENSORIAL EXPERIENCE AMONG YOUNG HINDUSTANI WOMEN

Caribbean Hinduism is an 'ethnic religion' (Vertovec and Van der Veer 1992: 149) which blurs the boundaries of culture, religion and ethnicity to form a Hindu identity that can be contextualised within current theories of aesthetics. For example, Meyer and Verrips (2008: 21) move away from the Kantian notion of aesthetics as 'disinterested beauty' and attempt to realign contemporary 'aesthetics' with the Aristotlean concept *aisthesis* (Meyer and Verrips 2008: 21; Meyer 2009: 6), which has most significantly been developed by Merleau-Ponty (1964). As Meyer and Verrips (2008) argue, *aisthesis* should be understood as a discussion of the issues in Aristotle's *De Anima*: 'Our corporeal capability on the basis of a power given in our psyche to perceive objects in the world via our five different sensorial modes, thus in a kind of analytical way, and at the same time as a specific constellation of sensations as a whole' (Meyer and Verrips 2008: 21).

This has in turn inspired a specific theorisation of 'diaspora aesthetics'. Werbner and Fumanti (2013) define diaspora aesthetics as: 'the sensual and performative medium through which diasporeans enact their felt autonomy while laying claims to "ownership" of the places and nations in which they settle' (Werbner and Fumanti 2013: 149). Diaspora aesthetics point out that authenticity and truth are ever-fluid concepts, so we cannot point to one 'original' source (Werbner and Fumanti 2013: 151).

Diaspora aesthetics are transnational and point to processes more complex than simple mimesis or nostalgia. The appropriation and re-construction of sartorial styles, literary and artistic objects, foods, and media are transformative processes that bring about shifting contexts and meanings, new objects and styles that are hybrid and in-between (Werbner and Fumanti 2013: 151; Bhabha 1994).

'My mom doesn't care about wearing saris, but I want to [wear them]', a young respondent wistfully told me. This difference of opinion within a family unit is not uncommon. I found that many of my respondents were interested in Indian cooking, visiting temples, keeping a vegetarian diet and developing an Indianised style of dress without any pressure from their parents. What is more, my respondents were often the only members of the family who engaged in these embodied practices.

As one young woman told me, she is 'basically just a Dutch girl' in relation to the way she thinks about her daily life and her social interactions, but her religion is 'Indian'. Rather than separating the two, or viewing them as conflicting, my young respondents easily reconcile their religious practices and everyday life in the Netherlands. They are also quick to point out what is 'practical' or 'impossible' to do in the Netherlands and easily justify abandoning such practices (such as visiting the temple more than once a week, or speaking fluent Hindi) while still recognising that these are ideal and valuable practices for Hindus in principle. At the same time, many of my respondents are quick to emphasise that certain embodied practices that are easily integrated in their daily life such as food and dress habits are 'more important that rituals'.

These categories of diaspora, newly emerging Hindu-Indian identity and aesthetics are the three main frameworks my respondents use when embodying their Hindu identity through ways of dress and style. Below, I lay out four ethnographic narratives that contextualise these categories and demonstrate how young Hindustani women use clothing and dress to embody an Indianised Hindu identity.

ETHNOGRAPHIC NARRATIVES

Saskia[6] is a 23-year-old who lives in the Netherlands close to Utrecht, but who travels to Amsterdam to attend the RK mandir in Osdorp. She approached me as I sat observing the Tuesday night prayers in the temple one evening. When I told her that both of my parents came from South India, she was quick to say 'We [Surinamers] also come from India.'

One day she asked to visit an Indian clothing store in the east of Amsterdam, as she was 'curious' about what they sold. She was particularly interested in the items that I found beautiful, often asking me

'Would you wear this to your wedding'? Again, it was interesting to see how she trusted my judgement on Indian clothing because I had mentioned to her that I have Indian parents and have visited India many times. The clothing sold in the shop we visited was very different from the traditional South Indian styles that I was brought up with and despite telling her so, she was still insistent that I give my opinion on the clothing she chose.

Saskia also spoke about the importance of Indian clothing in relation to her wedding. Like many young Surinamese Hindu women, Saskia expressed the view that marriage is a time where 'tradition' reigns: Indian clothing, Indian food, and a Hindu ceremony are all non-negotiable factors that contribute to an 'authentic' Indian wedding. She had searched various websites about how a traditional bride should be dressed and told me she was determined to wear 'all the items' that make for a traditional bridal ensemble in a Hindu wedding. Rather than consult Hindustani websites, which she said were difficult to find in the first place, she said she 'trusted' Indian websites when it came to matters of dress. Saskia attended a few weddings and social functions over the course of our interviews. When I asked her what she planned to wear, she would always say 'Western clothing', as she maintained that, even though beautiful, 'Indian clothing does not sit [feel] comfortable' on her. Although she felt more comfortable in western clothing, she took care to wear Indian accessories, such as *bindis, churia* (thin bangles), and other pieces of Indian jewellery to compliment her outfits at weddings and social occasions to give her outfit an 'Indian' look. While she had been to weddings where the bride and groom had worn 'Western' clothing, she firmly asserted that she would never do such a thing at her own wedding, although she did maintain that the concept was 'interesting'. However, she said that these weddings were 'not traditional'.

Saskia negotiated between her ideals about wearing Indian clothing and the practicality of certain styles. Her approach to Indian clothing at weddings was not unlike what I saw and heard from many of my young female respondents: Indian clothing is absolutely necessary if you are the bride or someone close to her, but for practical reasons when not closely related to the bride they opted to wear dresses and skirts to such events. However, accessorising becomes the way in which these young women add an 'Indian flavour' to their outfits, therefore making them 'appropriate' for a religious occasion such as a wedding. What is more, the accessories become as important as the outfit itself, as they represent the 'traditional' elements of dress that should be worn during a religious ceremony or occasion.

Although Saskia watched Bollywood films and was exposed to Indian TV, she did not expressly model her style upon what she saw in those films. She found websites about traditional modes of dress to be helpful, but always integrated those styles within her own personal take on 'dressing Indian'. While she knew the way she dressed at weddings and her visits to the temple was not the way Indians in India may dress, she felt that it represented her own style as a 'Dutch Hindu girl'. Saskia, like many other young women I have spoken to, negotiate their clothing choices carefully, vacillating between practicality and tradition – in Saskia's case, the two are not mutually exclusive. While she idealises Indian clothing as the 'traditional' way to dress during a wedding or temple service, she rejects the need to always wear Indian clothing as impractical and instead accessorises in order to mobilise her Indian Hindu identity. While she is preoccupied with Indian ways of dressing, especially when it comes to weddings, she is also firmly rooted in a diasporic style that neither mimics nor rejects, but constructs a sense of style that is Indianised, traditional, and diasporic in its aesthetics.

'I DON'T CARE WHAT I WEAR': REETU AND 'ANTI-STYLE'

I first met Reetu, a 20-year-old woman living in Osdorp, Amsterdam, in the RK temple on a Tuesday evening. She stood out not only because she was one of the younger people there, but she dressed very casually and simply compared to other young women, wearing a pair of pants and a T-shirt, sporting an unkempt hairstyle that caught my attention as soon as I came into the temple. Over the course of our meetings, she spoke to me often of meditation, renunciation and spiritual aspects of life. Unlike most of the young women that I spoke to, Reetu was much more interested in spirituality. However, much like the other young women I spoke to, she used media, particularly the Internet, to seek out episodes of the popular Indian television drama *Devon Ke Dev ... Mahadev* ('The Lord of All Lords ... Mahadev [Shiva]'), based on the mythology of Shiva. Although she spoke intently of the messages and the stories that she gleaned from each episode, it became apparent that she also paid close attention to the aesthetics and habits of Lord Shiva as depicted in the series, and sought to emulate them in her own life. She mentioned repeatedly that 'she didn't comb her hair' because she wanted to resemble Lord Shiva who is notorious for being unkempt, with a head of dreadlocks. Although she also apologised to me for 'not caring about her hair', she also seemed to be very proud of the fact that she was unembarrassed to leave her hair uncombed.

She was much less enthusiastic about fancy Indian clothing than other girls her age, showing little interest in the latest fashions she saw in Bollywood films or on the Internet. When I asked her if she liked wearing Indian clothes, she immediately cut me off and said that she wished she could 'wear a simple white shirt and white pants', as she was more concerned with 'giving away material things' and 'living like Shiv *bhagwan* [Lord Shiva]'. She also mentioned that the idea of abandoning fashion and material things was originally 'Indian', and she was suspicious of Hindustani gurus or renunciants because they 'are driven by money'. For Reetu, the lifestyle of renunciation is not only Hindu, but Indian. She was concerned that it was 'too difficult' to be a Hindu in the Netherlands because of the European 'lifestyle', which not only included eating meat, but it encouraged one to pay too much attention to physical appearance and fashion, which 'went against' the teachings of Shiva. '[Real] Hindus are not concerned with how they look', she told me. On the one hand, Reetu told me she was uninterested in fashion and wished she could wear simple white clothing for the rest of her life. On the other hand, she told me that she 'always wore her Indian cricket shirt' so that people 'knew where she comes from' when she was at the gym. She equated both her commitment to the spiritual pursuit of Hinduism as well as her Indian identity with the way she dressed and styled herself.

Reetu's engagement with 'Indian' fashion is unique among my female respondents, but her reasons for constructing and mobilising an 'Indian-Hindu' way of dressing is strikingly similar to Saskia's. Much like Saskia, Reetu relies on images circulated through the Internet in order to construct her own, idealised way of dressing that mobilises an Indian-Hindu identity. She, much like Saskia, does not go to lengths to perfectly mimic Lord Shiva's dress, but appropriates aspects of his mediated image as her own distinct Hindu-Indian style. Furthermore, she saw the renunciant's way of dressing in simple white cloth as an *ideal* to aspire to, representing an authentic and traditional way of Hindu dress, but instead was satisfied mobilising an Indian and Hindu identity through a style that was readily accessible – such as simple jeans and T-shirts at the temple, and uncombed hair.

'KEEP CALM AND LOVE DEEPIKA': BOLLYWOOD FANDOM STYLE

I also carried out fieldwork in a small temple established in 2011 in the southeast of Amsterdam. The temple is known for elaborate celebrations during Hindu festivals, which are rich, aesthetic performances that involve a diverse Hindu community. During an anniversary celebration of its opening, I observed Hindus of Afghan, Surinamese, Punjabi, Gujarati and South Indian backgrounds, as well as a few members of the Hare Krishna community come together to perform worship, share communal meals and participate in a lively singing and dance competition.

While the temple usually attracts a mix of backgrounds, most often people are distinguished as either 'Hindustani' or 'Indian': it is relatively easy to make the distinction between the two based on the way young women are dressed. Indian (mostly Punjabi Hindu) young women wear full *salwar kameez* or *anarkali* suits, and very rarely an older woman will come dressed in a *sari*. The Hindustani women usually come in pants and long shirts that resemble *kurtha* tops, long skirts and shirts, or some variation of modest clothing such as a long shirt with a round collar (resembling a *kurtha*) over leggings.

At the anniversary celebration I observed a young Hindustani woman named Reshmi who earlier was wearing a pair of jeans with a cream coloured *kurtha* top over them. As people piled into the temple and the temperature rose, she pulled off her *kurtha* to reveal a T-shirt that had a picture of Bollywood superstar Deepika Padukone. The back of the shirt read: 'KEEP CALM AND LOVE DEEPIKA'.

I already knew that Reshmi had a strong attachment to Bollywood culture – her mother told me she insisted on visiting Mumbai to 'see Bollywood', and that she often took her daughter to hear playback singers in concert in the Netherlands. Reshmi had proudly shown me pictures she had taken with playback singer stars as well as the background pictures on her phone of Deepika and other Bollywood celebrities. For Reshmi, not only films, plot lines and fashions were significant: she was wholly caught up in a fan-culture which venerated actors, actresses and singers as measures of Indian culture themselves. However, Reshmi's attachment to Bollywood culture was embodied much differently than the other young women I had interviewed. Rather than appropriate aspects of a style she observed in films, she constructed an embodied practice out of her devotion to a particular Bollywood personality. Rather than dress according to styles she had consumed in media, she created her own way to dress that represented her highly personalised attachment to Deepika Padukone. Her own admiration for Deepika did not manifest itself as it does for many other Hindustani girls her age – those who ask for Indian outfits that look like something the starlet had worn to an event or in a film. Unlike other instances of queer fandom that are outlined in this volume (see Chapter 3), the desire to *be* Deepika struck me as less important to Reshmi than showing to others at the temple how her simple Deepika t-shirt was part of her Hindu style. It may therefore be useful to think through the 'Deepika shirt' as a material object of fandom. While scholars have noted that the aspects of collecting, replicating and commodifying 'things' of fandom is often reduced to a commerical material practice (Hills 2014), the affective and nonmaterial aspects of such material culture should not be underestimated (Hills 2014; Rehak 2012). I see Reshmi's T-shirt as a creative and highly personalised form of mimesis that negotiates and rejects the desire to 'be Deepika' with (and ultimately in favour of) the desire to publicly 'admire Deepika'. It forms a sharp contrast to the reductive observations that consuming Bollywood culture among young Hindustanis is to mimic what is seen on screen: Reshmi's love for Deepika demonstrates that the films and stars she sees are part of an elaborate, aestheticised world that she would rather celebrate than directly emulate in terms of style. As a consumer and fan of Bollywood cinema, she negotiates her own style that can express her love for Bollywood and stars like Deepika. What is more, she can extend and perform her personal take on 'Bollywood culture' alongside more mimetic or other performative forms of fandom in the Hindu diaspora in the Netherlands.

Reshmi had worn her T-shirt on a day where Indian culture was being celebrated alongside a milestone for the Hindu community in Amsterdam: many young children chose to perform Bollywood inspired dances to popular songs. The judges of the dance competition, visibly irritated by the overwhelming amount of Bollywood as opposed to 'classical' Indian dances, gave a stern lecture that stated Bollywood stars 'trained first as Classical dancers'. Although her faded T-shirt was a far cry from the more elaborate outfits at the anniversary celebrations, it fitted comfortably within the event that vacillated between lively devotion to the gods and goddesses of the temple and devotion and celebration of Indianised, Bollywood culture as it was embodied through song and dance.

ADOPTING TRADITIONS, ADAPTING STYLE: DRESSING FOR *KARVA CHAUTH*

Karva Chauth, taking place in the Autumn season, is one of the major celebrations in one of the temples in the southeast of Amsterdam because of the large Punjabi Hindu community that attends regularly. Although many of my respondents had not heard of the festival as it is not traditionally practised in Suriname, I was surprised to hear that there was a growing number of Hindustani women beginning to organise *Karva Chauth* celebrations themselves. At the temple, the emphasis on Hindu Punjabi festivals and forms of worship meant that the celebration was elaborate and well-attended, attracting many Punjabi but also quite a few young Hindustani women.

Women who participate in *Karva Chauth* do more than simply fast; a key component is dressing up in elaborate, formal clothing, jewellery and make-up. At the temple, reminders of the festival were circulated through social media, directed to the 'beautiful ladies', who were asked to appear dressed in their finery on the day of the festival. I observed that the majority of women attending *Karva Chauth* wear *anarkali* or *salwar kameez* suits with mirror work and heavy stitching in bright colours. However, among the few Hindustani women there, very few were dressed like the Punjabi women who attended. Many came in the outfits that they wear to other festivals and celebrations in the temple – such as long skirts and shirts and leggings and long *kurtha* tops. Only one or two older women who sat at the sides of the temple observing the fast were actually wearing saris. It appeared that the popular style was to wear *salwar kameez* or *anarkali* suits. I saw a woman wearing a long summer dress with her shoulders covered by a shawl to create an Indianised outfit resembling a *lengha* or *sari*. Women were dressed formally and beautifully, with jewellery and make-up to accompany their outfits.

The young woman and her Indianised outfit represents how newly emerging traditions and rituals are appropriated according to one's own styles and tastes. Rather than treat the festival as 'Punjabi', this young woman, and others who were dressed similarly, chose to negotiate the aesthetics of the fast (especially sartorial style) according to their own constructions of how an 'Indian' festival with 'Indian' clothing should be embodied, rather than look to the Punjabi women as measures of 'authentic' style for *Karva Chauth*.

CONCLUSION

For my respondents, Hindu identity in their diasporic context is something they actively construct. The young women I interviewed and observed view India as a 'spiritual homeland', and set out to embody a Hindu identity that is Indianised, a trend that has been previously addressed in scholarship on Indo-Caribbean and Hindu diaspora communities. Yet, the cases of the young women that I present here offer us more than the well-rehearsed narratives of diasporic mimesis or romanticisation: they all require a rethinking of how style aesthetic may be creatively adapted and personally designed to fit in the particular experiences of a diasporic subject. While I do not deny that regimes of value that circulate across Hindu diasporic communities have a role in how these styles are, in the first place, consumed and performed, they demonstrate how young women in the diaspora play with the relationship that is drawn between ideal womanhood and expressions of Indianness as they strive to style themselves as Surinamese Hindus in Amsterdam. The relationship between Indianness and Hinduness may not be reduced to a singular reading of Hindu interests or frameworks: the way that Indianised culture is invoked across these cases through style and media means that we must look at different angles to frame this relationship in the case of these ethnographic vignettes. My ethnographic narratives seek to capture an emerging attitude towards clothing and Hindu identity not only to demonstrate the diversity in styles that are 'Hindu' but also to point to the greater trend of using fashion strategically as a way to mobilise Hindu identity in the Netherlands. Such mobilisations also include paying attention to Dutch or 'European' aesthetic values and qualities such as comfort in order to develop a style that is diasporic. By focusing on narratives that bring in media other than Bollywood films, this study also attempts to problematise the reductive notion that Hindustanis embody a 'Bollywood culture', and highlights the various mediatised fashions and styles that often conflict with or undermine styles seen in popular films.

The theoretical implications of my study urge researchers to continue to explore how diaspora identity is strategically mobilised by individuals and groups, rather than something that involves mere repetition of rituals and styles. By paying attention to fashion as a part of the larger discussion of diaspora aesthetics, researchers can develop insights into how diasporic youth actively engage and embody a religious and cultural identity that may differ radically from previous generations.

NOTES

1. For a thorough discussion of the relationship between Indians and Hindustanis in the Netherlands, see Lynnebakke 2007.
2. As this chapter stemmed out of a larger project on Hindu identity in the Netherlands, my contact with Christian and Muslim Hindustanis has been limited. Future research that explores the category of Indianness vis-à-vis styles and fashions among these other Hindustani religious groups would open up the observations made here to rich points of comparison.
3. This includes extensive and immersive participant observation at various temples in Amsterdam as well as extensive semi-structured interviews and informal conversations.

4. While the conflation of 'Indianness' and 'Hinduness' has often been described in the language of Hindu nationalism and Hindutva discourse, I argue that this is not strictly the case here. There is more of an indirect reference, in some cases, to grey literature on the Internet that reinforces this relationship between Hinduism and India through frameworks of Hindutva revisionist histories (cf. Thapar 1992). In most cases, and certainly among all the respondents whose voices are represented in this chapter, there is no mention or acknowledgement of Hindu nationalist groups as influential. Indeed, traditionally strong diasporic Hindutva organisations such as the Vishva Hindu Parishad (VHP) or Rashtriya Swayamsevak Sangh (RSS) are only minimally active in the Netherlands, and respondents have told me that since the mid 1990s these groups have seen a large drop in active membership. However, because many of my respondents rely on websites and web searches to find their information on Hinduism, there are no doubt some instances where Hindu nationalist views trickle into the information they consume and then actively transmit.
5. One particular image was of a North Indian-style wedding ensemble for males. It is interesting to note that 'Indian' or 'India' is usually constructed as a homogenous, North Indian identity, as members of the Surinamese Hindu diaspora are largely unaware of the sharp cultural and religious distinctions regionally.
6. All the names of my respondents have been changed.

REFERENCES

Appadurai, A. (1996) *Modernity at Large*, Minnesota: University of Minnesota Press.
Bhabha, H. (1994) *The Location of Culture*, London: Routledge.
Brubaker, R. (2005) 'The "Diaspora" Diaspora', *Ethnic and Racial Studies* 28(1): 1–19.
Choenni, C. (2011) *Integration Hindostani Style? On the Migration, History and Diaspora of Hindustanis*, Amsterdam: VU Amsterdam.
——— (2015) *Hindostaanse Surinamers in Nederland 1973–2003* [Hindustani Surinamers in the Netherlands 1973–2003], Arnhem: LM Publishers.
Gowricharn, R. (2009) 'Changing Forms of Transnationalism', *Ethnic and Racial Studies*, 32(9): 1619–1638.
Hills, M. (2014) 'From Dalek Half Balls to Daft Punk Helmets: Mimetic Fandom and the Crafting of Replicas', *Transformative Works and Cultures* 16.
Hoefte, R. (1998) *In Place of Slavery: A Social History of British Indian and Javanese Laborers in Suriname*, Gainsville: University Press of Florida.
Khan, A. (1995) 'Homeland, Motherland: Authenticity, Legitimacy, and Ideologies of Place among Muslims in Trinidad', in Peter van der Veer (ed.), *Nation and Migration: The Politics of Space in the South Asian Diaspora*, Philadelphia: University of Pennsylvania Press.
Kurien, P. (2007) *A Place at the Multicultural Table: The Development of an American Hinduism*, New Brunswick: Rutgers University Press.
Lynnebakke, B. (2007) 'Contested Equality: Social Relations Between Indian and Surinamese Hindus in Amsterdam', in G. Oonk (ed.), *Global Indian Diasporas:*

Exploring the Trajectories of Migration and Theory, Amsterdam: Amsterdam University Press, pp. 235–263.
Maira, S. (2002) Desis in the House. Indian American Youth Culture in New York City, Philadelphia: Temple University Press.
Mankekar, P. (2002) 'India Shopping: Indian Grocery Stores and Transnational Configurations of Belonging', Ethnos 67(1): 75–97.
Merleau-Ponty, M. (1964) Primacy of Perception, Illinois: Northwestern University Press.
Meyer, B. (2009) 'Introduction: From Imagined Communities to Aesthetic Formations: Religious Mediations, Sensational Forms, and Styles of Binding', in B. Meyer (ed.), Aesthetic Formations, New York: Palgrave Macmillan.
Meyer, B. and Verrips, J. (2008) 'Aesthetics', in D. Morgen (ed.), Keywords in Religion, Media, and Culture, New York and London: Routledge.
Pocock, D. (1976) 'Preservation of the Religious Life: Hindu Immigrants in England', Contributions to Indian Sociology 10: 341–365.
Rehak, B. (2012) 'Materializing Monsters: Aurora Models, Garage Kits and the Object Practices of Horror Fandom', International Journal of Francophone Studies, 1(1): 27–45.
Sökefeld, M. (2006) 'Mobilizing in Transnational Space: A Social Movement Approach to the Formation of Diaspora', Global Networks 6(3): 265–284.
Thapar, R. (1992) 'Imagined Religious Communities? Ancient History and the Modern Search for a Hindu Identity', in Interpreting Early India, Delhi: Oxford University Press, pp. 60–89.
Verma, N. (2000) '"Arrival, Survival and Beyond Survival": Indo-Trinidadian Quest for Political and Cultural Ascendancy', PhD Dissertation. Department of Sociology, University of Toronto.
Verstappen, S. (2005) Jong in Dollywood: Hindoestanse Jongeren en Indiase Films, Amsterdam: Het Spinhuis.
Verstappen, S. and Rutten, M. (2007) 'Bollywood and the Indian Diaspora: Reception of Indian Cinema among Hindustani Youth in the Netherlands', in G. Oonk (ed.), Global Indian Diasporas: Exploring Trajectories of Migration and Theory, Amsterdam: Amsterdam University Press.
Vertovec, S. (1994) 'Official and "Popular" Hinduism in Diaspora: Historical and Contemporary Trends in Surinam, Trinidad, and Guyana', Contributions to Indian Sociology 28(123): 123–147.
——— (2000) Hindu Diaspora: Comparative Patterns, Oxford: Oxford University Press.
Vertovec, S. and Van der Veer, P. (1992) 'Brahmanism Abroad: On Caribbean Hinduism as an Ethnic Religion', Ethnology 30(2): 149–166.
Warikoo, N. (2005) 'Gender and Ethnic Identity among Second-Generation Indo-Caribbeans', Ethnic and Racial Studies 28(5): 803–831.
Werbner, P. and Fumanti, M. (2013) 'The Aesthetics of Diaspora: Ownership and Appropriation', Ethnos 78(2): 149–174.

11

BRAS ARE NOT FOR BURNING

The Bra and Young Urban Women in Delhi and Bombay

Lipi Begum

INTRODUCTION

Within studies of Indian dress, the closest thing to a bra is usually the *choli* (*sari* blouse) (Fabri 1960; Kumar 2005). Bras, generally classified as western,[1] are rarely included. When the bra does appear in studies of Indian women's dress, it is incorporated into wider discussions of the general growth of women's western clothes and underwear retailing in India (Agarwal 2013; Sharma 2009; Technopak 2013). Scholars of Indian cinema (Banaji 2006; Dwyer 2001; Wilkinson-Weber 2014) have analysed the meanings of western outer-clothes worn by women in India, however these studies seldom discuss the semi-hidden bra. Whereas the panty through the Pink Chaddis campaign appeared in public as a symbolic tool of female power and protest, the relationship between power and the bra in India remains ambiguous.

This chapter focuses on the significance of the bra in India in relation to its proximity to the Indian woman's body. I focus on the ambiguity of the bra to investigate the tensions of the sexualised female body and changing ideals of Indian femininity (Fields 2007; Sukumar 2007). The bra is hidden under clothes, but has effects on the dressed female body that are publicly viewed, highlighting issues that western outer garments cannot always reveal. It is the inherently western and sexualised connotations of the bra that set the backdrop in which the power meanings of the bra for young (18–24) urban Indian women living in Delhi and Bombay[2] are to be explored.

I discuss how the bra lends insight into the paradoxical battleground between emerging bi-cultural identities and the increase in moral policing of young urban Indian women's sartorial behaviour in public spaces, as India begins to rapidly urbanise. I discuss how the tensions surrounding western dress in India re-circulate patriarchal and nationalistic anxieties concerning western modernity dating back to the Indian independence movement. And, through a Foucauldian analysis of power, I reveal how the bra is a technology of the young urban Indian woman's self and an embodiment of her ambivalent identity – one which evolves with the city and oscillates between practices of domination and practices of resistance.

The findings in this chapter are taken from a wider study that applied a qualitative research methodology. Primary research was undertaken from 2011–2014 and consisted of semi-structured surveys, interviews and focus groups conducted in shopping malls with the highest target consumers of underwear[3] in Delhi and Bombay. A sample size of approximately thirty women from each city was surveyed including ten in-depth interviews and two focus groups (one in Delhi and one in Bombay). Due to limited research on the bra in India, a multi-stage research approach was undertaken. This included further stages of research utilising online surveys and textual analysis of bra and lingerie representation in magazine advertising and in Indian cinema. To contextualise the study and add to the limited body of academic research on the bra in India, meanings of western dress in India, market growth factors of the bra, as well as existing studies of the bra and lingerie[4] are discussed in the remaining sections.

SELF-STYLISATION, THE BRA AND POWER

There is no such thing as a subject outside of the social discursive and political framework. And there is nothing outside the web of power

(Foucault 1978: 93). Central to Foucauldian power is the relationship between power and knowledge, where techniques of domination depend on the knowledge that classifies individuals and the power that the knowledge is derived from. Foucault's work did not look at fashion. However previous studies (Amy-Chinn 2006; Fields 2007; Jantzen et al. 2006) of the bra and lingerie have drawn on the contributions of Foucault's works (1977, 1978, 1988) to conceptualise the ways in which historical power relations and disciplinary regimes of surveillance shape and control our body and sexuality.

Applying Foucault's later works on the 'Technologies of the Self' (1988), I emphasise that instead of viewing biopower solely as a constraining force it should also be looked at in the light of its productive sides; how it produces knowledge and pleasure, where practices of domination go hand in hand with practices of self-production or of taking care of the self (Foucault 1988). A basis to understand the bra as a technology is to emphasise the role of bra as a power dressing tool useful for conducting the body in certain ways that both discipline the body and pleasure the flesh (Entwistle 2000) and a tool to construct inter-psychological (public identity based on an external world of shared values and symbols which direct identity construction) and intra-psychological (private identity, directed towards an internal world of longings, feelings and bodily representations) identity (Jantzen et al. 2006). In these respects, in the Foucauldian sense, the bra serves as a technology of the self.

A Foucauldian analysis acknowledges the gendered, social and political dimensions embodied within bra wearing practices and how the overarching relationship to power and undergarments is an oscillation between seizing control and being controlled (Jantzen et al. 2006: 179). Yet previous discussions that have applied this analysis, like the Danish study by Jantzen et al. (2006), can usefully be extended to consider the meanings of underwear in the context of globalised fashion consumption and mediation in India. The Indian context complicates previous applications of Foucauldian power and brings into view additional social and political power relationships of colonial, postcolonial and national struggles. The Hindu nationalist narrative of modernisation in India which equates western capitalism (increase in western fashions like the bra) with the perceived inadequacy of western moral values, such as a lack of sexual constraint and hyper-sexualised female identities, complicates the study by Jantzen et al. (2006) of the inter- and intra-psychological meanings of the bra along the lines of East/West power relations. This ambiguity calls for the questioning of the meanings of the bra in urban India from a postcolonial perspective. A postcolonial view allows me to address the ways in which meanings of the bra for women in India are not static, but are linked to meanings of western dress socially and culturally produced through a web of power connected to colonial and nationalist views of modernity.

This complex relationship of multiple modernisms that creates room for self-reflexivity and self-stylisation capable of challenging the dichotomies of ruler and ruled, oppressors and oppressed, East and West. This chapter focuses on the findings which revealed a mixture of both implicit and explicit personal views of the participants who challenged popular understandings of modernity, that modern does not equate to western and traditional to Indian. It explores the ambivalent space where a garment can move through space and time and has the potential to shift from one category to another, where positive meanings emerge out of the processes of appropriation, adaptation and transformation (Appadurai 1996; Ashcroft 2009; Bhabha 1997; Phillips and Steiner 1999). In order to understand this ambivalent space, the following section discusses the colonial and national tensions which give rise to the self-reflexive power meanings attached to the bra in urban India.

ANXIETIES SURROUNDING WESTERN DRESS IN INDIA

The anxiety surrounding western clothing in India coalesced as a political focus during the Indian independence movement. During the *Swadesi* (liberation) movement (1920–1947) (Tarlo 1996; Trivedi 2007), Gandhi formed essentialist views of the West arguing that western secular rational enquiry encouraged anarchist individualistic bohemian lifestyles with a lack of sexual inhibition (Hardiman 2003: 21). In contrast, Gandhi demanded puritanical ideals of restraint of mental and physical sexual desires for both Indian men and women. This included dress and adornment. Indian men and women were asked to boycott foreign British goods such as western clothing. These types of foreign goods were seen as symbolic of material desires and believed to be affecting the livelihood of Indian businesses and Indian cultural identities (Cohn 1996: 109). According to Gandhi, modernity was inseparable from western capitalism and colonialism and he sought liberation from both.

Gandhi's views on western modernity made a big impact, but also faced opposition. For example the influential Indian poet Rabindranath Tagore shared Gandhi's anxieties about globalisation and its universalising effects (Hardiman 2003), but challenged Gandhi's idea of nationalism and was supportive of globalisation. Unlike Gandhi's essentialist and conservative views about identity, Tagore was cosmopolitan and progressive (Bhushan and Garfield 2014). For Tagore, national growth required transnational integration; he advocated neither total insulation from nor a complete adoption of foreign western culture. However, in the strong pursuit for Indian independence from the British, Tagore's cosmopolitan views were dominated by Gandhi's nationalistic views. Certain strands of Hindu nationalism today deploy their own version of what they present as a Gandhian view, in their attempts to govern and shape mainstream public attitudes towards women's wearing of western clothing.

For Indian women, essentialist views about western modernity were complicated by patriarchal attitudes that positioned women as the guardians of traditional culture and chastity, so that whilst men widely adopted western dress after independence, women were slower to adopt western dress (Tarlo 1996; Banerjee and Miller 2003). These patriarchal moral attitudes also heightened the shamelessness and eroticisation popularly associated with western clothing. This is seen in the Indian cinema of Bollywood pre- and post-independence, where female characters of low repute wore gaudy western styles and revealed their bras (Wilkinson-Weber 2014), whilst virtuous wives and heroines wore Indian styles (Tarlo 1996). This trend still dominates Bollywood today. Actresses wearing western clothes are often associated with moral failings, seen as vices of western modernity, sexual promiscuity, shamelessness and sexual violence, whilst actresses wearing Indian dress are mostly associated with tradition, safety and chastity (Banaji 2006;

Banerjee and Miller 2003; Begum and Dasgupta 2015; Dwyer 2001; Wilkinson-Weber 2014). These attitudes have also re-surfaced outside of cinema and into mainstream political media through incidents like the Mangalore attacks, Miss India protests and anti-rape protests across India.

In 1998 Miss India pageants were met with hostility by far right Hindu groups who protested that western clothing like lingerie and swimsuits are symbols of western lifestyles and a threat to national identities (Dewey 2008; Oza 2001). In February 2009 a string of violent attacks against women in Mangalore[5] pubs took place. Forty male activists from the Hindu right wing group Sri Rama Sena (SRS) barged into a pub in Mangalore, South India, and dragged out and beat up a group of young women, claiming that the women were violating Indian traditional values by shamefully displaying romantic affection in public spaces, smoking, drinking alcohol and wearing western clothes. This was linked to populist Hindu right views that western modernity is a contaminating force against Indian traditions.

Such incidents have led to an increase in women's campaigns and protests across India and widespread media frenzy. Media coverage has ranged from patriarchal and nationalistic far right Hindu views against Indian women wearing western clothing to far leftist feminist views supporting the right to choose what to wear, including western clothing in public. Since then western clothing including undergarments have gained attention as symbolic tools of protest against patriarchal and nationalistic views that restrict Indian women's sexual identity to bearers of chastity and tradition (Oza 2001; Thapan 2004). Particularly in response to the 2009 Mangalore attacks, underwear has been appropriated to coin the name for the women's rights campaign Pink Chaddis (pink panties). A group of women came together through the Facebook consortium named 'Pub-Going, Loose and Forward Women' and urged women across India to send their pink panties through the letter boxes of SRS activists in time for Valentine's Day. Over five hundred panties were said to have been couriered, making it a landmark protest against moral codes of shame, sexism and Hindu conservatism in India (thepinkchaddicampaign.blogspot 2009). Furthermore, in 2011 the first western style SlutWalk format, named *Besharmi Morcha* (without shame), took place in New Delhi, India (*The Hindu* 2011). Unlike western iterations, the Indian *Besharmi Morcha* did not include provocative clothing such as bras as markers of protest (Valenti 2011), and was somewhat different to the historical context[6] of the SlutWalk movements where the bra was famously associated with the term 'bra burning'[7] to symbolise the rejection of objects of male oppression (Valenti 2011).

In India the symbolic meaning of the bra is ambiguous. Bras have not been specifically discussed as symbolic markers of female empowerment like *chaddis*, nor directly as objects of male sexual oppression as in the West. Yet they have been consistently referenced in relation to themes of postcoloniality, shame and the evolving identity of an Indian woman and her body (Bannerji 2001; Cohn 1996; Sukumar 2007). However, these themes have not been fully explored in relation to the meanings of specifically western clothing in the contemporary context, nor the rapidly changing liberalised global economic context within which the increasing consumption of bras are taking place. This is discussed in the following section.

THE CITY LIFE OF BRAS

Rapid urbanisation visible in the form of standardised[8] fashion retailing and greater entrance of Indian women into urbanised public spaces provides insight into the power meanings of the bra. Since the first standardised shopping mall opened in Delhi in 2003, British brand Marks and Spencer (M&S) and French brand Enamor (Keys 2003) increased their entry into the Indian underwear market. For the first time, these brands became available through retail concessions in department stores such as Shoppers' Stop, Lifestyle, Pantaloons, Westside, Globus, Piramyd and Globus (Franchiseindia.com 2008; Images F&R research 2007; Peer 2014) across big cities like Delhi and Bombay.

These standardised underwear retailers began to capitalise on changes in the lifestyle of urban Indian women. Increasing visibility outside of the home and in public spaces, such as the workplace, public transport to work, bars, clubs and shopping malls, paradoxically demanded that women signal success through clothing and increased the need for privacy within rapidly industrialising and uncertain public spaces. Retailers therefore targeted the increasing number of professional women entering the workforce[9] with higher disposable incomes employed within the secondary and tertiary sectors of India's tier one cities.[10] These retail spaces empowered Indian women who traditionally purchased their bra and lingerie in un-organised fragmented stores with male attendants (Keys 2003). Being able to purchase bras at their own ease and discretion allowed them to sidestep the disorder of rapid urbanisation which can give rise to patriarchal threats to intimacy in public places (Wilson 2011) such as the male-gaze and eve teasing[11] (Sukumar 2007). This need for ease and discretion however varies amongst age groups and it is these age differentials that provide further insight into the meanings of the bra in India.

While older women (24–35 year olds) are perceived to look for discretion and status in their bra wearing and shopping practices, younger women (18–24 year olds) are perceived to be less influenced by discretion and status. Young urban Indian women are understood to be more concerned with affordable and fashionable styles (Jadhav and Pati 2012). These younger urban women are from the post-liberalisation generation.[12] The liberalisation of the economy exposed greater numbers of Indians to global consumer goods including western fashion brands and global fashion media. Young urban women faced a greater choice of western fashion retailers and began to frequently mix and match traditional Indian styles with western styles (*sari* and *salwar kameez* with western jeans and T-shirts). This is seen amongst young urban Indian women who are increasingly adapting their bra to a growing number of sartorial choices (T-shirt bras for tight fitting *salwar kameez* and western-style tops and *choli* bras). Thus, underwear retailers aside from capitalising on the need for ease and discretion when bra shopping, also offered various styles and colours of underwear to capture retail growth.[13]

This cosmopolitan approach to fashion amongst Indian youth is increasingly reflected in Bollywood films. Unlike the meanings of western dress frequently potrayed in earlier mainstream Bollywood films, western styles in films post-liberalisation are more fluid and less restricted to women of low repute. Revealing bra straps, lingerie and bikini styles are increasingly worn by heroines on screen and young college girls off screen[14] (Dwyer 2001; Wilkinson-Weber 2014). Post-liberalisation films feature heroes and heroines similarly associated with western dress. For example, film characters depicted living abroad are shown mediating their Indian identities in the West by embracing traditional family arrangements and actively encouraging a youthful 'bicultural identity ... one rooted in global culture and one rooted in local culture' (Ghadially 2007: 29). Western dress situated within a bi-cultural identity is not always gender specific, neither anti-western nor condemning of Bollywood's portrayals of women in scantily clad and tight fitting clothes (Banaji 2006; Wilkinson-Weber 2014). Instead western clothes can also provide a fantasy space which epitomises the escapist nature of Bollywood, neither negative nor positive and potentially empowering and liberatory (Banaji 2006: 168).

This filmic embrace of a bi-cultural identity is also reflected in the choice of celebrity ambassadors for global bra brands in India. In May 2014, youth fashion icon and ex MTV 'Rock On' VJ and model-turned-Bollywood-actress Lisa Haydon unveiled M&S's first stand-alone store in Bombay; as of 2018, twenty stores are now open. (Fashionunited.in 2014). Haydon in her films is mostly situated within a bi-cultural identity through the wearing of Indian and western fashions. Although Haydon's onscreen Indian identity is not always free from cultural stereotypes, the roles she plays in her films are often neither hypersexualised (prostitute or vamp) nor desexualised and are firmly associated with unashamed sexiness, fantasy, independence and a working identity (*Queen*, dir: Bahl 2014). She is portrayed as emblematic of the post-liberalisation generation; typical of an aspirational, educated, middle-class, bi-cultural youth and fashion identity (*Aisha*, dir: Ojha 2010). Similar to Tagore's sceptical yet optimistic view of globalisation, bi-cultural identities created for and cultivated by stars like Haydon are not free from the nationalistic tensions surrounding western modernity, rather they demonstrate a critical engagement with multiple possibilities both of freedom and resistance. Notably, this tension between freedom and resistance is complicated by the fantasy space within which bi-cultural identities operate. This is seen in the Bollywood film *Fashion* (dir: Bhandarkar 2008) where the bra is symbolic of both the allure and the threat of western modernity.

In *Fashion*, wearing western lingerie is instrumental to the protagonist Meghna's career as a successful international supermodel and is symbolic of her self-determination, fulfilling friendships, romantic relationships.

On the other hand, the dangers of modernity are allegorised by the trials undergone by Meghna as a result of her being too modern (western). This is seen in scenes where her career as a western lingerie model leads her down the individualistic path of cultural rejection (by family), hedonism (excessive alcohol consumption, smoking, drugs), lack of sexual restraint (relationship break-ups, one-night stands) and an emotional breakdown (despair of her career in the fashion industry). Yet it is the empowering potential of fantasy, situated within her bi-cultural identity that rejects the nationalistic view of western modernity for Indian women as a moral problem. These meanings of fantasy and pleasure heighten the paradox of fashion during periods of urbanisation (Wilson 2011).

The variety of choice attached to clothing styles and the variation in desired body image/size across age groups, regions and marital status (from goddess-like curves to fitness bodies) makes self-power ambiguous within a pluralistic, multi-lingual and multi-ethnic country made up of 42 cities. In the context of bra consumption in India, the increase in standardised bra retailers is as much about avoiding eve teasing at traditional outdoor public vendors, as it is about aesthetic and pragmatic choice, empowering and changing means of expression. This ambiguity of power is discussed through the findings of the study in the following section.

FINDINGS: BESHARMI[15] BRAS

Younger (18–24-year-old) urban Indian women living in the cities of Delhi and Bombay differed in their attitudes to older urban Indian women (25 years and over). Where older working women purchased bras to generate a sense of freedom and control in the private space of their bedrooms with their partners, younger working women purchased bras to generate a sense of sexual freedom and control in public spaces. This was revealed in both the purchasing behaviour of younger women and the discussions that took place during the interviews and focus groups.

During the fieldwork, Malika (24 years old) wore a T-shirt and jeans and talked to me in a Delhi food court. Malika told me that 'women in

India are more confident about speaking up about lingerie', whilst in the 'earlier days they were too shy or concerned'. She also said that 'rape is a big thing in India', and that 'every girl is always cautious' which is why women do not talk about their bras. However, Malika went on to say that this mindset is changing amongst younger women and that they are a 'new generation' who 'speak about these things'. I asked her whom she was referring to as this 'new generation' and she stated the 'college girls'. College girl is a term that Malika gave to unmarried women who engaged with women's rights campaigns while studying at university or shortly after graduating from university. College girls in her opinion were also not shy about openly shopping for the latest bras in 'Chinese stalls' with their friends. In my study, younger urban women such as Malika expressed opinions about themselves and other young urban women who mostly shopped at unlicensed vendors which they called 'Chinese markets' – vendors who sold fake designer bras at significantly lower prices than the original retailers. Although this was linked to lower income levels of younger women in the study, a closer analysis revealed that young educated urban women were also patronising the Chinese market. Having acquired greater intellectual freedom through better education, young urban women through their shopping practices at unlicensed vendors were breaking down and resisting patriarchal and populist Hindu national codes of shame. Young urban Indian women studied were not ashamed of openly talking about their bras and their bodies. These liberal attitudes towards sexuality were supported by their responses to the growth of bra consumption in India. The younger and older urban women I studied all attributed the growth in bra and lingerie consumption to growing liberal attitudes amongst the younger generation and namely the college girls.

It became apparent through our discussions that my study was creating an opportunity for participants to privately and openly discuss their feelings and resistance towards the policing of female sexuality in India. In my interview with Surma (24 years old) in Bombay, the conversation about her bra led to a discussion on codes of shame in bra and other fashion advertising, recalling the controversial advert from 1995 in India for 'Tuff Shoes'. The advert created controversy amongst Hindu women's groups for the depiction of real life couple Madhu Sapre and Milind Somand naked, save for their Tuff shoes, with a python around their neck. Whilst women's groups protested against the advert for its obscene and shameful depiction of Indian femininity and degradation to Indian moral values, she herself liked it for the good-looking models and its 'boldness', the ability to 'not be ashamed of expressing yourself and your body freely' and to 'dare to dream'. She went on to explain that the attitude towards female sexuality is 'slowly beginning to change in India'; whilst there was controversy in the 1990s about Indian models advertising underwear, she believes 'now there is less shame'. Currently there is 'greater visibility of Indian women in bra advertising, because of an increase in liberal sexual attitudes and increase in the level of body awareness, body fitness and health-education' amongst Indian youth.

Due to the sexualised nature of discussing the bra in India, it became clear that references to health-education were a code for sexual-health education. According to my respondents, improved health-education (sexual-health) was an important reason for the increase in consumption of bras. For Surma, in the Jantzen et al. (2006) sense discussed earlier, her inter-psychological identity related to health and body awareness was linked to her intra-psychological identity related to feelings of boldness and confidence. Here meanings of health and comfort attached to the bra broke down Hindu nationalist opinions that western clothing causes cultural shame and hyper-sexualises Indian women. During a focus group Sameera (23 years old) in Delhi commented:

> Women want to feel good from inside out. Women are also becoming more aware of their own bodies and realise that it needs some pampering. The majority of women do not look into the mirror to see their boobs or sexual organs, they just have no connection to those parts of their body. Ask them to name different parts of their genitals and they will only come out with words that are commonly used as abuse.
>
> (Sameera, focus group)

Through codes of health it can be seen that Sameera's construction of her identity was directed by her intra-psychological identity (Jantzen et al. 2006), her longing to practice better self-care and self-esteem.

For Sameera the bra signified better attitudes towards sexual health and the breaking down of codes of shame and taboos attached to female sexuality.

It is clear from Sushma, Malika and Sameera's response and other responses obtained from the wider field research that the bra in urban India is mostly associated with sexual choice and freedom and not with male oppression. In a country where public display of affection and discussing sex in public are considered taboo, growth in the consumption of bras for these urban women became a symbolic marker of a young generation of Indian women negotiating power through greater practices of self-care and self-stylisation. This was revealed in the form of increased body awareness: less shame of their bodies meant that they could openly discuss and purchase bras in public. Despite the desire to discuss and display sexuality in public, the bra still remained a discreet topic of conversation because the perceived risk of sexual harassment and shaming from displaying bra straps in public spaces continued to be a real concern. According to the respondents this shaming is perpetuated by the public discourse surrounding female sexual identity in India, specifically the way in which underwear is advertised in public spaces of India.

Both younger and older respondents openly challenged Hindu national attitudes towards western garments (bra) through their response to bra advertising in India. Patriarchal codes of shame were perpetuated by bra brand advertising message strategies in India. Underwear advertising frequently represented both Indian and white western models as hyper-sexualised and objects of male pleasure. Beena (36 years old) commented that bra adverts in India are mostly 'vulgar, pornographic and for male pleasure'. However, there was an understanding between younger women compared to the older women surveyed that this was not the case for editorial fashion shoots in international or up-to-date fashion magazines. Ambika (19 years old) commented that 'in the past only desperate and B grade actresses and models would appear in adverts, now younger women are more confident with their bodies and appearing in bra, swimwear and lingerie adverts'.

There was a consensus among younger women surveyed that bra adverts in local fashion magazines (e.g. *Femina India*) in contrast to international fashion magazines (e.g. *Vogue India*) focused more on depicting female pleasure for the sake of male pleasure. They commented that this is frequently seen through the use of hyper-sexualised poses for white models and the absence of Indian women models. Indian models were often absent from lingerie advertising in *Femina India*, as they were culturally expected to retain their chastity by keeping their bodies away from the public gaze. According to Ambika, local Indian bra advertising, similar to western studies of lingerie advertising (Amy-Chinn 2006), was perceived to be 'lagging behind lingerie fashion shoots and editorials as seen in *Vogue India* and similar' because these magazines, unlike local bra advertising, placed female pleasure and fantasy at the centre of the message strategy. Among younger respondents there was an oppositional gaze evident, where younger respondents were able to interrogate and question the male gaze; and in doing so, by cultivating awareness, opened up the possibility to resist and assert agency (Hooks 1992).

These western-style magazine adverts for global brand lingerie did not always avoid recirculating orientalist legacies, mostly promoting western fashion aesthetics. However, they moved away from Hindu patriarchal national stereotypes of the hyper-sexualised white woman and the chaste Indian woman, by placing both Indian and white models in poses that were deemed to be not hypersexual. These poses were within both western and eastern fantasy holiday locations, and the models in these shoots were seen wearing a mix of local and global-western underwear brands, therefore blurring the hierarchy between global-western and local brands. Here then we see an increasing shift towards transnational representations of female identity in underwear advertising, neither a rejection nor a complete adoption of westernisation. Additionally, we see ways opening up in which younger respondents are capable of self-producing agency and pleasure through their own female gaze and ideas of sexuality and shame, agency that abandons patriarchal and nationalistic representations of sexuality and shame.

OSCILLATING IDENTITIES

In conclusion, the bra in India for young urban professional working women is a technology of the self (Foucault 1988), instrumental to generating a sense of power through inter- and intra-psychological comfort (Jantzen et al. 2006). In the Indian context, this sense of comfort is also an embodied desire to control and resist patriarchal Hindu nationalist forces of power caught up within the tensions of western colonialism. In the Foucauldian sense, although young urban Indian women were not always conscious of these forces of power shaping their sartorial identity, it was clear that young women through their bra wearing practices were entangled within networks of power, which they were both controlled by and in control of. It is within these inescapable meanings of being in control and being controlled that the bra embodies Indian women's ambivalent identity, one that is both oscillating and evolving. On the one hand, this is seen in the naming of the Pink Chaddis campaign, The word *Chaddi* which literally translates to shorts was used rather than panty, which 'simultaneously desexualised and un-gendered the garment' (Menon 2012), providing an example of how young urban Indian women remain entangled within controlling forces of power. Furthermore, the organiser of the *Besharmi Morcha*[16] requested participants to avoid 'sexualised clothing', mindful of the moral judgement that they would face from conservative groups. On the other hand, the young women studied were capable of negotiating a sense of agency. For them, the bra also became a technology of the self (Foucault 1988), instrumental to generating a sense of freedom and power whilst moving through private and public spaces. The bra can be seen as a garment capable of producing pleasure and practicing self-care without shame. It was clear through meanings of the bra that younger urban women in Delhi and Bombay are becoming increasingly comfortable with a bi-cultural identity and expressing liberal sexual attitudes, even if they do not always have the freedom to do so openly and in public.

The wider study also revealed that these meanings were complicated by historical and pre-colonial British feminine identities and orientalist fashion legacies. Female sexuality through moral codes of shame linked to the covering and un-covering of breasts has been scrutinised throughout Indian history, marking Indian womanhood as ambivalent. In the pre-colonial era, women went bare-chested and upper-class Brahmin women were often seen wearing *saris* without a blouse as a sign of purity and status (Bannerji 2001; Fabri 1960). The slow eroticisation and covering of the breasts in India began when the Moghuls introduced modest Islamic dress codes, and when the middle-class Anglo-Christian missionaries introduced virtuous dress codes.[17] This is seen in the fragmented documentation of various changes in sartorial identity related to the dressing of the breasts, such as covering of the bare chest (Fabri 1960); low-cut cleavage enhancing *cholis* of the Hindu dancers; long-sleeved Victorian inspired *sari* blouses worn by middle-class Bengali women; T-shirt bras that enhance the shape of the breasts; and the visible rise in global brand lingerie consumption.

What is evident from the study is the ways in which ideals surrounding Indian women's sexuality, its shape and form, signified through fashions is changing. Yet what is constant is the ambivalence of Indian womanhood, the ways in which these ideals keep oscillating from open (pre-colonial) to closed (colonial) and back to open (liberalised consumer).

NOTES

1. It is the widespread mass manufacturing of the bra in the West and later across the world by western companies and popularisation by Hollywood (Fields 2007) that lends to the perceived inherently western connotations of the bra across the world and in India. The bra appeared as an alternative to the uncomfortable corset in the 1900s and first patented by Mary Phelps Jacobs in New York 1914 under the name Caresse Crosby calling her invention 'the backless brassiere'. Mary sold her rights to the Warner Brothers Corset Company who went on to sell the most popular brassiere in the next 30 years (Fields 2007). India's oldest lingerie brand Groversons Paris Beauty (since 1953) began mass manufacturing bras for Indian women who aspired to western fashions (hence the naming Paris) and were used to getting them imported from the West or tailored (Groversons India 2013). Nowadays, the bra is associated with the rise in western clothing and western fashion retailing in India.
2. The city of Bombay was officially renamed Mumbai in November 1995 by the BJP-Shiv Sena coalition government (a political right and far right Hindu group coalition) (Mehta 2005; Prakash 2011). I use Bombay instead of Mumbai to dissociate from far right Hindu claims to the city. Others still use Bombay instead of Mumbai to honour the imagination and hopes associated with a cosmopolitan Bombay, a 'maximum city' (Mehta 2005), a 'jigsaw puzzle of distinct neighbourhoods marked by community, language, religion, dress and cuisine' (Prakash 2011: 11).
3. Select City Walk (Delhi); Inorbit Mall (Bombay); DLF Emporium (Delhi); High Street Phoenix Mall (Bombay); Atria the Millennium Mall (Bombay); La Senza (Delhi and Bombay) and M&S (Delhi and Bombay).
4. 'Bra' and 'lingerie' are used interchangeably by my respondents. The terms both refer to an intimate piece of apparel which signifies the sexualised female body

and changing ideals of Indian femininity (Fields 2007; Jantzen et al. 2006). Furthermore, during the field research respondents used both terms interchangeably. A precise definition of what constitutes lingerie or the bra is subjective to the wearer – underwear that one woman considers to be lingerie may be conceived as an everyday bra by another women (Begum 2012).
5. Mangalore is India's eighth largest port city, an urban and industrial city and considered a growing metro city with an airport and in close proximity to Bangalore, India's third largest metropolitan city.
6. The SlutWalk movement draws inspiration from the 'second wave' of the feminist movement and anti-rape movements of the 1960s and 1970s (mostly taking place in the USA, eventually spreading throughout the West and the rest of the world) (Carr 2013).
7. Bras were thrown (not actually burnt) into the trash can alongside other beauty products.
8. Organised and standardised refers to licensed retailing formats such as branded malls, hypermarkets and global retail outlets that are large privately-owned businesses. Unorganised retail sector refers to fragmented un-licensed stores, market stalls, cart vendors and family owned general stores.
9. The labour market situation is mixed in India. It is predicted to remain the same or less between 2015 and 2018 for men and the youth population, while the overall employment rate for women is predicted to increase from 30.7 million in 2015 to 31 million in 2018 (International Labour Organisation 2014: 60).
10. Urbanised metropolitan cities of Delhi, Bombay, Bangalore, Chennai and Kolkata.
11. Eve teasing is the term for unwanted sexual remarks, indecent molestations and sexual harassment in public spaces in India.
12. Post-liberalisation refers to the historic decision made in 2002 to permit foreign direct investment in the media (Prasad 2008), a period which allowed greater room for the promotion of global consumer culture and exposed middle-class urban Indian youth to global media.
13. In 2009 lingerie growth rate was predicted at 45 per cent yearly and one of the biggest areas alongside women's western clothing, going from a market worth Rs. 870 crores (£119 million) to almost double that at Rs. 1,645 crores (£225 million) by 2010 (Sharma 2009). Since 2009, there has been an explosion of media interest indicating the growing number of both offline and online lingerie retailers in India.
14. An overtly modern middle-class girl who has university education (Wilkinson-Weber 2014: 115) and is often at the forefront of student politics, women's rights campaigns and protests.
15. Without shame, shameless or nothing to be ashamed of.
16. Debates on restricting provocative western clothes took place during the *Besharmi Morchas*. The outcome was defined as a 'modest affair' (Hindu 2011) by many and bloggers and newspapers commented that this was to avoid backlash from conservative groups (thealternativein 2011).

17. During the Channar Revolt lower class women in Travancore, South India protested against being denied breast cloths. They were made to go bare-chested to retain their marker of respect to upper-class women who had newly converted to Christianity, and therefore were allowed to wear breast cloths as a symbol of virtuosity (Cohn 1996).

REFERENCES

Agarwal, P. (2013) *Indian Intimate Wear Sector Current and Emerging Landscape*, Mumbai: Peppermint Communications Pvt Ltd.

Aisha (2010) Directed by Vikas Bahl, Studio: PVR Pictures, India.

Amy-Chinn, D. (2006) 'This is Just for Me(n): How the Regulation of Post-feminist Lingerie Advertising Perpetuates Woman as Objects', *Journal of Consumer Culture* 6(2): 155–175.

Appadurai, A. (1996) *Modernity at Large: Cultural Dimensions of Globalization*, Minneapolis: University of Minnesota Press.

Ashcroft, B. (2009) 'Beyond the Nation: Post-Colonial Hope', *Journal of the European Association of Studies of Australia* 1(17). Available at http://www.easa-australianstudies.net/files/jeasa1aashcroft.pdf (accessed on 18 September 2017).

Banaji, S. (2006) *Reading 'Bollywood': The Young Audience and Hindi Films*, London: Palgrave Macmillan.

Banerjee, M. and Miller, D. (2003) *The Sari*. Oxford: Berg.

Bannerji H (2001) *Inventing Subjects Studies in Hegemony, Patriarchy and Colonialism*, Tulika India.

Begum, L. (2012) 'Lingerie Brand Advertising through Saidian Logic', *Working Papers in Fashion Studies* (2), University of the Arts London.

Begum, L. and Dasgupta, R.K. (2015) 'Contemporary South Asian Youth Cultures and the Fashion Landscape', *International Journal of Fashion Studies* 2(1).

Bhabha, H.K. (1997) 'Signs Taken for Wonders: Questions of Ambivalence and Authority under a Tree Outside Delhi May 1817', *The Location of Culture*, London: Routledge, pp. 102–122.

Bhushan, N. and Garfield, L.J. (2014) 'Swaraj and Swadeshi: Gandhi and Tagore on Ethics, Development and Freedom', Smith College, Yale University. Available at http://jaygarfield.commons.yale-nus.edu.sg/wp-content/uploads/sites/24/2014/01/garfield_swaraj.pdf (accessed on 3 July 2015).

Carr, L.J. (2013) 'The SlutWalk Movement: A Study in Transnational Feminist Activism', *Journal of Feminist Scholarship*, Spring (4).

Cohn, B. (1996) *Colonialism and Its Forms of Knowledge: The British in India*, Princeton: Princeton University Press.

Dewey, S. (2008) *Making Miss India Miss World: Constructing Gender, Power, and the Nation in Post-Liberalization India*, Syracuse: Syracuse University Press.

Dwyer, R. (2001) 'The Erotic of the Wet Sari in Hindi Films', *South Asia: Journal of South Asian Studies*, XXIII (1): 143–159.

Entwistle, J. (2000) *The Fashioned Body: Fashion, Dress and Modern Social Theory*, Cambridge: Polity Press.

Fashion (2008) Directed by M. Bhandarkar, UTV Motion Picutures: India.

Fabri, C. (1960) *Indian Dress: A Brief History*, New Delhi: Sangam Books.

Fashionunited.in (2014) 'M&S Separates Lingerie into New Format', fashionunited.in. Available at http://www.fashionunited.in/news/apparel/ms-separates-lingerie-into-new-format-160520147052 (accessed on 2 May 2014).

Fields, J. (2007) *An Intimate Affair, Women Lingerie, and Sexuality*, Berkeley: University of California Press.

Foucault, M. (1977) *Discipline and Punish*, Harmondsworth: Penguin.

——— (1978) *The History of Sexuality: Volume I, Introduction*, Harmondsworth: Penguin.

——— (1988) 'Technologies of the Self', in H.Luther, M.G. Huck and P.H. Hutton (eds), *Technologies of the Self: A Seminar with Michel Foucault*, Amherst, MA: The University of Massachusetts Press, pp. 16–49.

FranchiseIndia.com (2008) 'Foreign Lingerie Brands in India', *Franchise India Magazine*. Available at http://www.franchiseindia.com/magazine/2008/may/Foreign-lingerie-brands-in-India_39-2-3/ (accessed on 2 May 2014).

Ghadially, R. (ed.) (2007) *Urban Women in Contemporary India: A Reader*. India: Sage Publications.

Groversons India (2013) 'About Us: History'. Available at http://www.groversonsindia.com/about.html (accessed on 2 May 2015).

Hardiman, D. (2003) *Gandhi: In His Time and Ours, the Global Legacy of His Ideas*. New York: Columbia University Press.

Hooks, B (1992) 'The Oppositional Gaze: Black Female Spectators', *Black Looks: Race and Representation*, Boston: South End Press. Chapter Seven, pp. 115–131.

Images F&R research (2007) 'India Retail Report', *An Images F & R Research*. India Retail Forum, India: New Delhi.

International Labour Organisation (2014) Global Employment Trends 2014. International Labour Office, Geneva. Available at http://www.ilo.org/wcmsp5/groups/public/--dgreports/--dcomm/--publ/documents/publication/wcms_233953.pdf (accessed on 18 September 2017).

Jadhav, P.S. and Pati, S.A. (2012) 'Consumer Behaviour Regarding Women's Decisions Concerning Fashion in the Emerging Market'. Available at http://www.aygrt.isrj.net/UploadedData/992.pdf (accessed on 13 February 2014).

Jantzen, C., Østegaard, P. and Vieria-Sucena, C. (2006) 'Becoming a Woman to the Backbone Lingerie Consumption and the Experience of Feminine Identity', *Journal of Consumer Culture* 6(2): 177–202.

Keys, L. (2003) 'French Lingerie Market Targets a Land Without Undies', Seattlepi. Available at http://www.seattlepi.com/national/130401_lingerie11.html (accessed on 17 October 2009).

Kumar, R. (2005) *Costumes and Textiles of Royal India*, Antique Collectors Club Ltd.

Mehta, S. (2005) *Bombay Lost and Found*, Fifth Edition, Headline Review.

Menon, N. (2012) *Seeing Like a Feminist*, India: Zubaan.

Oza, R. (2001) 'Showcasing India: Gender, Geography, and Globalization', *Signs: Journal of Women in Culture and Society* 26(4): 1067–1095, Chicago: The University of Chicago Press.

Peer, N. (2014) 'Adult Private Shopping Online in Vogue in India', Techcircle.in. Available at http://techcircle.vccircle.com/2014/05/16/adult-private-shopping-online-in-vogue-in-india/ (accessed on 16 May 2014).

Phillips, R.B. and Steiner, C.B. (1999) *Unpacking Culture: Art and Commodity in Colonial and Postcolonial Worlds*, Berkeley: University of California Press.

Prakash, G. (2011) *Mumbai Fables: History of an Enchanted City*, Princeton: Princeton University Press.

Prasad, K. (2008) 'The False Promise of Media Liberalization in India', *Free Markets Free Media? Reflections on the Political Economy of the Press in Asia*, AIMC.

Queen (2014) Directed by Vikas Bahl, Studio: Viacom 18 Motion, India.

Sharma, R. (2009) 'Indian Lingerie Industry: Unleashing the Growth Potential', *Koncept Analytics*. Available at http://www.techexchange.com/thelibrary/indian.html (accessed on 1 July 2009).

Sukumar, S. (2007) 'The Bra and the Indian Woman's Notion of Sexuality', *Journal of Creative Communications*, 2(3): 267–278.

Tarlo, E. (1996) *Clothing Matters: Dress and Identity in India*, London: Hurst & Co.

Technopak (2013) 'Apparel E-tailing in India'. Available at http://www.technopak.com/files/Apparel_E-tailing_in_India.pdf (accessed on 2 May 2014).

Thapan, M. (2004) 'Embodiment and Identity in Contemporary Society: Femina and the New Indian Woman', *Contributions to Indian Sociology* 38(3): 411–444, Delhi: Thousand Oaks.

Thealternative.in (2011) 'Besharmi Morcha: Little Slut, Even Lesser Walk, and No Message'. Available at http://www.thealternative.in/lifestyle/besharmi-morcha-little-slut-lesser-walk-message/ (accessed on 18 September 2017).

The Hindu (2011) 'SlutWalk Makes a Modest Entry in Delhi'. Available at http://www.thehindu.com/todays-paper/slutwalk-makes-a-modest-entry-in-delhi/article2312105.ece (accessed on 18 September 2017).

Thepinkchaddicampaignblogspot (2009) 'Pink Chaddis Campaign'. Available at http://thepinkchaddicampaign.blogspot.co.uk/ (accessed on 22 October 2014).

Trivedi, L. (2007) *Clothing Gandhi's Nation: Homespun and Modern India*, Indiana: Indiana University Press.

Valenti, J. (2011) 'SlutWalks and the Future of Feminism', 3 June. Available at http://www.washingtonpost.com/opinions/slutwalks-and-the-future-of-feminism/2011/06/01/AGjB9LIH_story.html (accessed on 6 June 2015).

Wilkinson-Weber, C.M. (2014) *Fashioning Bollywood the Making and Meaning of Hindi Film Costume*, London: Bloomsbury.

Wilson, E. (2011) *Adorned in Dreams Fashion and Modernity*, London: I.B.Tauris.

INDEX

abayas, 126, 138, 139–41, 142–3
Abu-Lughod, Lila, 140
accessories, 38
advertising, 212–15
affordability, of clothes, 141, 148, 151
agricultural workers, 149
Althusser, Louis, 82
American Hindu families, 187
Amila (FTZ worker), 134–5
Amin, S., 128
Amsterdam, Hindustani women, 183–99
anarkali suits, 195
androgynous style, 65
androgyny, 70
anklets, 30, 43
Anusha, JNU (Singh), Pl.10, 100
Appadurai, A., 166
Arekti Premer Golpo/Just Another Love Story (film), 67, 70, 71, 73–4
Aristotle, De Anima, 190
arranged marriages, Kathmandu, 20–1, 165–80
artistic nationalism, 102–5
Asian influences, 156–7
Azrak show (Valaya), 103

Bakshi, Kaustav, 18, 77
Bal, Rohit, 102
Bandopadhyay, Manabi, 81
bands, music, 117
Bangladesh, 16–17
Bangladeshi communities, 89
bangles (churia), 192
banyans, 43
beanie hats, 90
Begum, Lipi, 16, 18–19, 69, 86–95
belts, 146, 147
Bengal, 65–82
Berry, J., 46
Besharmi Morcha, 207–8, 216
Bhaduri, Chapal, 81
Bhootsavaar (brand), 105, 106, 108–9, 111, 113, 115–18
Bhutan
  national attire, 146–7, 149, 155, 158–60
Bhutan Street Fashion Project, 13, 147, 149, 154
Bhutanese Youth and Fashion Magazine, 149
bindis, 192
bisexuality, Pl.4, Pl.8, 89–90, 93

blogs, 16, 32, 37, 149
  See also Manou, wearabout (blogger)
blouses, 130, 143, 147, 202, 217
Bodu Bala Sena (Buddhist Power Force), 139, 140, 141
Bollywood culture, 184–5, 195–7
Bollywood films, 13–14, 106, 187–8, 193, 206, 209–11
  See also individual films
Bombay, 202–17
Bosnian Muslim refugee women, 142
Botswana, 128
Bourdieu, P., 167–8
Brahmin women, 216
'Brand India', 108–9, 110
brands, global, 16, 25, 33, 129, 208, 215
bras, urban women and, 202–17
Brick Lane, London, 89
British Asian Fashion Network, 17
'brown' ways of being, 91, 93
Brubaker, Rogers, 186
Buddhism, 125, 146, 160
Butler, Judith, 168

Cahun, Claude, 98
Cambridge, Duchess of, 150
camel traders, 39
capes, 150
capitalist systems, 119
castes, 7, 60, 61–2, 62, 185–6
catcallers, 124–5, 133, 138–9
cēri, 61–2
chaddis, 208, 216
chappals, 30
chastity, 55
Chatterjee, Partha, *The Nation and its Fragments*, 3–4
Chauhan, Nitin Bal, 105, 109, 110, 111, 113, 118

Chennai, 49–63
Chinese fashion, 156, 179
Chitrangada: A Crowning Wish (film), 73, 74, 79
Chokher Bali/A Passion Play (film), 67, 72–3
cholis, 30, 43, 129, 202
'Christopher Street' (Sunil), 97
churia (bangles), 192
cinema, Indian, 69, 71, 99, 106
Citton, Yves, 112
CK Jeans, 44
class system, 7–8, 155
  'distinction', 167–8
  'position taking', 168
coats, 159
code-switching, 9–10, 15, 20
college, and fashion, 50–3
college culture, 51–2, 54
'college girls', 212
colonialism, 40, 68–70
colours, in fashion, 71, 93, 133
comfort, importance of, 159
communities
  Bangladeshi, 89
  building, 133–4
  India, 38
  Pakistani, 90, 92
  Punjabi Hindu, 195, 197–8
  tribal communities, 40
community building, 133–4
consumer-citizens, 104, 108, 119, 121, 208–11
Converse sneakers, 92
corporate social responsibility (CSR), 120
costumes, film, 71
counterfeit goods, 50, 129, 131, 212
creativity, 106, 108, 127

INDEX

cropped pants, 125
cross-dressing, 77

Dalit settlements, India, 61
Das, Amoha, 81
Das, Sabarni, 76
Das, Tista, 81
Dasgupta, Rohit K., 18, 69, 86–95
Datta, Kallol, 31
Delhi, 30–1, 202–17
Delphi, 96
department stores, 208
derogatory terms, 77, 138
desi street style, 32–7
designers, 15, 105, 109–10, 156
Devon Ke Dev ... Mahadev (Indian TV drama), 194
Dharmapala, Anagarika, 130
Dhee (lesbian comic strip), 12
dhotis, 43, 69
diaspora, Hindu, 186–9
digital platforms, 15, 24
directions, future, 23–5
disposable income, 105, 209
Dissanayake, Wimal, 67
'distinction' (class system), 167–8
'doing style', 8, 53–6
Dorji, S.S. Pek-, 155
dress codes, 13, 128, 146–7, 165–80, 197–8, 216
dress practices, 8–9, 20, 38, 42, 141, 142
dresses
  length, 125, 146
  style, 31, 127, 129–32, 132, 136
  work, 130
Driglam Namzha (Bhutan cultural code), 147, 148
dupattas, 75, 76

Durkheim, E., *Elementary Forms of Religious Life*, 113
Dutta, Sharbari, 65, 70, 76, 79–80
Dyer, Richard, 68, 71

East India Company, 151
Ebong Rituparno (talk show), 75–6
Edensor, T., 43, 45–6
elite class, 33–4, 58, 59, 102–3
Elson, D., 160
Enamor, 208
Entwistle, J., 167
ethical values, 16, 119, 120
ethnic minorities, 148
ethnic style, 58, 76
'eve teasing', 59–62
Exiles (Gupta), 97

Fabindia, 44, 58
Facebook, 147, 154, 175, 207
factory workers, Sri Lanka, 124–43
fantasy, 50, 101
fashion
  capitals, 32, 36, 37
  crazes, 130
  fusion, 43
  implications, 158–60
  perception of, 154–5
  retail, 34, 208–11
Fashion (film), 210–11
fashion shows, 38, 112–13, 120–1
fashion weeks, 12–13, 30–1, 44, 78
Femina India (magazine), 214–15
femininity, 59, 68, 69, 71, 99
feminism, 90, 207, 212–13
Fernandes, Leela, 35, 103
festivals, Indian, 116

films, 49, 67, 70–4, 79, 80, 99, 210–11
 See also Bollywood films
Fischer, Hal, 98–9
flâneur, 45–6
flirtation, 56, 59, 60, 134
footwear, 159
 sandals, 58, 131, 134
 shoes, 31, 129, 150, 212–13
 sneakers, 92
Forever 21, 33
Foucault, Michel, 204, 216
Free Trade Zone (FTZ) factory workers, Sri Lanka, 20, 124–43
Fumanti, M., 190
fusion, fashion, 43

gamchas, 43
Gandhi, Mahatma, 9, 69, 205–6
Gay Semiotics (Fischer), 98–9
Gen-X market, 105, 111
Gen Z ('zippies'), 105, 106, 113, 116
gender, and style, 53–7, 127–8
gender roles, 97, 168, 171–2, 176, 180
ghaghras, 30, 38
 gagra cholis, 129, 131, 133
Ghare Baire (film), 70
ghos, 146, 147, 150, 158, 159
Ghosh & Company (talk show), 67
Ghosh, Rituparno, 18, 65–8, 70–82, 74, 78, 80
Girl in Hijab (Kabir), Pl.4, Pl.8
global nationalism, 51
globalisation, 41–2
Goffman, E., 168
goni billa, 138
Gopinath, Gayatri, 70
Gowricharn, R., 187

Gujarati culture, 190
Gujarati Indians, 93
Gupta, Sunil (SG), 18, 96–101

hairstyles, 131, 136, 143, 193
handbags, 31, 50, 131
Haney, P., 130
'hanging around', 9, 22, 54–5, 59
Hashim, Kabeer, 140
hats, beanie, 90
haute couture, 50, 102–3
Hauz Khas, Delhi, 57–8
Haydon, Lisa, 210
Hazra, Anindya, 76, 77
Hewamanne, Sandya, 20
hijabs, Pl.4, Pl.8, 89
hijras, 97, 99
Hijras, Giriyas and Others (Singh), 96–7
Hindman, H., 167
Hindu cultures, 69, 187, 190
Hindu mythology, 69, 73, 101, 194–5
Hindu Punjabi festivals, 197–8
Hindustani women, Amsterdam, 183–99
Hiphop Tamizha (band), 55
Holliday, Ruth, 72
'home clothes', 136–7
homosexuality, 75
Hondagneu-Sotelo, P., 141–2
Hong Kong fashion, 156
honour (ijat), 9, 55, 167, 173–4, 176
hoodies, 90
Huisman, K, 141–2
hybrid dressing, 89

identity, constructing, 86–95
identity politics, 66, 126, 129
immigrants, 89, 148, 148, 183–99
implications, fashion, 158–60

In/visible Space (Kabir), Pl.1–9, 86–95
India
  communities in, 38
  cultural heritage, 186–7
  financial reforms, 34
  independence, 9, 205
Indian fashion, 156, 179, 191–2
Indian-Hindu identity, 194–5
'Indianised' style, 184
indigenous people, 40
inequality, wealth, 45, 153
Instagram, 147, 154
International Fashion Showcase, London, 12
Islamic cultures, 69
Islamophobia, 90, 126, 140–1

jackets, 92, 147, 149, 150, 159
Jantzen, C., 204–5, 213
Japanese fashion, 156
Jawaharlal Nehru University, New Delhi, 57, 100
jeans
  affordable, 141
  Asian, 57, 58, 157, 170
  designer, 44
  FTZ workers, 125, 134, 137–8, 142
  western, 90, 136
Jetsun Pema, Queen, 152, 154, 155, 160
jewellery, 70, 192
  anklets, 30, 43
  gold, 73, 131
  Hindu male gods, 69
  tribal, 31
jholas, 75
jodhpurs, 31
Johnson-Hanks, J., 169
Jones, C., 41
journalists, fashion, 32–3

Kabir, Raisa S., 19, 86–95
Kabra, Anand, 44
Kalaiselvi (athlete), 61
kalisan, 125
Kant, Rajni, 59
Kapur, R., 55, 60
'Karma' (Bhutan), 159
Karva Chauth celebrations, 197–8
Kathmandu, 165–80
Kaye, John William, 40
kedia tops, 31
Kerala, 129
keras, 147
khadis, 69
Kiki (sex worker), 93
'Kinley' (Bhutan), 159
kiras, 146, 147, 149
Koechin, Kalki, 106–7, 107
kolhapuri sandals, 58
komos, 146
Kondo, Dorinne, 41, 128, 132
kothis, 97, 99
Kothis, Hijras, Giriyas and Others (Singh), Pl.13–16, 98, 99
Krishnan, Sneha, 128, 129
Kuldova, Tereza, 5, 23
Kumar, Ritu, 41, 102
kurta surawels, 170–1, 178
kurt(h)as, 57, 75, 90, 195, 198

labouring class, 32, 37
LBTQ youth, South Asian, 11–12, 86–95
leggings, 50, 195, 198
lengas, 132
lesbians, 12, 87, 90, 93
Leshkowich, A.M., 41
Lewis, Reina, 17
liberalisation, economic, 13, 45, 66, 96, 209
Liechty, M., 167, 174

Lindquist, J., 128
lingerie *see* bras, urban women and; underwear
literacy, 152
Lo, J., 147
Louis Vuitton bags, 31
'Lovemarks', 112–13
lower class, 32
lower middle-class, 9, 50, 57, 58, 59, 60
Lukose, R., 129
Lulla, Neeta, 15
lungis, 43
Lynes, George Platt, 98

Maffesoli, M., 110–11
magazines, fashion, 32, 36, 154
   Bhutanese Youth and Fashion Magazine, 149
   Femina India, 214–15
   Vogue India, 15, 214–15
   Yeewong, 152, 153
Mahabharata, 69
makeup, 71, 99, 129, 131, 134
Malaysia, 128
Malhotra, Manish, 15
'Malika' (Delhi), 211–12
Mangalore attacks (2009), 207
Mankekar, P., 51, 187
Manna, Sayak, 80
Manou, *wearabout* (blogger), 32, 38–40, 39, 42, 44, 46
marketing, fashion, 24–5, 116
Marks and Spencer (M&S), 208
marriages, arranged, Nepal, 165–80
Maryam (gay woman), 90–3
Maryam (Kabir), Pl.3
masculine-of-centre-identifying lesbian, 93

masculinity, 69
matchmakers, marriage, 174
material practices, 112
material wealth, 155
Mazarella, W., 7, 25
media, influence of, 98, 99
Memories in March (film) 80
men, young, 53, 65–82, 69, 97
Merleau-Ponty, M., 190
metrosexual look, 99
Meyer, B., 190
middle class, 34, 35, 120
   South Asian, 51, 66, 129, 142, 167
   status, 7–8, 59, 127–8, 171
migrants, 126, 129, 136
Miller, S., 174–6
Misener, J., 154
Misra, Santu, *devil wore* (blogger), 32
Miss India pageants (1998), 207
mobile phones, 7, 13, 14, 15
models, 213, 215
modernity, 25, 69, 170, 177–9
monks, 155
moral codes, 92, 119, 169, 202, 206, 216
mosques, 90–1
Motsemme, N., 128
Mr Malhotra's Party (Gupta), Pl.9–12, 96, 98–9, 100
Mukherjee, Sabyasachi, 41, 102
multimedia, 68, 147, 188, 193–4, 207
Mumbai, 34, 37
music culture, 14, 50, 111, 117
Muslim consumers, 24–5
Muslim Council of Sri Lanka, 140
Muslim men, 138–9
Muslim women, 90–1, 128, 138–9, 142

Nakassis, C.V., 52, 53–4, 57
national attire, Bhutan, 146–7, 149, 155, 158–60
national identity, 3, 68, 147, 148, 207
nationalism, 3, 51, 102–5, 113, 143, 204–7
Naval, Deepti, 80
neoliberalism, 5
Nepalese fashion, 13, 156, 165–80
Nepali women, 171–2
Netherlands, 184, 186
Netting, N.S., 175
New Delhi, 34, 37
'New Documents Show' (MoMA), 97
Nigah (organisation), 100
Nikita, Pl.5, 93
Nisbett, N., 7
non-Bhutanese clothing, Bhutan, 148–50
non-binary persons, 92
non-traditional clothing, 159
Nor Black Nor White (NBNW), 15
'Norbu' (Bhutan), 156
nose rings, 43
nostalgia, Indian, 41–3

off-the-street display, 34, 36
O'Neill, A., 33
Ong, A., 128
Oor sutharathu, 53
Oppenheim, R., 167
Osella, C., 8, 54, 56, 60
Osella, F., 8, 54, 56, 60
Oxford shoes, 31

Padukone, Deepika, 195–6
Pakeezah (film), 99
Pakistan, 17

Pakistani communities, 90, 92
pants, 125, 193
parental influence, 92
Paul & Joe (designers), 150
payals, 30
Peiss, Kathy, 129
Pek-Dorji, S.S., 155
'Pema' (Bhutan), 157–8
'Penam' (Bhutan), 155
The People of India (Watson and Kaye), 40
Péro (brand), 31
Phadke, S., 54
phones, mobile, 7, 13, 14, 15
photographic
  essays, Pl.1–9, 86–95
  shoots, 87, 90
photography, 18, 40, 97, 98
Pink Chaddis campaign, 202, 207
Pinney, C., 40
Pocock, David, 189
'position taking' (class system), 168
postcolonialism, 205
pottu, 129, 143
Pragati Maidan, New Delhi, 30
pre-colonial dressing, 69–70, 216
Prohibition of Eve Teasing Act (1998), 60
Punjabi Hindu community, 195, 197–8
pyjamas, 57, 75

'q-wearing', 92–3
queer looks, of India, 96–101
queer spaces, 86–94

Radha Krishna temple, Amsterdam, 189, 191, 193
Raj, Rishi, 115
Rajasthani, India, 37
Raju (Kabir), Pl.6–7, 93–4
Ramani, Bina, 57–8

Ramayana, 69
Rankin, K.N., 174
re-orientalism, Indian, 41–3
rebellion, symbols of, 105–6, 121, 134–5
'Reetu' (Amsterdam), 193–5
Rekha (actress), 79
religion, 6–7, 90, 126, 159, 189–91, 195
'Reshmi' (Amsterdam), 195–7
retail, fashion, 34, 208–11
Rich Mix (community art centre), London, 87–8
ritual practices, 128
rituals, staged, 112–13
Roberts, Kevin, 112
robes, 147
Rocamora, A., 33
Rogers, M., 59
royal chic, 102–3
royal fashion, 151, 155
royal weddings, 149–50, 153, 160
rural villagers, 37, 54
rural women, 125, 132–3, 136–7
'Ruy' (Bhutan), 156

salwar kameez, 125, 195, 198
same-sex relationships, 97
'Sameera' (Delhi), 213–14
sandals, 58, 131, 134
Sandhu, Arti, 22
Sapre, Madhu, 212–13
saris, 31, 38, 169–70, 178
sartorial codes, 65–82
'Saskia' (Amsterdam), 191–3
satchels, 31
scarves, 31, 147
scene podarathu, 58–9
Schuman, Scott, Sartorialist (blogger), 32
seamstresses, 130, 131

Secret Closet (online brand), 15
self-identified women, 86
self-orientalisation, 41–3
Serazio, Michael, 120
sex workers, 93, 130–1
sexual harassment, 59, 60
sexual-health education, 213–14
sexualisation, of female body, 54, 60, 202, 213
sexuality, female, 15, 212–15, 216
Shah, Darshan, 80
Shah Jahan Mosque, Surrey, 90
Shahni, Parmesh, 72
shalwar kameez, 92
shalwars, 129, 131, 133
shame-fear, 9, 125, 207, 214
Shantiniketani men's style, 75
Sharangpani, M., 175
sharing clothes, 159–60
Shepherd-Manandhar, Sarah, 20–1
shirts, 134
Shivan and Naresh (designers), 15
shoes, 31, 129, 150, 212–13
shopping malls, 108, 203, 208
Shoreditch, London, 90
shringar, 73
sight adikkarathu, 57, 61
Singh, Charan (CS), 96–101
Singh, Ritika, 18, 117
Sinhalese Buddhists, 126, 130, 141
Sinhalese women, 138–9
Sita (Kabir), Pl.1, 88, 93
skin colour, 132
skirts, 130, 143, 170
skirts, male, 31
skorts, 31
'slightly damaged' garments, 135
SlutWalk movements, 207–8
social media, 14–16, 55, 147, 189, 197, 207
Sökefeld, M., 188

INDEX

Somand, Milind, 213
'Sonam' (Bhutan), 155, 156, 159
South Asia, region of, 2–4
South Asians, UK, 89–93
Spivak, G., 3
Sri Chaitanya, 70
Sri Lanka, 124–43
Sri Rama Sena (SRS), 207
Sri Ramakrishna, 70
steampunk, 103
stockings, 31
Stonewall Inn, New York, 97
straight-up shots, 33
Strain, E., 40
street photography, 97
street styles, 32–7, 147, 154
Strickland, Paul, 21, 150
studio photography, 98
styles, 37–41, 50, 53–7, 62–3
subcultures, 10, 103–4, 109, 119, 127
subversion, 96–101, 119–20
suits, 195, 198
Suriname, 183, 186–7
'Surma' (Bombay), 212, 213
sustainability, 16–17, 24, 107, 120
Swadesi movement, 9, 205
Swaminarayan movement, Britain, 189–90
Swamy, Priya, 19

T-shirts
  bras, 209
  choice of, 170, 179, 193
  as fandom, 195, 196–7
  unisex, 100
Tagore, Rabindranath, *Chokher Bali*/, 65, 70, 73, 75, 206
Tahiliani, Tarun, 102
Tamil workers, 143
Tarlo, Emma, 4, 57–8, 82

'Tashi' (Bhutan), 157
temples, Hindu, 189, 191, 193, 195
textile industry, 16, 146, 153, 160
'Thinley' (Bhutan), 158, 159
third class, 126–9
'Titanic dresses', 130
toegos, 147
topi, 90
Topman, 44
tourism, 151, 153, 157
tradition, 165–80
transgender non-binary persons, 86
transport, 171
transsexual/transwomen, 97
transvestism, 71
tribal communities, 40
tribal dress, 37, 38
trips, factory worker, 133–4
trousers, 124–6, 125, 139–41
'Tshering' (Bhutan), 157
'Tshewang' (Bhutan), 159
Tsui, C., 157
Tuff shoes, 212–13
tunics, 50, 58
turbans, 37
Turkish fashion, 158–9
Turquoise Cottage (Vasant Vihar bar), 116
TV, influence of, 98, 99, 188

'Ugen' (Bhutan), 159
Umrao Jaan (film), 99
underwear, 15, 150, 159, 202–17
Ungendering Prayer (Kabir), Pl.2, 88, 91
uniforms, 57, 170
unique styles, 128, 129
unisex styles, 96, 100
United Arab Emirates fashion, 158–9
Untitled, 2 (Singh), 100

Untitled, 6 (Singh), 98
upper-middle class
  photography, 98
  style, 33, 34
  youth, 57, 58–9, 105, 120
urban classes, 34, 35, 41, 105, 202–17
  See also Free Trade Zone (FTZ) factory workers, Sri Lanka
uttariyas, 69, 70, 75, 76

Valaya, JJ, 41, 102
Vanita, Ruth, *Masculinity and its Challenges in India*, 69
Varghese, M., 5
Vathikutchi (film), 49
veils, 128
Verrips, J., 190
visual media, 34–5
Vogue India (magazine), 15, 214–15

Wangchuck Dynasty, 151, 152
Wangchuck, Jigme Khesar Namgyel, 151, 152, 155
Wangchuk, Karma, 149
Warikoo, N., 187
watches, 131
Watson, John Forbes, 40

weddings, 149–50, 153, 160, 192
Werbner, P., 190
western clothing, anxieties surrounding, 205–8
western culture, 36, 42, 114, 116, 136, 148
  influence of, 150, 151–2, 157–8, 159, 203
Willis, P., 127
Wills Lifestyle India Fashion Week (WLIFW), 30–1, 38, 103
women, young, 9
wonjus, 147
working-class fashion, 124–43
workwear, 30, 37, 124–43, 130, 149

'Y' (bisexual woman), Pl.4, Pl.8, 89–90
'Yebar' (Bhutan), 159
Yeewong (magazine), 152, 153
youth population, Bhutan, 152–4
youth, views of, 154–60
YouTube, 55, 189

Zara (brand), 31, 33
zippies (Gen Z), 105, 106, 113, 116

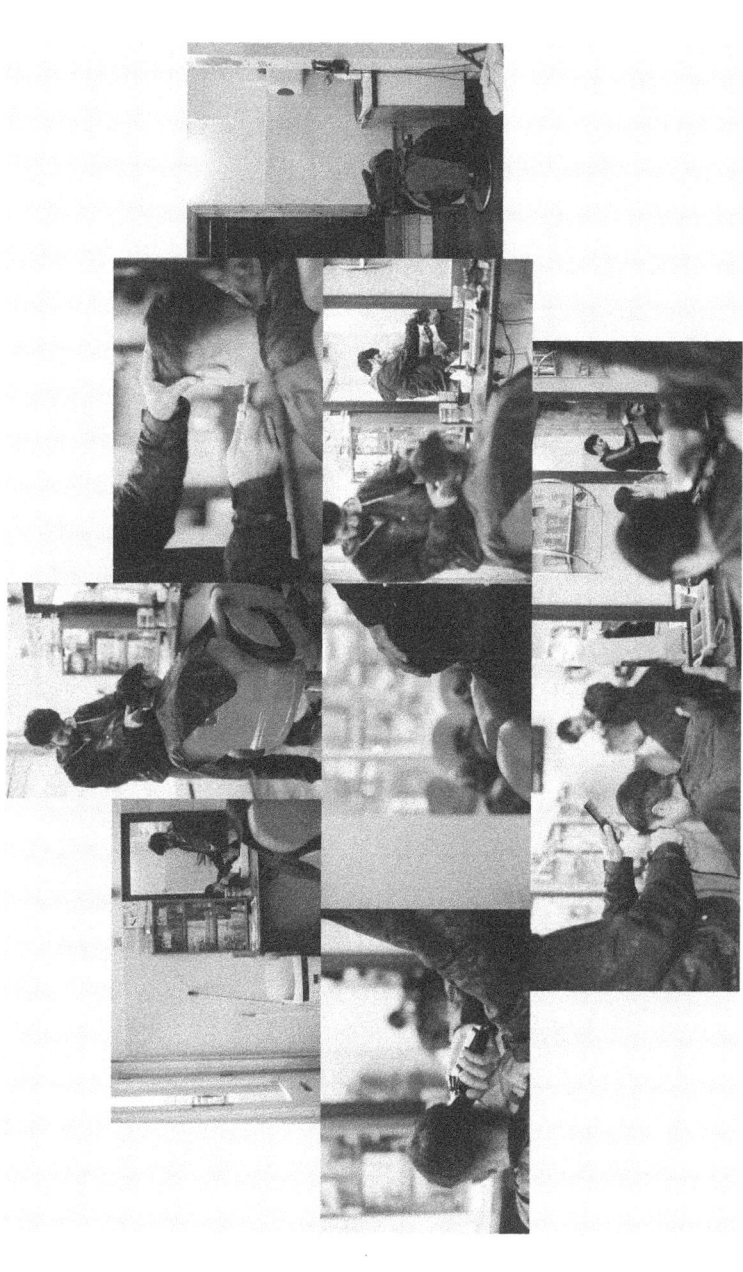

Plate 1 *Sita*, Raisa Kabir, 2014. 35mm film, type C prints, paper montage, 64 cm × 45 cm, from the series *(In)visible Space*. Courtesy of Raisa Kabir.

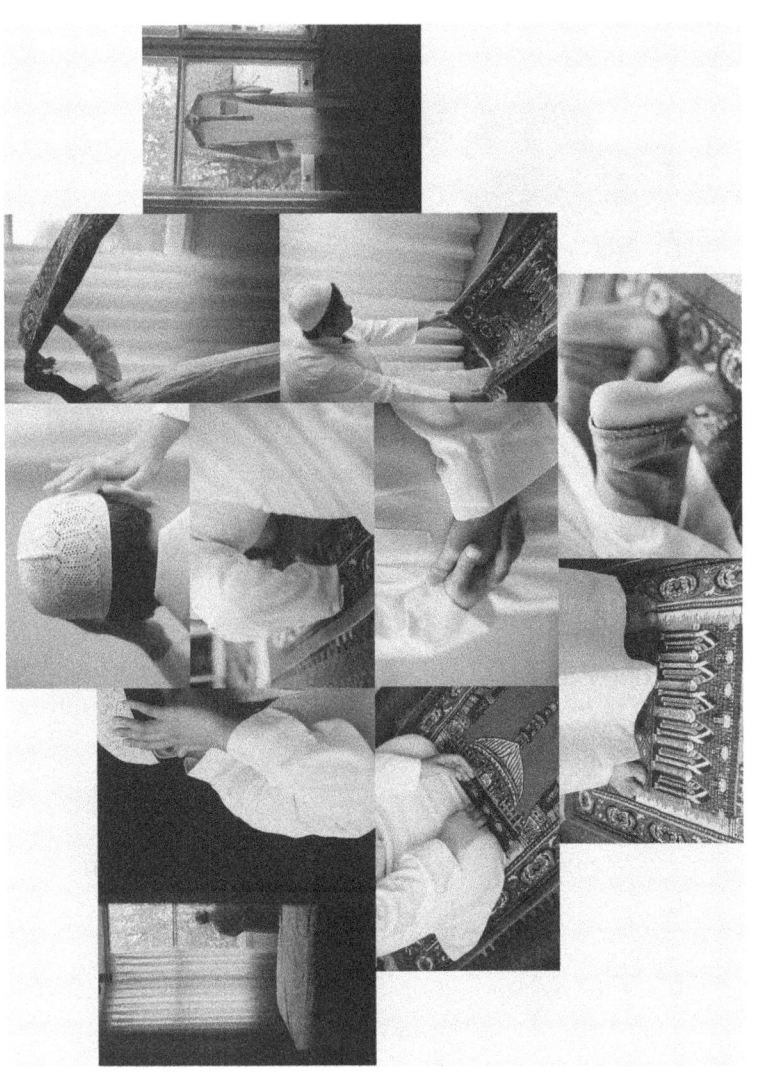

Plate 2 Ungendering Prayer, Raisa Kabir, 2014. 35mm film, type C prints, paper montage, 64 cm × 45 cm, from the series (In)visible Space. Courtesy of Raisa Kabir.

Plate 3 *Muryum*, Raisa Kabir, 2014. 35mm film, type C prints, paper montage, 64 cm × 45 cm, from the series (In)visible Space. Courtesy of Raisa Kabir.

Plate 4 *Girl in Hijab*, Raisa Kabir, 2014. 35mm film, type C prints, paper montage, 64 cm × 45 cm, from the series *(In)visible Space*. Courtesy of Raisa Kabir.

Plate 5 Nikita, Raisa Kabir, 2014. 35mm film, type C prints, paper montage, 64 cm × 45 cm, from the series (In)visible Space. Courtesy of Raisa Kabir.

Plate 6 *Raju*, Raisa Kabir, 2014. 35mm film, type C prints, paper montage, 64 cm × 45 cm, from the series *(In)visible Space*. Courtesy of Raisa Kabir.

Plate 7 *Raju detail*, Raisa Kabir, 2014. 35mm film, type C prints, paper montage, 64 cm × 45 cm, from the series *(In)visible Space*. Courtesy of Raisa Kabir.

Plate 8 *Yasmin/Girl with Hijab detail*, Raisa Kabir, 2014. 35mm film, type C prints, paper montage, 64 cm × 45 cm, from the series *(In)visible Space*. Courtesy of Raisa Kabir.

Plate 9 *Arti, Greater Kailash, M-Block Market*, from the series *Mr Malhotra's Party*, Sunil Gupta, 2007–2012. Courtesy of the artist and SepiaEye.

Plate 10 *Anusha, Jawaharlal Nehru University*, from the series *Mr Malhotra's Party*, Sunil Gupta, 2007–2012. Courtesy of the artist and SepiaEye.

Plate 11 *Mario, Golf View Apartments*, from the series *Mr Malhotra's Party*, Sunil Gupta, 2007–2012. Courtesy of the artist and SepiaEye.

Plate 12 *Sonal, Yusuf Sarai*, from the series *Mr Malhotra's Party*, Sunil Gupta, 2007–2012. Courtesy of the artist and SepiaEye.

Plate 13 *Untitled #5*, from the series *Kothis, Hijras, Giriyas and Others*, Charan Singh, 2013–2014. Courtesy of the artist and SepiaEye.

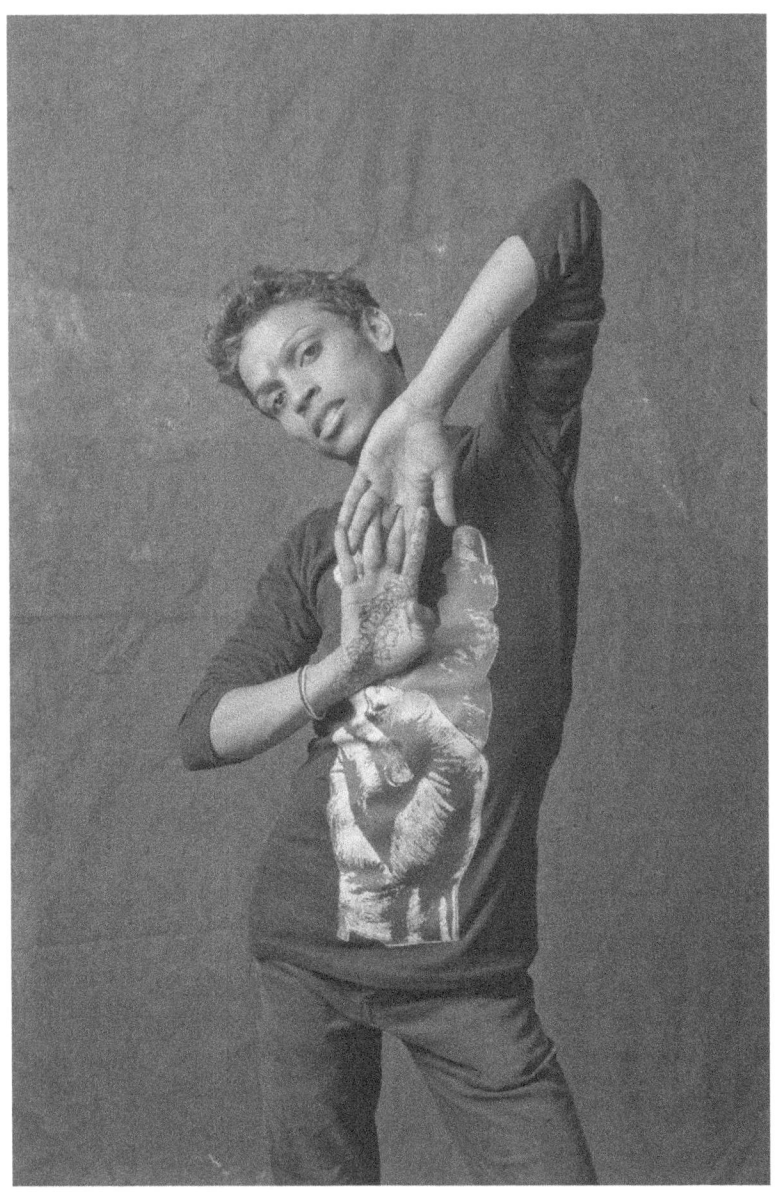

Plate 14 *Untitled #6*, from the series *Kothis, Hijras, Giriyas and Others*, Charan Singh, 2013–2014. Courtesy of the artist and SepiaEye.

Plate 15 *Untitled #1*, from the series *Kothis, Hijras, Giriyas and Others*, Charan Singh, 2013–2014. Courtesy of the artist and SepiaEye.

Plate 16 *Untitled #2*, from the series *Kothis, Hijras, Giriyas and Others*, Charan Singh, 2013–2014. Courtesy of the artist and SepiaEye.

Lightning Source UK Ltd.
Milton Keynes UK
UKHW042309300520
364119UK00007B/703